Areas of Knowledge: Competance

1. Investments
2. Banking (small/regional)
3. Services   Mod
    a) Medical   High
    b) Telecom   Mod
4. Energy
5. Fundemental use products
    - Food   low
    - Beverages   high
    - Home Building   low
6. Real Estate   Mod
7. Insurance   High

ROBERT G. HAGSTROM

THE
ESSENTIAL
BUFFETT

ROBERT G. HAGSTROM

THE ESSENTIAL BUFFETT

TIMELESS PRINCIPLES FOR
THE NEW ECONOMY

 JOHN WILEY & SONS, INC.

New York   Chichester   Weinheim   Brisbane   Singapore   Toronto

FOREWORD

Investing is context dependent. The best investment advice is general and timeless, but not very helpful if you have to figure out what to do today. "Buy low, sell high" is advice that works in all investing environments. It doesn't matter if it's the twenty-first century and you're Warren Buffett buying junk bonds, or the nineteenth century and you're a Rothschild taking advantage of the panic surrounding Waterloo, or 500 B.C. and you're the pre-Socratic philosopher Thales of Miletus, making his fortune in commodity markets. The trouble with that advice, though, is that if you know what's low and what's high, you don't need it. If you don't know, you don't need it either, since you won't be able to use it.

The more specific the advice, the more its use depends on the current environment and how it evolves. The answer to almost every investment question is the same: It depends. Are technology stocks a good investment? They were from 1996 through 1999, but in 2000 they had their biggest yearly decline in history.

Are stocks a better long-term investment than bonds? It depends. Does your long term start in the late 1920s and end in the late 1940s? Then the answer is "no." Or does it start in the late 1940s and end in the late 1960s? In that case, the answer is "of course." The amount of time is the same; the result is totally different. When the answer is "it depends," the question is context dependent.

Context dependence is why so much investment writing is useless after a few weeks. The more specific the advice, the quicker it becomes dated. No one reads last year's investment "strategy" pieces from the major Wall Street firms to get insight about what to do. The demand for investment books is context dependent, too. Books about monetary crises dominated the bestseller lists in the early to mid-1970s, inflation titles were the rage in the early 1980s, and books about the Internet just finished their brief flurry of fame.

The list of perennially useful investment books is short. *Reminiscences of a Stock Operator* is a book most professional investors and nearly every successful trader has read and found worthwhile. It is the thinly veiled story of legendary stock operator Jesse Livermore, told in his own words and transcribed by Edwin Lefèvre, who is listed as the author. Its value lies in its descriptions of situations that recur in every investment era, and the strategies Livermore used to deal with them. He became adept at recognizing recurring patterns and profiting from them. He was not so adept at recognizing that superficially similar patterns can turn out to be substantially different. He made and lost several fortunes; the last loss led him to shooting himself in the men's room of the Sherry Netherland hotel.

Another fine investment book is known more by its title than its contents. *Where Are the Customers' Yachts?* by Fred Shwed is interesting as a period piece—an amusing picture of a mostly vanished world.

The rarest investment books are those that can be profitably read by everyone interested in the craft of investing: books that inform, illuminate, and teach, that can be reread in different periods and contexts and that will deepen our understanding or provide new insights into the current situation.

For value investors, one classic is Ben Graham's *The Intelligent Investor*. First published in the late 1940s, it reflects *Security Analysis,* his pioneering text, without the heavy lifting. You can be a good investor and never have read *The Intelligent Investor,* but you'll be a better one if you have. Graham inspired and shaped the thinking of a generation of value investors, the best known, of course, being Warren Buffett.

I first became aware of Warren Buffett in the mid-1970s through Adam Smith's now out of print *Super Money,* the sequel to his best-selling tale of the late 1960s bull market, *The Money Game.* Written after the severe declines of 1969 and 1970 and the bankruptcy of the Penn Central Railroad, *Super Money* introduced Buffett in Chapter 5, titled "Somebody Must Have Done Something Right: The Lessons of the Master." The chapter was about Graham's principles of margin of safety and intrinsic value, illustrated through the activities of Warren Buffett, then in his early forties and comfortably rich. Unlike the famous fund managers of the 1960s such as Fred Carr, Fred Mates, and Gerry Tsai, Buffett avoided the collapse, disbanding his partnership when speculative excess removed the margin of safety he deemed necessary to continue investing in public markets.

I was then in my mid-twenties and what immediately got my attention was that Buffett's initial capital rounded to zero, but when he ended the partnership at 39 he had $25 million. The way "Adam Smith" told it, Buffett got some money from friends and family, and "sat in his bedroom office, reading through the manuals . . ." He bought "quiet simple stocks, easy to understand, with a lot of time left over for the kids, for handball, for listening to the tall corn grow." Having an almost infinite capacity for indolence, I thought this sounded pretty good. Start with nothing, read some stuff, buy a few stocks, wait, get rich, and then hang it up before 40.

I read Ben Graham and began looking around for stuff on Buffett. I got some money from friends and began buying stocks, simple, easy-to-understand companies trading at low price-earnings multiples, preferably with lots of hard assets and a good current ratio. I looked for net/nets, just as Graham advised. It was a little more work than the method Nicholas Darvas advocated in *How I Made $2,000,000 in the Stock Market,* which involved drawing boxes around the pattern of price action of a stock, as I recall, but I figured if it was too easy then others might get the excess returns before I did.

I need not have worried. Twenty-five years later, it seems people are just as eager to avoid thinking about the businesses underlying the stocks they buy as they ever were. Markets behave pretty much as they have since the time of Thales. Most people prefer to buy what *is* going up rather than what *will* go up. Peter Lynch has often said people will do more research on a $1,000 purchase of a refrigerator than they will before they spend $10,000 on a stock.

Today's markets are larger, deeper, offer more investment choices, move more quickly, and are accompanied by much more noise than the markets of the past. Markets have become democratized; more people own stocks than ever before, and governments cannot ignore markets as they once thought they could.

Markets are all about value. Their function is to price assets and, despite their shortcomings, no better system has been devised. Value is rarely overlooked for long. That is true in the market for books, as well as in the market for stocks.

I have always been mystified by the desire to write books. If you are unknown to the public, writing must surely have among the lowest probabilities of achieving an adequate economic return of any activity. We are fortunate that Robert Hagstrom writes books the way I eat cottage fries at the Post House in New York: compulsively. His compulsion, unlike mine, is good for you.

The Essential Buffett revises, updates, and expands Robert's analysis of Warren Buffett's investment methodology. It covers both stock selection and Buffett's style of portfolio management, which Robert calls *focus investing*. It also contains much new material about how to think about and apply Buffett's approach to the "New Economy."

One of the challenges for investors who believe intrinsic value and margin of safety are the keys to investment success is how to use those concepts in a world that seems increasingly without firm valuation moorings. Many of the old rules no longer work. It used to be that stocks were unattractive relative to bonds when their yields exceeded those of bonds. That valuation rule always worked until it stopped working in the late 1950s, and it hasn't worked since. It used to be that the market was cheap at book value and a sale at twice book or more. That worked until it didn't. It used to be that if stock yields fell below 3 percent, stocks were overvalued. That always worked until it stopped working in the early 1990s.

As Robert Hagstrom ably demonstrates, Warren Buffett's investment thinking evolved, partly from his own experience and partly under the prodding of Charlie Munger. The evolution has been one of method, not one of temperament. The same timeless principles endure, the tenets are always applicable. It is only the environment, the context, which changes.

BILL MILLER
Legg Mason Value Trust

PREFACE

With each passing year, the noise level in the stock market rises. Television commentators, financial writers, analysts, and market strategists are all overtalking each other to get investors' attention. At the same time, individual investors, immersed in chat rooms and message boards, are exchanging questionable and often misleading tips. Yet, despite all this available information, investors find it increasingly difficult to profit. Some are hard-pressed even to continue. Stock prices skyrocket with little reason, then plummet just as quickly, and people who have turned to investing for their children's education and their own retirement become frightened. There appears to be no rhyme or reason to the market, only folly.

Far above this market madness stand the wisdom and counsel of Warren Buffett. In an environment that seems to favor the speculator over the investor, Warren Buffett's investment advice has proven, time and again, to be a safe harbor for millions of lost investors.

Over the years, critics have argued that Warren Buffett's idiosyncratic approach to investing is impossible to duplicate. I wouldn't disagree that his approach is unique—in a market that emphasizes the frenetic buying and selling of securities, Buffett's buy-and-hold philosophy is an anomaly. But I do take issue with those who say that only Buffett can do what Buffett does.

The goal of this book is to showcase Buffett's entire methodology: to make it accessible and useful to all investors—individuals and professionals alike—and to demonstrate how

Buffett's thinking can be applied successfully in the New Economy.

To do all of this, I have culled the best from two earlier books and highlighted their core principles: *The Warren Buffett Way,* which describes how Buffett analyzes companies and selects stocks, and *The Warren Buffett Portfolio,* which describes the guidelines by which he manages the Berkshire portfolio. Throughout, fundamental Buffett principles are called out, to detail and clarify Buffett's four-part investment strategy:

1. Analyze a stock as a business.
2. Demand a margin of safety for each purchase.
3. Manage a focus portfolio.
4. Protect yourself from the speculative and emotional forces of the market.

With that background as your framework, you will learn how the Buffett principles can be, and successfully have been, applied in three areas Buffett has traditionally not explored: technology, small-cap, and international stocks. Chapter 8, "New Opportunities, Timeless Principles," gives you an inside look at how three successful investors are applying Warren Buffett's investment principles in their special areas of expertise. Bill Miller, manager of the Legg Mason Value Trust, explains how he has extended Buffett's methodology into the technology arena. Wally Weitz, manager of the Weitz Value Funds, discusses how he uses Buffett's approach to invest in small- and mid-capitalization stocks. Mason Hawkins, manager of the Longleaf Funds, demonstrates how he uses Buffett's principles to invest in foreign companies.

Many people are aware of Buffett's long-standing decision to avoid technology stocks. However, it is important to realize that Buffett's unwillingness to invest in technology is not a statement that technology stocks are unanalyzable. As he confessed during Berkshire's 2000 annual meeting, "It is not that we don't understand a technology business or its product. The reason we don't invest is because we can't understand the predictability of the economics ten years hence." It is this lack of economic predictability that has prevented Buffett from venturing into the technology world. But it has not prevented others from applying Buffett's investment tenets to technology companies, with much success.

In fact, I would argue that what is missing in many analytical reports on technology companies is a businessperson's understanding of how the company operates, how it generates profits, and how a businessperson would then value the technology company. As you will discover in the chapters on portfolio management, one way to compensate for the lack of economic predictability in any company is to reduce its weighting in your portfolio, and another is to require a larger margin of safety with that purchase. The key point is: Warren Buffett's investment tenets are the only sensible way to invest in *any* company, technology or otherwise.

Is there a "New Economy"? While thoughtful people disagree on this question, I believe the answer is yes. We moved from an agriculture-based economy in the nineteenth century to a manufacturing-based economy in the twentieth. Now, in the twenty-first century, it is easy to observe our economy rapidly evolving into one dominated by technology. Broadly speaking, "technology" encompasses many different businesses and industries. Hardware machines fitted with software applications manipulate bytes of information that are then transported around the world to other hardware machines and software applications. In a nutshell, this instantaneous transmission of information is a technological revolution, and it is changing the entire business landscape.

The New Economy is also having a profound impact on the behavior of individual investors. Today, investors have a full menu of stocks to choose from. They can purchase small-capitalization stocks that only yesterday were venture capital investments. They can purchase shares of foreign companies in markets around the world, and obviously they can purchase technology stocks if they so choose. In the New Economy, individuals have easy access to information that only a short while ago was considered so highly valued and proprietary that it was available only to professional investors. Never before has so much information been so readily available to so many investors. In the New Economy, individuals no longer have to rely on investment professionals. They can now electronically trade stocks with a push of a button, or personally change their 401(k) retirement plan on a daily basis, if they wish.

In a world littered with information, the scarce resource is *understanding*. Information itself is not enough to ensure investment success. What is required is an understanding of how best to use the information to achieve the desired goals. We are indeed operating in a New Economy, but the rules of investing have not changed. Businesses still require profits to operate, and investors still calculate these profits to determine value. At first glance, Warren Buffett, who makes no bones about staying away from technology companies, may appear far removed from the New Economy, but a closer inspection will reveal that his investment principles are timeless.

The Chairman's Letters that Warren Buffett writes to shareholders in the Berkshire annual reports are famous; in the early days of my career, they were a profound influence. Taken together, these letters form the best investing textbook I could possibly imagine.

Here is one succinct and powerful lesson, from the 1996 report: "Your goal as an investor should be simply to purchase, at a rational price, a part interest in an easily understood business whose earnings are virtually certain to be materially higher, five, ten, and twenty years from now. Over time, you will find only a few companies that meet those standards—so when you see one that qualifies, you should buy a meaningful amount of stock."

Whatever level of funds you have available for investing, whatever industry or company you are interested in, you cannot find a better touchstone than that.

ROBERT G. HAGSTROM

Wayne, Pennsylvania
February 2001

CONTENTS

Contents

CHAPTER 1

THE UNREASONABLE MAN

Forty-five years ago, Warren Buffett began a career managing money. At the relatively young age of 25 and with a relatively small amount of capital (his own investment was only $100), Buffett started an investment partnership. With the support of family members and a few close friends, the Buffett Partnership began operations, on day one, with $105,000 and seven limited partners.

Buffett set himself a tough goal: to beat the Dow Jones Industrial Average by ten percentage points each year. He achieved that and more. From 1956 until 1969, the year the partnership disbanded, Buffett generated an average annual return that was 22 percentage points higher than the Dow. Along the way, the partnership took a controlling interest in a small textile company called Berkshire Hathaway. Over a 35-year period, Buffett grew its book value from $19 per share to $37,987 per share. That works out to a rate of 24 percent compounded annually. It is not surprising that Warren Buffett was recently voted the greatest investor of the twentieth century.

When we look back on the life of Warren Buffett, we can identify several important experiences that helped him become

1

successful. He was raised in a loving home under the moral guidance of two parents who exemplified midwestern values. His father, a stockbroker and U.S. Congressman, stressed both honesty and integrity in all his dealings with clients and the public. Young Buffett had an entrepreneurial streak from the beginning; he quickly learned to appreciate the value of a dollar and, just as important, the value of growing a dollar. Taken together, Buffett's early personal experiences helped provide him with a lifelong moral compass.

In addition to this strong moral foundation, Buffett possessed a seemingly inexhaustible appetite for knowledge. While working at his father's brokerage firm, he devoured all the investment books he could find, which led him ultimately to one of the greatest investment books ever written: Ben Graham's *The Intelligent Investor*.

But it is not enough to say that Buffett's investment success is simply a result of good character and a good education. To this we must add the all-important characteristics of courage and self-confidence. Buffett deeply believed in the lessons taught by his father and by Ben Graham, so he was unafraid when he found himself at odds with the more popular Wall Street view. This quality, which we might call "intelligent contrarianism," has most helped Warren Buffett achieve remarkable success.

"The reasonable man adapts himself to the world," wrote George Bernard Shaw. "The unreasonable one persists in trying to adapt the world to himself. Therefore all progress depends on the unreasonable man."[1] Shall we conclude that Warren Buffett is "the unreasonable man"? To do so presumes that his investment approach represents progress in the financial world, an assumption I strongly make. For when we look at the recent achievements of "reasonable" men, we see, at best, mediocrity and at worst, disaster.

After the 1973–1974 bear market, the U.S. economy endured several difficult years. Not until 1981 were we able to finally throw off the shackles of high inflation and high interest rates, setting the stage for a new bull market. And did we ever have one! In the past 20 years, we have seen the Dow Jones Industrial Average rise from 1,000 to over 10,000.

Another interesting trend during this extraordinary period of price appreciation is the increased activity and interest level of individual investors. Using Individual Retirement Accounts, self-directed 401(k) plans, discount brokers, and electronic trading, individuals have taken a much more hands-on role in managing their own financial affairs. The net effect has been to shift a large portion of financial assets and decision making away from professional investors.

This in no way implies that professional investors have been left with little to do. On the contrary, they have kept themselves busy inventing program trading, leveraged buyouts, derivative securities, and index futures. And they have launched hundreds of hedge funds at a dizzying pace. These funds have shown the ability to roll financial markets, crush foreign currencies, and put to risk the economies of entire countries. This constant game of "I can design a more complex strategy than you can," played at a feverish pace in order to generate the highest return in the shortest period of time, has frightened many investors.

Today, the distinction between one money manager and another has faded. Fundamental research has been replaced by the whir of computers. Black boxes have replaced management interviews and company investigations. Automation has replaced intuition. As a consequence, professional money managers have put more distance between the financial securities we own and the businesses these securities represent. No wonder the average investor is becoming more of a do-it-yourselfer. No wonder passive index investing has increased in popularity. With most money managers unable to add value to their clients' accounts, active money management is increasingly viewed as a "satellite" strategy, a smaller adjunct to the much larger indexing strategy.

Throughout the past few decades, money managers have flirted with many different investment approaches: small capitalization, large capitalization, growth, value, momentum, thematic, and sector rotation. At some point, each has proved financially rewarding, and each has stranded its followers in periods of mediocrity.

Buffett is the exception. He has rarely suffered periods of underperformance. His investment performance, documented over the past 45 years, has been consistently superior. What makes his record all the more remarkable is that, despite the market's ever-changing landscape, his investment strategy has changed very little. While other investors and speculators, over time, have been distracted by fads and have toyed with many esoteric approaches to investing, Buffett's consistent common-sense approach has helped him amass a multibillion-dollar fortune.

How did he do it?

When we study Buffett's success and compare his approach with the practices of a majority of other investors, we can easily distill critical differences in three areas. The differences have to do with the way Buffett:

1. Analyzes stocks.
2. Manages a portfolio.
3. Thinks about the stock market.

LESSON 1

Analyze Stocks as Businesses

When Buffett invests, he sees a business. When he looks at a stock, he quickly moves past the share price and begins to analyze the attributes of the business. One by one, he weighs them against the business tenets, the management tenets, and the financial tenets that represent the core of his investment analysis (see page 79). Next, he calculates what the business is worth. Only then does he take a look at the stock price.

Most other investors look *only* at the stock price. They spend far too much time and effort watching, predicting, and anticipating price changes, and far too little time understanding the business. And even when investors do try to gauge the value of a stock, they use single-factor models like price-to-earnings ratios, book values, and dividend yields. But these simple metrics, as we shall see, tell us nothing about the value of the company.

I am convinced this is a critical variable that helps to explain Buffett's investment success. Most people look only at stock factors; Buffett analyzes only business factors.

Buffett's unique combination of business experiences gives him an advantage that separates him from all other investors. He gained hands-on experience by owning and managing a wide variety of businesses while simultaneously investing in common stocks. He has experienced both success and failure in his business ventures, and he has applied to the stock market the lessons he learned.

Other professional investors have not had the same kind of education. While they were busy studying capital asset pricing models, beta, and modern portfolio theory, Buffett studied the income statements, balance sheets, capital reinvestment requirements, and cash-generating abilities of his companies.

That kind of direct experience offers insights that can be learned only from doing. As Buffett himself puts it, "Can you really explain to a fish what it's like to walk on land? One day on land is worth a thousand years of talking about it, and one day running a business has exactly the same kind of value."[2]

Owning and operating businesses has given Buffett a distinct advantage. But I do not mean to suggest that to be successful using the Warren Buffett tenets you first have to manage a business. What is most important for all investors, whether they have ever managed a business or not, is to think about the stock as if they actually had to manage the business.

LOOK AT THE STOCK AS A BUSINESS

Look at the company's economics, and look as intently as if you were taking over as CEO tomorrow. Then *check the price.*

Buffett believes the investor and the businessperson should look at the company in the same way because they both want essentially the same thing. The businessperson wants to buy the entire company, and the investor wants to buy portions of the company. If you ask businesspeople what they think about when purchasing a company, the most frequent answer is: "How much cash can be generated from the business?" Finance theory dictates that, over time, there is direct correlation between the value of the company and its cash-generating ability. Theoretically, then, the businessperson and the investor should be looking at the same variables.

"In our view," says Buffett, "investment students need only two well-taught courses: How to Value a Business, and How to Think About Market Prices."[3]

The necessary first step for anyone who wants to emulate Warren Buffett's approach is to think about stocks first and foremost as businesses. "Whenever Charlie [Munger] and I buy common stocks for Berkshire," Buffett has said, "we approach the transaction as if we were buying into a private business. We look at the economic prospects of the business, the people in charge of running it, and the price we must pay."[4]

LESSON 2

Manage a Focused, Low-Turnover Portfolio

In 1996, Stephen Jay Gould, the noted biologist, prolific writer, and lifelong Yankees fan, published *Full House: The Spread of Excellence from Plato to Darwin*. Gould is fascinated by the complex nature of life, and he studies intensely the variations of different systems. In this illuminating book, he talks about, among other things, the death of .400 hitting in major league baseball.

The record books say that between 1901 and 1930, a span of 30 years, there were nine seasons in which at least one player achieved a batting average better than .400. But in the 68 years that followed, only one player reached that milestone: Ted Williams hit .406 in 1941.

From those statistics, we might conclude that batting skills, over time, have deteriorated. But Gould wants us to consider the ease with which statistics can be misread. He believes another force is at work. Hitting is not getting worse, but, overall, defensive play is getting better. The pitching is more sophisticated, the fielding skills are better, and the team's ability to develop a full defense against strong hitting is much advanced. Gould the scientist explains, "As play improves and the bell curve marches toward the right wall, variation must shrink at the right tail. [And] .400 hitting disappears as a consequence of increasing excellence in play."[5]

Peter L. Bernstein, founding editor of the *Journal of Portfolio Management* and author of two outstanding works on finance—*Capital Ideas: The Improbable Origins of Modern Wall Street* and *Against the Gods: The Remarkable Story of Risk*—takes Gould's thesis on .400 hitting and applies it to the business of portfolio management. "The performance data for equity portfolio managers," he says, "reveals patterns that are astonishingly similar to what has happened in baseball."[6] Bernstein reasons that a lack of above-average performance by professional money managers is a result of the ever-increasing level of investment management education and knowledge. As more and more people become more and more skilled at investing, the odds of a breakout performance by a few superstars diminish.

It is an intriguing analogy. Following this argument to the end, one could conclude that heavy hitters like Warren Buffett will gradually be displaced completely by an efficient market of well-informed, intelligent investors. Indeed, Bernstein points out that Berkshire Hathaway's record, when compared against the S&P 500, was better in the 1960s and 1970s than in the 1980s and 1990s. However, I would argue: considering that the stock market is more competitive today and that Berkshire's enlarged capital base becomes a relative handicap in this kind of comparison, Warren Buffett still qualifies as a .400 hitter.

In his article (titled "Where, Oh Where Are the .400 Hitters of Yesteryear?"), Bernstein willingly left the back door unlocked in his performance analysis. He wrote that, to become a .400 hitter, the portfolio manager must be *"willing to make the kinds of concentrated bets that are essential if the aim is to provide high excess returns"* (emphasis added).[7] To my mind, "concentrated bets" equate to a focused portfolio of no more than 20 stocks. Never mind that Bernstein believes the risk of tracking error and high standard deviation would dissuade any portfolio manager from taking on a focus portfolio. The fact still remains: A focus portfolio stands the best chance of beating a market rate of return, and providing the "high excess returns" that only the .400 hitters can deliver.

Not surprisingly, if we open Bernstein's back door and look out, whom do we see? Brilliant financial thinkers: John Maynard Keynes, Phil Fisher, Warren Buffett, Charlie Munger, Lou Simpson, and Bill Ruane, all of whom we shall meet later. Just as a young rookie might have intently watched Ted Williams, we can learn a great deal by studying the batting stance and swing of these .400 hitters. As Buffett once said, "The key to life is to figure out who to be the batboy for."[8]

*B*est way to hit a home run: Don't swing at everything; wait for a fat pitch.

* * *

*B*est way to outperform the market: Don't load up on hundreds of stocks; wait for the few outstanding opportunities.

How many stocks should an investor own? Buffett would tell you it depends on your investment approach. If you have the ability to analyze and value businesses, then you are not likely to need many stocks. As a buyer of businesses, there is no law that requires you to own a stock from every major industry. And you are not required to include 40, 50, or 100 stocks in your portfolio to achieve adequate diversification. Even the high priests of modern finance have discovered that, on average, "85 percent of the available diversification is achieved with a fifteen-stock portfolio and increases to 95 percent with a thirty-stock portfolio."[9]

Buffett believes that the only investors who need wide diversification are those who do not understand what they are doing. If "know-nothing" investors want to own common stocks, they should own a large number of equities and space out their purchases over time. In other words, they should use an index fund and dollar-cost average their purchases. There is nothing shameful about this simple technique. In fact, Buffett points out, the index investor will actually outperform the majority of investment professionals. "Paradoxically," he notes, "when 'dumb' money acknowledges its limitations, it ceases to be dumb."[10]

A BETTER YARDSTICK

If adapting Buffett's investment strategy required only a change in perspective, then probably more investors would follow his lead. Unfortunately, applying Buffett's approach requires changing not only perspective but also how performance is evaluated and communicated.

The traditional yardstick for measuring performance is price change: the difference between the price originally paid for the stock and its market price today. In the long run, the market price should approximate the change in the value of the business. However, in the short run, prices gyrate widely above and below a company's value; they are dependent on factors other than the progress of the business. The problem remains that most investors use short-term price changes to gauge the success or failure of their investment approach. Unfortunately, these short-term price changes often have little to do with the changing economic value of the business and much to do with anticipating the behavior of other investors.

In addition, professional investors are required by their clients to report performance in quarterly periods. Frequently, clients become impatient while waiting for the price of their portfolio to advance at some predetermined rate. If they aren't seeing short-term performance gains, clients become dissatisfied and skeptical of the investment professional's ability. Knowing that they must improve short-term performance or risk losing clients, professional investors become obsessed with chasing stock prices.

Buffett believes it is foolish to use short-term prices to judge a company's success. Instead, he lets his companies report their value to him via their economic progress. Once a year, he checks several variables, including return on equity, changes in operating margins, debt levels, capital expenditure needs, and, lastly, the company's growth in cash earnings. If these economic measurements are improving, he knows the share price, over the long term, should reflect this improvement. What happens to the stock price in the short run is inconsequential.

Don't judge a company's success by short-term change in the price of its stock. Instead, consider the business fundamentals.

The difficulty of using economic measurements as yardsticks for success is that communicating performance in this manner is not customary. Clients and investment professionals alike are programmed to follow prices. The stock market reports price changes daily. The client's account statement reflects price changes monthly, and the investment professional is measured on the same basis quarterly. The answer to this dilemma may lie in employing Buffett's concept of "look-through" earnings, described in Chapter 6. The goal of the business owner, Buffett explains, is to create a portfolio of companies that, in 10 years, will produce the highest level of look-through earnings.

When growth of look-through earnings replaces price changes as the highest priority in your portfolio, many things begin to change. First, you are less likely to sell your best businesses just because you have a profit. Ironically, corporate managers understand this when they focus on their own business operation. "A parent company," Buffett explains, "that owns a subsidiary with superb long-term economics is not likely to sell that entity regardless of price."[11] A CEO wanting to increase the value of his or her business will not sell the company's crown jewel. Yet this same CEO will impulsively sell stocks in his or her personal portfolio with little more logic than "You can't go broke taking a profit." "In our view," Buffett explains, "what makes sense in business also makes sense in stocks: An investor should ordinarily hold a small piece of an outstanding business with the same tenacity that an owner would exhibit if he owned all the business."[12]

> *See yourself as owning a portfolio of businesses, not a portfolio of stocks.*

Now that you are managing a portfolio of businesses, not only will you avoid selling your best businesses, you will exercise much greater care when you pick new businesses for purchase. As the manager of a portfolio of businesses, you must resist the temptation to purchase a marginal company just because you have cash reserves. If the company does not pass your tenet screen, do not purchase it. Be patient and wait for the right business. It is wrong to assume that if you are not buying and selling, you are not making progress. In Buffett's mind, it is too difficult to make hundreds of smart decisions in a lifetime. He would rather position his portfolio so he has to make only a few smart decisions.

Ty Cobb once said, "Ted Williams sees more of the ball than any man alive—but he demands a perfect pitch." That intense discipline may explain why Williams is the only .400 hitter in the past seven decades. Warren Buffett is a great admirer of Ted Williams and, on several occasions, has shared Williams's disciplined approach with Berkshire's shareholders. In *The Science of Hitting*, Williams explained his technique. He divided the strike zone into seventy-seven cells, each representing the size of a baseball. Now, said Buffett, "Swinging only at the ball in his 'best' cell, Williams knew, would allow him to hit .400; reaching for the balls in the 'worst' spot, the low outside corner of the strike zone, would reduce him to .230."[13]

The investment analogy of Williams's hitting advice is obvious. For Buffett, investing is a series of "business" pitches, and, to achieve above-average performance, he must wait until a business comes across the strike zone in the "best" cell. Buffett believes investors too often swing at bad pitches, and their performance suffers. Perhaps it is not that investors are unable to recognize a good pitch—a good business—when they see one; maybe the difficulty lies in the fact that investors can't resist swinging the bat.

Don't be tempted to swing at the pitches that are low and outside. Learn to wait for the fat pitch. Williams, waiting for his best pitch, took risks of striking out. In that regard, investors have it easier, Buffett says. Unlike Williams, "We can't be called out if we resist three pitches that are barely in the strike zone."[14]

LESSON 3

Understand the Difference Between Investment and Speculation

What separates an investor from a speculator? This old but persistent debate has passionate proponents on both sides. Several great financial thinkers, including John Maynard Keynes, Ben Graham, and Warren Buffett, have all taken a turn at explaining the difference between investment and speculation.

According to Keynes, "Investment is an activity of forecasting the yield over the life of the asset; speculation is the activity of forecasting the psychology of the market."[15] For Graham, "An investment operation is one which, upon thorough analysis, promises safety of principal and a satisfactory return. Operations not meeting this requirement are speculative."[16] Buffett believes: "If you're an investor, you're looking at what the asset—in our case, businesses—will do. If you're a speculator, you're primarily forecasting on what the price will do independent of the business." (OID)[17]

Generally, they all agree that speculators are obsessed with guessing future prices, while investors focus on the underlying asset, knowing that future prices are tied closely to the economic performance of the asset. If they are correct, it would appear that much of the activity that dominates the financial markets today is speculation, not investing.

Perhaps we have been looking at this question the wrong way. Instead of getting into a shouting contest about what is investment and what is speculation, maybe we should concern ourselves more with the element of knowledge.[18]

I have come to believe that as we gain more understanding about how businesses work and how stock prices behave; as we begin to understand that focus portfolios, as opposed to broadly diversified portfolios, give the best chance of outperforming index funds; as we begin to appreciate that high-turnover portfolios increase our investment cost while low-turnover portfolios increase our potential return, then we have begun to lay the bricks of knowledge that drive us toward a focus investment approach.

Just as important, when we begin to understand the mathematical impossibility of predicting the future behavior of the stock market, we begin to look suspiciously at any speculative strategy that seeks to profit from anticipated changes in stock prices.

And when we understand the ill effects of the psychology of misjudgment, so pointedly emphasized by Charlie Munger (and discussed fully in Chapter 7), we also protect ourselves from making foolish mistakes. The psychology involved in investing is all-important, and Munger has done a great service to all investors by insisting that we pay attention to it. We can get the economics right and get the probabilities right, but if we allow our emotions to override our good judgment, there will be no benefit to the focus investment approach—or any other investment approach, for that matter.

It is important to remember that the focus investment approach is not for everyone. It is a unique style that is often at odds with how the majority of people think about investing. "Each person," says Charlie, "has to play the game given his marginal utility considerations and in a way that takes into account his own psychology. If losses are going to make you miserable—and some losses are inevitable—you might be wise to utilize a very conservative pattern of investment and savings all your life." (OID)[19]

Buffett would concur. As long as you have a long-term investment horizon, the risk of focus investing, says Buffett, "becomes the risk of yourself—of whether you're able to retain your belief in the real fundamentals of the business and not get too concerned about the stock market." (OID)[20]

THE SEARCH FOR PATTERNS

"Something about the mind, wired to find patterns both real and imaginary, rebels at the notion of fundamental disorder."[21] Those words, written by George Johnson in his book *Fire in the Mind,* reveal the dilemma that all investors face. The mind craves patterns, argues Johnson; patterns suggest order, which allows us to plan and make sense of our resources.

What we have come to understand is that Warren Buffett is seeking patterns—the patterns that can be found when analyzing a business. He also knows these business patterns will, at some point, reveal the future pattern of the stock price. Of course, a stock price pattern will not obligingly follow every change in the business pattern, but if your time horizon is long enough, it is remarkable how the price patterns eventually match up with the business patterns.

Too many investors are seeking patterns in the wrong place. They are certain that there is some predictable pattern for gauging short-term price changes. But they are mistaken. There simply are no predictable patterns for guessing the future direction of the stock market. The exact patterns do not repeat. Still, these investors keep trying.

15

How do investors maneuver in a world that lacks pattern recognition? By looking in the right place at the right level. Although the economy and the market as a whole are too complex and too large to be predictable, there are recognizable patterns at the company level. Inside each company, there are business patterns, management patterns, and financial patterns.

If you study those patterns, in most cases you can make a reasonable prediction about the future of that company. Warren Buffett focuses on those patterns, not on the unpredictable behavioral patterns of millions of investors. "I have always found it easier to evaluate weights dictated by fundamentals than votes dictated by psychology," he says.[22]

Always recognize the difference between investment and speculation, and develop the discipline never to cross the line.

One thing we can say with certainty is that knowledge works to increase our investment return and reduces overall risk. I believe we can also make the case that knowledge is what defines the difference between investment and speculation. In the end, the greater your level of knowledge, the less likely that pure speculation will dominate your thinking and your actions.

Ron Chernow, a talented financial writer, claims that "financial systems reflect the values of societies."[23] I believe that is largely true. From time to time, we seem to misplace our values, and then our markets succumb to speculative forces. Soon, we right ourselves and continue on with our financial walk, only to trip and fall back into destructive habits. One way to stop this vicious cycle is to educate ourselves about what works and what does not.

Early in his career, Warren Buffett drew an intellectual line between investment and speculation. His success has come from not only recognizing the difference between investment and speculation but having the discipline never to cross the line.

WHY HAS WALL STREET IGNORED WARREN BUFFETT?

The field of money management has, for several reasons, evolved into an antithesis of Warren Buffett. Amazingly, in an industry noteworthy for copying success, Wall Street has somehow managed to disregard focus investing, even though its practitioners have enjoyed phenomenal results. Given the documented success of Buffett's performance and the simplicity of his methodology, the question we must ask is: Why haven't more investors—professionals and individuals alike—applied his approach?

The answer, I believe, is twofold. It is linked partly to how society at large processes new ideas, and partly to how we as individuals embrace or resist change. For the first, we turn to Thomas Kuhn.

Kuhn, who died in 1996, was a physicist turned philosopher. His 1962 masterpiece, *The Structure of Scientific Revolutions,* is considered one of the most, if not *the* most, influential philosophical works of the latter half of the twentieth century. In this book, which has sold over a million copies, Kuhn described his theory of scientific evolution and introduced the concept of paradigms and the now-familiar phrase: "paradigm shifts."

Kuhn contended that progress in science does not always happen smoothly. Sometimes, it is triggered by crisis—tearing down the intellectual fabric of the prevailing model or paradigm, and then constructing a brand-new model. History gives us many examples; here are but two: The Copernican revolution replaced the idea of Earth's centrality, and Einstein's general theory of relativity unseated Euclidean geometry. In each case, before there was a paradigm shift, explained Kuhn, there was a crisis period. Some people believe that the current intellectual tug-of-war between broadly diversified portfolios and focus portfolios is such a crisis.

You might think that, in today's world, scientists would readily accept new and even contradictory information and then work collegially to construct a new paradigm. Nothing could be further from the truth, said Kuhn. "Though they [the proponents of the current paradigm] may begin to lose faith and then consider alternatives, they do not renounce the paradigm that has led them into crisis."[24] They tenaciously hold on to the old paradigm because they have invested so much personal intellectual capital in it. Accepting the new would be tantamount to admitting failure, and that is a risk not worth taking.

Something of the same dynamic is at work on the personal level for investors. Individually and collectively, we have become accustomed to one way of thinking about investing, and we are not interested in changing, especially if it means we would have to wait for a payoff. We have been seduced by the very qualities that make investing speculative: we want quicker solutions and quicker rewards. We want to see action today, not tomorrow.

According to Kuhn, the first step in a paradigm shift occurs when an anomaly is introduced. For years, academicians attempted to explain Buffett as an anomaly, or what statisticians call a five-sigma event. In their view, Buffett was so unusual that his success would occur only rarely and could be duplicated only by chance. Some economists used the classic orangutan analogy: If you put enough orangutans in a room, statistically one of them has to be able to pick stocks as well as Buffett. But if that is so, how are we to explain the success of John Maynard Keynes, Phil Fisher, Charlie Munger, Lou Simpson, and Bill Ruane?

A DIFFERENT WAY OF THINKING

Over the past several years, I have had the great fortune to study and write about the investment lessons of Warren Buffett and Charlie Munger. I have also had a chance to conduct original research on focus investing, and the front-line experience of managing a focus portfolio. The Legg Mason Focus Trust, which I have run since its inception in 1995, has given me invaluable experience on what it is like to manage a focus portfolio. During these years of interacting with shareholders, clients, consultants, analysts, other portfolio managers, and the financial media, I have learned that focus investors operate in a world far different from the one that dominates the investment industry. The simple truth is: They think *differently*.

Charlie Munger helped me to understand this pattern of thinking by using the very powerful metaphor of *a latticework of metal models*.[25] In 1995, Munger delivered a lecture entitled "Investing Expertise as a Subdivision of Elementary, Worldly Wisdom" to Professor Guilford Babcock's student investment seminar at the University of Southern California School of Business. The lecture, which was reprinted in *Outstanding Investor Digest*, was particularly fun for Charlie because it centered around a topic that he considers especially important: how people achieve true understanding, or what he calls "worldly wisdom."

Wisdom is not reflected in the simple exercise of compiling and quoting facts and figures. Rather, Munger explains, <u>wisdom is very much about how facts align and combine.</u> He believes that the only way to achieve wisdom is to be able to hang life's experiences across a broad cross-section of mental models. "You've got to have models in your head," he explained, "and you've got to array your experience—both vicarious and direct—on this latticework of models." (OID)[26]

The first rule to learn, says Charlie, is that you must carry multiple models in your mind. Not only do you need more than a few, but you need to embrace models from several different disciplines. Becoming a successful investor, he explains, requires a multidisciplinary approach to your thinking.

That approach will put you in a different place from almost everyone else, Charlie points out, because the world is not multidisciplinary. Business professors typically don't include physics in their lectures, and physics teachers don't talk about biology, and biology teachers don't include mathematics, and mathematics professors don't teach psychology. But Charlie believes we must ignore these "intellectual jurisdictional boundaries" and include all models in our latticework design.

"I think it is undeniably true that the human brain must work in models," says Charlie. "The trick is to have your brain work better than the other person's brain because it understands the most fundamental models—ones that will do the most work per unit." (OID)[27]

It is clear to me that focus investing does not fit neatly within the narrowly constructed models popularized and used in our investment culture. To receive the full benefit of the focus approach, we will have to add a few more concepts, a few more models, to our thinking. You will never be content with investing until you understand the behavior models that come from psychology. You will not know how to optimize a portfolio without learning the model of statistical probabilities.

The investigation need not be overwhelming. "You don't have to become a huge expert in any one of these fields," explains Charlie. "All you have to do is take the really big ideas and learn them early and learn them well." (OID)[28] The exciting part of this exercise, Charlie points out, is the insight that is possible when several models combine and begin operating in the same direction.

The most detailed model that focus investors have to learn is the model for picking stocks and managing portfolios. In the following chapters of this book, these models will be provided to you. Then we need to add just a few more simple models to complete our education. But we are not alone. We have Warren Buffett's and Charlie Munger's wisdom to guide us, and we have their accumulated experience at Berkshire Hathaway. Typically, these two visionaries credit not themselves personally but their organization, which they describe as a "didactic enterprise teaching the right systems of thought, of which the chief lessons are that a few big ideas really work." (OID)[29]

"Berkshire is basically a very old-fashioned kind of place," Charlie Munger said, "and we try to exert discipline to stay that way. I don't mean old-fashion stupid. I mean the eternal verities: basic mathematics, basic horse sense, basic fear, basic diagnosis of human nature making possible predictions regarding human behavior. If you just do that with a certain amount of discipline, I think it's likely to work out quite well." (OID)[30]

CHAPTER 2

THE WORLD'S GREATEST INVESTOR

Every year, *Forbes* magazine publishes a list of the 400 richest people in America, the very elite Forbes 400. Individuals on the list come and go from year to year, as their personal circumstances change and their industries rise and fall, but some names are constant. Among those leading the list year in and year out are certain megabillionaires who trace their wealth to a product (computer software or hardware), a service (retailing), or lucky parentage (inheritance). Of those perennially in the top five, only one made his fortune through investment savvy. That one person is Warren Buffett.

In the early 1990s, he was number one. Then, for a few years, he seesawed between number one and number two with a youngster named Bill Gates. Even for the year 2000, when so much of the wealth represented by the Forbes 400 came from the phenomenal growth in the technology area, Buffett, who smilingly eschews high-tech anything, was firmly in the fourth position—still the only person in the top five for whom the "Source of Wealth" column reads "Stock market."

In 1956, he started his investment partnership with $100; after 13 years, he cashed out with $25 million. At this writing (late 2000), his personal net worth has increased to over $30 billion, the stock in his company is selling at $71,300 a share, and literally millions of investors around the world hang on his every word.

Evidence of his unmatched performance is everywhere. In late 1999, a leading financial consulting firm asked investment professionals to select the best money manager of the twentieth century. The not very surprising answer: 86.4 percent of the 300 who responded named Warren Buffett number one.[1]

To fully appreciate Warren Buffett, however, we have to go beyond the dollars, the performance accolades, and the reputation.

■ INVESTMENT BEGINNINGS

Warren Edward Buffett was born August 30, 1930, in Omaha, Nebraska. His grandfather owned a grocery store (and once employed a young Charlie Munger); his father was a local stockbroker. As a boy, Warren Buffett was always fascinated with numbers and could easily do complex mathematical calculations in his head. At age 8, he began reading his father's books on the stock market; at age 11, he marked the board at the brokerage house where his father worked. His early years were enlivened with a succession of entrepreneurial ventures, and he was so successful that he told his father he wanted to skip college and go directly into business. He was overruled.

Buffett attended the business school at the University of Nebraska, and while there read a new book on investing by a Columbia professor named Benjamin Graham. It was *The Intelligent Investor*. Buffett was so taken with Graham's ideas that he applied to Columbia Business School so that he could study directly with Graham. Bill Ruane, who now co-manages the Sequoia Fund, was in the same class. He recalls that there was an instantaneous mental chemistry between Graham and Buffett, and the rest of the class was primarily an audience.[2]

Not long after Buffett graduated from Columbia with a master's degree in economics, Graham invited his former student to join his company, the Graham-Newman Corporation. During his two-year tenure there, Buffett became fully immersed in his mentor's investment approach. Then, in 1956, Graham-Newman disbanded and Graham, at age 61, decided to retire. Buffett returned to Omaha. Armed with the knowledge he had acquired from Graham, with the financial backing of family and friends, and with $100 of his own money, Buffett began a limited investment partnership. He was 25 years old.

THE BUFFETT PARTNERSHIP, LTD.

The partnership began with seven limited partners who together contributed $105,000. The limited partners received 6 percent annually on their investment and 75 percent of the profits above this bogey; the remaining 25 percent went to Buffett, who as general partner had essentially free rein to invest the partnership's funds.

Over the next 13 years, Buffett compounded money at an annual rate of 29.5 percent.[3] It was no easy task. Although the Dow Jones Industrial Average declined in price during five of those years, Buffett's partnership never had a down year. Buffett, in fact, had begun the partnership with the very ambitious goal of outperforming the Dow by 10 points every year. And he did it—not by 10 points, but by 22!

As Buffett's reputation grew, more people asked him to manage their money. In 1962, Buffett moved the partnership office from his home to Kiewit Plaza in Omaha, where his office remains today. The next year, he made a stunning purchase.

Tainted by a scandal involving one of its clients, American Express saw its shares drop from $65 to $35 almost overnight. Buffett had learned Ben Graham's lesson well: when stocks of a strong company are selling below their intrinsic value, act decisively. Buffett made the very bold decision to put $13 million

25

(40 percent of the partnership's total assets) into American Express stock. Over the next two years, the shares tripled in price and the partners netted a cool $20 million in profit. It was pure Graham, and pure Buffett.

In the ensuing years, in addition to significant minority positions, Buffett bought controlling interests in several public and private companies, and in 1962, he began purchasing shares in an ailing textile company called Berkshire Hathaway.

In 1969, explaining that he found the market highly speculative and worthwhile values increasingly scarce, Buffett decided to end the investment partnership. When the partnership disbanded, investors received their proportional interests. Some of them, at Buffett's recommendation, sought out money manager Bill Ruane, his old classmate at Columbia. Ruane agreed to manage their money, and thus was born the Sequoia Fund. Others, including Buffett, invested their partnership revenues in Berkshire Hathaway. By that point Buffett's share of the partnership had grown to $25 million, and that was enough to give him control of Berkshire Hathaway.

THE EARLY DAYS OF BERKSHIRE HATHAWAY

When the Buffett Partnership took control of Berkshire Hathaway, stockholders' equity had dropped by half and loss from operations exceeded $10 million. Buffett and Ken Chace, who managed the textile group, labored intensely to turn the textile mills around. Results were disappointing; returns on equity struggled to reach double digits.

By the late 1970s, shareholders of Berkshire Hathaway, which by then had expanded its holdings into other industries through Buffett's investment of cash earnings, began to question the wisdom of retaining an investment in textiles. After a few more difficult years, Buffett closed the books on the textile

26

group in July 1985, thus ending a business that had begun some 100 years earlier.

Despite the misfortunes of the textile group, the experience was not a complete failure. First, Buffett learned <u>a valuable lesson about corporate turnarounds</u>: <u>They seldom succeed</u>. Second, the textile group did generate enough capital in the earlier years to buy an insurance company, and that is a much brighter story.

THE INSURANCE BUSINESS

In March 1967, Berkshire Hathaway purchased, for $8.6 million, the outstanding stock of two insurance companies headquartered in Omaha: National Indemnity Company and National Fire & Marine Insurance Company. It was the beginning of Berkshire Hathaway's phenomenal success story. Berkshire Hathaway the textile company would not long survive, but Berkshire Hathaway the investment company that encompassed it was about to take off.

To appreciate the phenomenon, we must recognize the true value of owning an insurance company. Sometimes insurance companies are good investments, sometimes not. They are, however, always terrific investment *vehicles*. Policyholders, by paying their premiums, provide a constant stream of cash; insurance companies invest this cash, known as the "float," until claims are filed. Because they cannot predict when claims will occur, insurance companies opt to invest in liquid marketable securities—primarily stocks and bonds. Thus, Warren Buffett had acquired not only two modestly healthy companies, but a cast-iron vehicle for managing investments.

For a seasoned stock picker like Buffett, it was a perfect match. In just two years, he increased the combined stock and bond portfolio of the two companies from $31.9 million to nearly $42 million. At the same time, the insurance businesses themselves were doing quite well. In just one year, the net income of National Indemnity rose from $1.6 million to $2.2 million. Buffett's early success in insurance led him to expand aggressively into this group. During the 1970s, he purchased three additional insurance companies and organized five more.

Warren Buffett understands the insurance business in a way that few others do. His success derives in large part from understanding the essential commodity nature of the industry, and elevating *his* insurance companies to the level of a franchise. In a commodity business, where the products of any one company are indistinguishable from those of its competitors, one common way to gain market share is to cut prices. Other companies were willing to sell insurance policies below the cost of doing business rather than risk losing market share. Buffett held firm: Berkshire's insurance operations would not move into unprofitable territory.

Unwilling to compete on price, Buffett instead seeks to distinguish Berkshire's insurance companies in two other ways. First, by financial strength. Today, Berkshire's net worth ranks second only to State Farm in the property/casualty industry. Additionally, the ratio of Berkshire's investment portfolio to its premium volume is three times the industry average.

The second method of differentiation involves Buffett's underwriting philosophy. His goal is simple: Always write large volumes of insurance but only at prices that make sense. If prices are low, he is quite content to do very little business. This philosophy was instilled at National Indemnity by its founder, Jack Ringwalt, and Berkshire has never wavered from this underwriting discipline. Buffett's approach is likened to a stabilizer for the insurance industry. When competitors vanish from the marketplace because they are frightened by recent losses, Berkshire stands by as a constant supplier of insurance—but only at prices that make sense.

Throughout the 1990s, the insurance industry as a whole endured very rough times: brutal price competition, continual underwriting losses, and poor investment results combined to produce a decidedly shaky picture. Buffett, as we shall see, was not deterred.

GEICO

Warren Buffett first became acquainted with GEICO— Government Employees Insurance Company—while a student at Columbia. His mentor, Ben Graham, was chairman of GEICO's board of directors. A favorite part of the Buffett lore is the now-familiar story of the young student's visit to the company's offices on a Saturday morning. He pounded on the door until a janitor let him in, then spent five hours getting an education in the insurance business from the only person working that day: Lorimer Davidson, an investment officer who eventually became the company's CEO. What he learned intrigued him.

GEICO had been founded on a couple of simple but fairly revolutionary concepts: If you insure only people with good driving records, you'll have fewer claims; and if you sell directly to customers, without agents, you keep overhead costs down.

Back home in Omaha and working for his father's brokerage firm, a very young Warren Buffett wrote a report of GEICO for a financial journal in which he noted, in what may be the understatement of that decade, "there is reason to believe the major portion of growth lies ahead."[4] Buffett himself put $10,282 in the company, then sold it the next year at 50 percent profit. But he always kept track of the company.

Throughout the 1950s and 1960s, GEICO prospered. But then it began to stumble. For several years the company had tried to expand its customer base by underpricing its policies and relaxing its eligibility requirements. Two years in a row, it seriously miscalculated the amount needed for reserves (out of which claims are paid). The combined effect of these mistakes was that, by the mid-1970s, the once-bright company was near bankruptcy.

When the stock price dropped from \$61 to \$2 a share in 1976, Warren Buffett started buying. Over a period of five years, with an unshakable belief that it was a strong company with its basic competitive advantages unchanged, he invested \$45.7 million in GEICO.

The very next year, 1977, the company was profitable again. Over the next two decades, GEICO had positive underwriting ratios—meaning that it took in more in premiums than it paid out in claims—in every year but one. In the industry, where negative ratios are the rule rather than the exception, that kind of record is almost unheard of. And that excess float gives GEICO tremendous resources for investments, which are brilliantly managed by a remarkable man named Lou Simpson, whom we shall meet again in Chapter 6.

By 1991, Berkshire owned nearly half (48 percent) of GEICO. The insurance company's impressive performance, and Buffett's interest in the company, continued to climb. In 1994, serious discussions about Berkshire's buying the entire company began; a year later, the final deal was announced. At that point, Berkshire owned 51 percent of GEICO and agreed to purchase the rest for \$2.3 billion—this at a time when most of the insurance industry struggled with profitability and most investors stayed away in droves. By the time all the paperwork was done, it was early 1996. At that point, GEICO officially became a wholly owned unit of Berkshire Hathaway, managed independently from Berkshire's other insurance holdings.

Buffett's trust in the basic concept of GEICO has been handsomely rewarded. From 1996 to 1999, the company increased its share of market from 2.7 percent to 4.1 percent. In 1999 alone, the customer base grew by 766,256, adding \$590 million in cash from operating earnings and the increase in float. Because its profit margins increase the longer policyholders stay with the company, GEICO focuses on building long-term relationships with customers, each of whom pays, on average, premiums of \$1,100 year after year but most of whom maintain excellent driving records. As Buffett points out, the economics of that formula are simple: "Cash is pouring in rather than going out."[5]

From the early bargain days of $2 a share in 1976, Buffett paid close to $70 a share for the rest of the company in 1996. He makes no apologies. He considers GEICO a unique company with unlimited potential, something worth paying a hefty price for. In this perspective—if you want the very best companies, you have to be willing to pay up when they become available— Buffett has been profoundly influenced by his partner, Charlie Munger, whom we shall meet in the next chapter.

Given their close working relationship, it's a fair bet that Munger had a lot to say about Berkshire's other big insurance decision of the 1990s.

General Re Corporation

In 1996, Buffett paid $2.3 billion to buy the half of GEICO he didn't already own; two years later, he paid *seven times* that amount—about $16 billion in Berkshire Hathaway stock—to acquire a reinsurance company called General Re.[6] It was his biggest acquisition by far.

Reinsurance is a sector of the insurance industry not well known to the general public, for it doesn't deal in the familiar products of life, homeowner's, or auto insurance. In simplest terms, reinsurers insure other insurance companies. Through a contract that spells out how the premiums and the losses are to be apportioned, a reinsurer takes on some percentage of the original company's risk. This allows the primary insurer to assume a higher level of risk, reduces its needs for operating capital, and moderates loss ratios.

For its part, the reinsurer receives a share of the premiums earned, and can invest them as it sees fit. At General Re, that investment has been primarily in bonds. This, as we shall see in a moment, was a key part of Buffett's strategy in buying the company.

Just after Berkshire bought General Re (GenRe), the company had one of its worst years. In 1999, GenRe paid claims resulting from natural disasters (a major hailstorm in Australia, earthquakes in Turkey, and a devastating series of storms in Europe), from the largest house fire in history ($20 million), and from high-profile movie flops (the company had insured box-office receipts). To make matters worse, GenRe was part of a grouping of several insurers and reinsurers that became ensnarled in a workers' compensation tangle that ended in multiple litigation and a loss exposure of approximately $275 million for two years running (1998 and 1999).

Warren Buffett, as is well known, takes the long view. The market strengths of General Re—in particular, their fit with the financial strengths of Berkshire Hathaway—produce the kind of synergy that significantly elevates the long-term future of both. As Buffett remarked in a press conference around the time of the merger announcement, "We're creating Fort Knox here."[7]

When Buffett acquired it, General Re owned approximately $19 billion in bonds, $5 billion in stocks, and $15 billion in float. By using Berkshire stock to buy the company (and its heavy bond portfolio), Buffett in one neat step shifted the balance of Berkshire's overall holdings from 80 percent stocks to 60 percent stocks. When the IRS ruled, late in 1998, that the merger involved no capital gains, that meant he had managed to "sell" almost 20 percent of Berkshire's equity holdings, thus deftly sidestepping the worst of price volatility, essentially tax-free.

The only significant staff change following the merger was the elimination of General Re's investment unit. Some 150 people had been in charge of deciding where to invest the company's funds; they were replaced with just one individual: Warren Buffett.

Buffett continually reminds shareholders that financial soundness and fiscal responsibility will make a significant difference for

Berkshire Hathaway. Nowhere is this more evident than in Berkshire's insurance holdings—a group that comprises 28 separate companies, including GEICO and General Re (each of which has many subsidiaries) and the two original Omaha-based companies. It's no wonder that Buffett notes, in his typical straightforward way, "Our main business is insurance."[8]

Berkshire's superior financial strength has distinguished its insurance operations from the rest of the industry. We can say, therefore, that the financial integrity that Buffett has imposed on Berkshire's insurance companies has created a franchise in what is otherwise a commodity business.

A MOSAIC OF OTHER BUSINESSES

Berkshire Hathaway, Inc., as it exists today, is best understood as a holding company. In addition to the insurance companies, it owns a newspaper, a candy company, an ice cream/hamburger chain, several furniture stores, a carpet manufacturer, a paint company, a building-products company, a company that provides private jets to businesses on a time-share basis, a jewelry store, an encyclopedia publisher, a vacuum cleaner business, a public utility, a couple of shoe companies, and a company that manufactures and distributes uniforms—among others.

Some of these companies, particularly the more recent acquisitions, are jewels that Buffett found in a typically Buffett-like way: he advertised for them in the Berkshire Hathaway annual reports.

His criteria are straightforward: a simple, understandable business with consistent earning power, good return on equity, little debt, and good management in place. He's interested in companies in the $5 billion to $20 billion range, the larger the better. He's not interested in turnarounds, hostile takeovers, or tentative situations where no asking price has been determined. He promises complete confidentiality and a quick response.

In Berkshire Hathaway's annual reports and in remarks to shareholders, he has often described his acquisition strategy this way: "It's very scientific. Charlie and I just sit around and wait for the phone to ring. Sometimes it's a wrong number."[9]

The strategy works. Through the public announcement in annual reports, and also through referrals from managers of current Berkshire companies, Buffett has acquired an amazing string of successful businesses. In this chapter, we have space for an abbreviated tour of just five of them.

The story of how Buffett came to acquire these diverse businesses is interesting in itself. Perhaps more to the point, the stories collectively give us valuable insight into Buffett's way of looking at companies. It will come as little surprise that he uses the same yardstick to evaluate companies for possible acquisitions as for additions to the Berkshire Hathaway stock portfolio.

See's Candy Shops

In 1921, a 71-year-old grandmother named Mary See opened a small neighborhood candy shop in Los Angeles, selling chocolates made from her own recipes. With the help of her son Charles and his partner, the business slowly grew into a small chain in southern and northern California. It survived the Depression, survived sugar rationing during World War II, and survived intense competition, through one unchanging strategy: never compromise the quality of the product.

Some 50 years later, See's had become the premier chain of candy shops on the West Coast, and Mary See's heirs were ready to move on to the next phase of their lives. Charles Huggins, who had joined the company 30 years earlier, was given the job of finding the best buyer and coordinating the sale. Several suitors came calling, but no engagement was announced.

Enter Warren Buffett. Late in 1971, an investment adviser to Blue Chip Stamps, of which Berkshire Hathaway was then the majority shareholder, proposed that Blue Chip should buy See's. After a quick look at the numbers, Buffett was ready to talk.

The asking price was $40 million, but because See's had $10 million in cash, the net price was actually $30 million. Buffett offered $25 million and the sellers accepted. When the purchase became final, early in 1972, Buffett, encouraged by his partner Charlie Munger, had paid three times book value. It was the first major shift away from Graham's philosophy of buying a company only when it was underpriced in relation to its hard book value. It was, Charlie Munger later remarked, "the first time we paid for quality."[10]

Ten years later, Buffett was offered $125 million to sell See's—five times the 1972 purchase price. He decided to pass. It was a wise decision. Between 1972 and 1999, the candy stores with the distinctive black-and-white decor and a logo featuring the likeness of Mary See earned $857 million pretax and required very little additional capital expenditures. In 1999, its pretax operating profit was $73 million, and its operating margin was a record 24 percent.[11]

Buffett gives 100 percent of the credit for this success to CEO Chuck Huggins. "Charlie and I put him in charge the day of our purchase, and his fanatical insistence on both product quality and friendly service has rewarded customers, employees, and owners. Chuck gets better every year. When he took charge of See's at age 46, the company's pretax profit, expressed in millions, was about 10 percent of his age. Today he's 74, and the ratio has increased to 100 percent. Having discovered this mathematical relationship—let's call it Huggins' Law—Charlie and I now become giddy at the mere thought of Chuck's birthday."[12]

Nebraska Furniture Mart

The Nebraska Furniture Mart (NFM), in Buffett's hometown of Omaha, is the largest single home furnishings complex in the country: 1.2 million square feet.

The business began in 1937. A Russian immigrant named Rose Blumkin, who had been selling furniture to friends and neighbors from her basement, put up $500 to open a small store. From the beginning, her business strategy was simple and straightforward: "Sell cheap and tell the truth." It worked.

After many years of admiring the store's success, Warren Buffett stopped in one day in 1983 and asked to speak to the owner. Mrs. B, as she was always known, later recounted the exchange:

"He said, 'Today's my birthday and I want to buy your store. How much do you want for it?' I tell him $60 million. He goes, gets a check, and comes right back."[13]

As it turned out, the family wanted to retain 20 percent of the store, so Buffett ended up paying $55 million for 80 percent ownership. Mrs. B's son Louie and his three sons were retained to manage the business. But Mrs. B, chairman of the board, remained where she had always been: right at the heart of the operation.

At the time Buffett bought NFM, Mrs. B was 90 years old and was still working seven days a week. Six years later, after squabbling with family members over plans to expand NFM's carpet department, she abruptly resigned and opened a competing store across the street. Three years later, Berkshire bought her out. Mrs. B was then age 99. She immediately returned to working 60 hours a week at NFM, scooting around the warehouse in her motorized golf cart, and terrorizing salespeople she thought were slacking off by bumping into them from behind.

Mrs. B died in August 1998, at the age of 104. A fearless dynamo just 4 feet 10 inches tall, she never attended school and never learned to read or write English. Yet she built a business that, at the time she sold it to Buffett, was generating $100 million in annual sales.

Even in those years when she was his competitor, Buffett's admiration for Mrs. B never wavered. More than once, he noted that business school students could learn a great deal more from watching Mrs. B for a few months than from years in graduate school.

Borsheim's

Soon after Mrs. B immigrated from Russia, her parents and five brothers and sisters followed. Rose's youngest sister, Rebecca, married Louis Friedman and together they purchased a small jewelry store in Omaha in 1948. Mr. Friedman's son, Ike, joined the family business in 1950. Eventually, Ike was followed by his son, Alan, and two sons-in-law, Donald Yale and Marvin Cohn. The Friedmans never changed the store's original name: Borsheim's.

What worked for the Blumkins in the furniture business worked for the Friedmans in the jewelry trade: "Sell cheap and tell the truth." Like the original Furniture Mart, Borsheim's jewelry store has one large location. For this reason, Borsheim's expense ratios are several points lower than those of most competitors. Borsheim's generates high sales volume and strong buying power. With an eye on expenses, and with store traffic that averages 2,500 on most Sundays and easily reaches 4,000 on seasonal buying days, the Friedmans have a recipe for success.

Also like the Nebraska Furniture Mart, Borsheim's has been able to widen its market share beyond Omaha. Some customers travel hundreds of miles to shop at Borsheim's. The company also has a strong mail-order business, which helps to keep operating costs low—18 percent of sales, compared to 40 percent of sales for most competitors. By keeping costs down, Borsheim's is able to sell at low prices and expand its market share. According to Buffett, Borsheim's store in Omaha does more jewelry business than any other store in the country, except for Tiffany's in New York City.

As to how Buffett came to acquire his interest in Borsheim's, the story goes that, while Christmas shopping in

December 1988, he was casually looking at a ring when Donald Yale, Irv Friedman's son-in-law, who later became Borsheim's CEO, spotted his famous customer. "Don't sell him the ring," he shouted, "sell him the store!"[14]

A few months later, Buffett asked if indeed the store might be for sale. After two brief meetings—one at Ike Friedman's house and one at Buffett's office—the sale was agreed upon, at a purchase price estimated at more than $60 million.

Donald Yale, who was present at both meetings, described the negotiations. "The substantive part of the talk was ten minutes. He asked us five questions and Ike had a price. The three of us met later at Buffett's office and Ike and Warren shook hands on the sale. The contract was short—the signatures were longer than the contract."[15]

Buffett's questions were:

1. What are sales?
2. What are gross profits?
3. What are expenses?
4. What's in inventory?
5. Are you willing to stay on?

In any other case, Buffett would also have asked about debt level, but he already knew that Borsheim's had none.

The Scott & Fetzer Company

The Scott & Fetzer Company (Scott Fetzer) is a conglomerate of 22 separate companies, including the makers of Kirby vacuum cleaners; *World Book* Encyclopedias; Wayne furnace burners and sump, utility, and sewage pumps; and Campbell Hausfeld air compressors, air tools, and painting systems. The company is headquartered in Westlake, Ohio, and is managed by Ralph Schey.

Buffett paid $315 million in cash for Scott Fetzer's businesses in January 1986. It was one of Berkshire's largest business acquisitions up to that point. Since that time, this purchase has exceeded his own optimistic expectations. The company has capably reduced its investment in both fixed assets and inventory, and achieves high levels of earnings with very little debt. In fact, Buffett calculates that Scott Fetzer's return on equity would easily place it among the top 1 percent of the Fortune 500.

Scott Fetzer's various companies make a range of rather esoteric (some would say boring) industrial products, but what they really make is money for Berkshire Hathaway. In 1998, for example, the company earned a record $96.5 million, aftertax, on its $112 million net worth—all with no leverage.

Look for companies that create high return on equity with minimal debt.

Executive Jet

Anyone who has observed Warren Buffett for any length of time knows about Berkshire Hathaway's corporate jet, named *The Indefensible* in wry acknowledgment of Charlie Munger's objections to the purchase. So strong was Buffett's affection for this one luxury that the investment world took careful note when he *sold* the jet a few years ago, explaining that he had found something better.

That something was a company called Executive Jet Aviation (EJA) and its program of fractional ownership of private jets, known as NetJets. It is the brainchild of CEO Rich Santulli, former head of the leasing division of Goldman Sachs and a mathematician by training. After leaving Goldman, Santulli took his leasing experience and formed a company that leased aircraft; in 1984, his leasing company acquired another company called Executive Jet, which had been created 20 years earlier by former Air Force officers but was, by that time, in serious difficulty. It gave Santulli the base he needed to try an idea he had been working on.

He knew that with commercial airlines, business travelers paid a premium price for mediocre service—the same crowded airports, flight delays, and lost luggage as recreation travelers paying far less for their tickets. The only alternative then available was owning or leasing private jets—an expense that only few could afford, and even more expensive considering how much it costs for those planes to sit on the ground. Santulli's idea was to sell shares in business-class jets—similar to time shares at vacation resorts—to provide individuals and businesses with the convenience of a private plane at a fraction of the cost.

Using his mathematics background, Santulli thoroughly analyzed the costs and worked out how many fractional owners he would need to acquire enough planes and pilots to guarantee owners a plane with four hours' notice. In 1986, NetJets opened for business. Santulli had, it was later remarked, created an entirely new industry.

After some rough going during the recession of the early 1990s, the NetJets program steadily grew. Then, in 1995, Warren Buffett became an owner. Buffett was introduced to the company by the manager of one of Berkshire's operating companies, and instantly recognized the strength of the concept. He bought a one-fourth interest in a Hawker 1000 and, for the next three years, publicly praised the idea, the company, and the man who had created it. He even sold the now-indefensible *Indefensible*.

In 1995, Santulli, searching for new sources of funds in order to expand into Europe, had sold part of the company to his former employer, Goldman Sachs. Three years later, Goldman began pressuring Santulli to take the company public. He was not thrilled with the prospect, but the cash infusion would

40

help him buy more planes and hire more pilots. Santulli went to one of his owners for advice.

"What do you think?" he asked Warren Buffett.

"Well," Buffett responded, "what if I buy the company?"[16]

And thus, for $725 million, Buffett acquired Executive Jet, which he confidently predicted would explode over the following decade. One measure of its success: imitation. Where once EJA was the only company offering fractional ownership, now several others have come on the scene. Executive Jet, however, with 75 percent of the market, still dominates the industry it essentially invented.

The mathematics of the concept are especially intriguing to Buffett. Since the customers own the planes, the company's capital involvement is low. Even modest operating margins can bring excellent return on equity. Berkshire receives what amounts to a stream of royalties, and uses the revenues to finance an aggressive expansion program.

After Buffett bought it, Executive Jet instantly became the fastest-growing division of Berkshire Hathaway. Its largest problem has been getting enough planes to fill the growing demand. In the 1999 Berkshire Hathaway annual report, Buffett wrote, "We now are taking delivery of about 8 percent of all business jets manufactured in the world, and we wish we could get a bigger share than that. Though EJA was supply-constrained in 1999, its recurring revenues—monthly management fees plus hourly flight fees—increased 46 percent."[17]

THE MAN AND HIS COMPANY

Warren Buffett is not easy to describe. Physically he is unremarkable, with looks often described as grandfatherly. Intellectually he is considered a genius, yet his down-to-earth relationship with people is truly uncomplicated. He is simple, straightforward, forthright, and honest. He displays an engaging combination of sophisticated dry wit and cornball humor. He has a profound reverence for all things logical and a foul distaste for imbecility. He embraces the simple and avoids the complicated.

Reading the annual reports, one is struck by how comfortable Buffett is quoting the Bible, John Maynard Keynes, or Mae West. The operable word here is "reading." Each report is 60 to 70 pages of dense information: no pictures, no color graphics, no charts. Those who are disciplined enough to start on page one and continue uninterrupted are rewarded with a healthy dose of financial acumen, folksy humor, and unabashed honesty. Buffett is very candid in his reporting. He emphasizes both the pluses and the minuses of Berkshire's businesses. He believes that people who own stock in Berkshire Hathaway are owners of the company, and he tells them as much as he would like to be told if he were in their shoes.

The company that Buffett directs, Berkshire Hathaway, is the embodiment of his personality, his business philosophy, and his own unique style. Looking at Berkshire, we can see Buffett's key principles in operation. All the qualities that Buffett looks for in companies he's considering buying are displayed in his own company. And here too, we see the Buffett philosophy reflected in some unusual and refreshing corporate policies. Two examples are the charity designation program, and the compensation program.

Executive compensation has become a source of heated debate between shareholders and management. Annual salaries of senior management can easily exceed $1 million. In addition to these lofty salaries, executives of publicly traded companies are customarily rewarded with fixed-price stock options, often tied to corporate earnings but very seldom tied to the executive's job performance.

This goes against the grain for Buffett. When stock options are passed out indiscriminately, he says, managers with below-average performance are rewarded on a par with managers who have had excellent performance. In Buffett's mind, even if your team wins the pennant, you don't offer a .350 hitter the same deal as a .150 hitter when it's contract-signing time.

At Berkshire, Buffett uses a compensation system that rewards managers for performance. The reward is not tied to the size of the enterprise, the individual's age, or Berkshire's overall profits. As far as Buffett is concerned, good unit performance should be rewarded whether Berkshire's stock price rises or falls. Instead, executives are compensated based on their success at meeting performance goals keyed to their area of responsibility. Some managers are rewarded for increasing sales, others for reducing expenses or curtailing capital expenditures. At the end of the year, Buffett does not hand out stock options; he writes checks. Some are quite large. Managers can use the cash as they please. Many purchase Berkshire stock, thereby ultimately taking the same risks as the owners.

Perhaps nothing so typifies Buffett's unique way of doing things as Berkshire's method of distributing charitable donations. It is called the *shareholder designation program*. Shareholders, based on the proportional number of shares they own, can designate the recipients of Berkshire's charitable contributions. At most corporations, the senior officers and board members select the charities that will benefit from corporate contributions. Often, they choose their own favorite charities, and shareholders—whose money is being given—have no input on this decision. Buffett rejects this system. "When A takes money from B to give to C," he says, "and A is a legislator, the process is called taxation. But when A is an officer or director of a corporation, it is called philanthropy."[18]

At Berkshire, the shareholder names the charity and Berkshire writes the check. In 1981, the first year of this program, Berkshire distributed $1.7 million to 675 charities. In 1999, more than $17 million was given to 3,850 charities. In those 19 years, Berkshire contributed more than $147 million to charities its shareholders named.

It is only one small measure of Berkshire's phenomenal financial success. When Buffett took control of Berkshire, the corporate net worth was $22 million. Thirty-five years later, it has grown to $69 billion, more than $20 billion of which represents the recent acquisition of General Re. It has long been Buffett's goal to increase the book value of Berkshire Hathaway at a 15 percent annual rate—well above the return achieved by the average American company. Since he took control of Berkshire in 1964, the gain has been much greater: book value per share has grown from $19 to $37,987, a rate of 24 percent compounded annually. This relative performance is all the more impressive when we consider that Berkshire is penalized by both income and capital gains taxes and the Standard & Poor's 500 returns are pretax.

On a year-by-year basis, Berkshire's returns have at times been volatile; changes in the stock market, and thus in the underlying stocks that Berkshire owns, create wide swings in per-share value (see Table 2.1). This was particularly evident in 1999, when the net increase in per share value was only 0.5 percent. This result originated from two factors: (1) poor return on consumer nondurables (Coca-Cola and Gillette) and (2) the outstanding performance of technology stocks, which Berkshire does not own. Speaking with the candor for which he is famous, Buffett admitted in the 1999 annual report that "truly large superiorities over the [S&P] index are a thing of the past."[19] Now his goal is to beat the S&P "modestly."

This in no way diminishes the overall track record, nor does it weaken the investment philosophy on which the long-term success was built. I believe that the fundamental principles that have so long guided Buffett's decisions are uncompromised, and that they still carry opportunities for careful investors to outperform the S&P 500. The purpose of this book is to present those principles in such a way that they can be understood and used by thoughtful investors.

Berkshire Hathaway, Inc., is complex but not complicated. It owns several businesses—the insurance companies and the other businesses described in this chapter, plus others not described due to space limitations—and, using the income stream from insurance premiums, it also buys shares in publicly traded

Table 2.1 Berkshire Hathway, Inc.

| Year | Annual Percentage Change | | |
	Per-Share Book Value of Berkshire Hathaway (1)	S&P 500 Index (2)	Relative Results (1)–(2)
1965	23.8	10.0	13.8
1966	20.3	−11.7	32.0
1967	11.0	30.9	−19.9
1968	19.0	11.0	8.0
1969	16.2	−8.4	24.6
1970	12.0	3.9	8.1
1971	16.4	14.6	1.8
1972	21.7	18.9	2.8
1973	4.7	−14.8	19.5
1974	5.5	−26.4	31.9
1975	21.9	37.2	−15.3
1976	59.3	23.6	35.7
1977	31.9	−7.4	39.3
1978	24.0	6.4	17.6
1979	35.7	18.2	17.5
1980	19.3	32.3	−13.0
1981	31.4	−5.0	36.4
1982	40.0	21.4	18.6
1983	32.3	22.4	9.9
1984	13.6	6.1	7.5
1985	48.2	31.6	16.6
1986	26.1	18.6	7.5
1987	19.5	5.1	14.4
1988	20.1	16.6	3.5
1989	44.4	31.7	12.7
1990	7.4	−3.1	10.5
1991	39.6	30.5	9.1
1992	20.3	7.6	12.7
1993	14.3	10.1	4.2
1994	13.9	1.3	12.6
1995	43.1	37.6	5.5
1996	31.8	23.0	8.8
1997	34.1	33.4	0.7
1998	48.3	28.6	19.7
1999	0.5	21.0	−20.5

Source: Berkshire Hathaway, Inc., 1999 Annual Report.

Notes: Data are for calendar years with these exceptions: 1965 and 1966, year ended 9/30; 1967, 15 months ended 12/31.

Starting in 1979, accounting rules required insurance companies to value the equity securities they hold at market rather than at the lower of cost or market, which was previously the requirement. In this table, Berkshire's results through 1978 have been restated to conform to the changed rules.

companies. Running through it all is Warren Buffett's down-to-earth way of looking at businesses: whether it be a business he's considering buying outright, a business he's evaluating for stock purchase, or the management of his own company. Those who would aspire to a measure of Buffett's success could do far worse than adopt his philosophy.

CHAPTER 3

LESSONS FROM THE THREE WISE MEN OF FINANCE

The education of Warren Buffett is best understood as a synthesis of three distinct investment philosophies from the minds of three powerful figures: Benjamin Graham, Philip Fisher, and Charles Munger.

The Graham influence on Buffett is well known and, in some instances, has been considered all-encompassing. This is not altogether surprising, considering the entwined histories of the two men. Buffett was first an interested reader of Graham, then a student, an employee, a collaborator, and, finally, Graham's peer. Graham molded Buffett's untrained mind. However, those who consider Buffett to be the singular product of Graham's teachings are ignoring the influence of two other towering financial minds: Philip Fisher and Charles Munger. We will study both of them later in this chapter.

◼ BENJAMIN GRAHAM

Graham is considered the dean of financial analysis. He was awarded that distinction because "before him there was no [financial analysis] profession and after him they began to call it that."[1] Graham's two most celebrated works are *Security Analysis*, coauthored with David Dodd and originally published in 1934; and *The Intelligent Investor*, originally published in 1949. *Security Analysis* appeared just a few years after the 1929 stock market crash and in the depths of the nation's worst depression. While other academicians sought to explain this economic phenomenon, Graham helped people regain their financial footing and proceed with a profitable course of action.

Graham was born in London on May 9, 1894. His parents emigrated to New York when he was an infant. Graham's earliest education was at Boys High, in Brooklyn. At age 20, he received a Bachelor of Science degree from Columbia University and election to Phi Beta Kappa. Graham was fluent in Greek and Latin and had a scholarly interest in mathematics and philosophy.

Despite his nonbusiness education, he began a career on Wall Street. He started as a messenger at the brokerage firm of Newburger, Henderson & Loeb, posting bond and stock prices on a blackboard for $12 a week. From messenger, he rose to writing research reports and soon was awarded a partnership in the firm. By 1919, at age 25, he was earning an annual salary of $600,000.

In 1926, Graham formed an investment partnership with Jerome Newman. It was this partnership that hired Buffett some 30 years later. Graham-Newman survived the 1929 crash, the Great Depression, World War II, and the Korean War, before it was dissolved in 1956.

From 1928 through 1956, while at Graham-Newman, Graham taught night courses in finance at Columbia. Few people know that Graham was financially ruined by the 1929 crash. For the second time in his life—the first being when his father died, leaving the family financially unprotected—Graham set about to rebuild his fortune. The haven of academia allowed Graham the opportunity for reflection and reevaluation. With the counsel of David Dodd, also a professor at Columbia, Graham produced what became the classic treatise on conservative investing.

Between them, Graham and Dodd had over 15 years of investment experience. It took them four years to complete *Security Analysis*. When the book first appeared, in 1934, Louis Rich wrote in *The New York Times:* "It is a full-bodied, mature, meticulous and wholly meritorious outgrowth of scholarly probing and practical sagacity. If this influence should ever exert itself, it will come about by causing the mind of the investor to dwell upon securities rather than upon the market."[2]

In the first edition, Graham and Dodd dedicated significant attention to corporate abuses. Prior to the Securities Acts of 1933 and 1934, corporate information was misleading and totally inadequate. Most industrial companies refused to divulge sales information, and the valuation of assets was frequently suspect. Corporate misinformation was used to manipulate the prices of securities, both in initial public offerings and in the aftermarkets.

After the Securities Acts, corporate reforms were slow but deliberate. By the time the third edition of the book appeared in 1951, references to corporate abuses were eliminated and, in their place, Graham and Dodd addressed the problems of stockholder-management relations—principally, management's competence and the policy on dividends.

The essence of *Security Analysis* is that a well-chosen diversified portfolio of common stocks, based on reasonable prices, can be a sound investment. Step by careful step, Graham helps investors to see the logic of his approach.

The first problem that Graham had to contend with was the lack of a single universal definition for *investment*. Quoting Justice Louis Brandeis, Graham pointed out that "investment is a word of many meanings." And the issue, he noted, does not turn on whether the item is a stock (and therefore speculative by definition) or a bond (and therefore an investment). The purchase of a poorly secured bond cannot be considered an investment just because it is a bond. Neither can a stock with a per-share price that is less than its net current assets be considered a speculation just because it is a stock. The decision to purchase a security with borrowed money, in hopes of making a quick profit, is speculation, regardless of whether the security is a bond or a stock. Here, Graham says, intention more than character will determine whether the security is an investment or a speculation.

ESSENTIAL GRAHAM

A true investment is that which thorough analysis shows will offer both safety of principal and a satisfactory return. Anything less is speculation.

Considering the complexities of the issue, Graham proposed his own definition: "An investment operation is one which, upon thorough analysis, promises safety of principal and a satisfactory return. Operations not meeting these requirements are speculative."[3] Graham preferred to speak of investment as an operation that precludes the purchase of a single issue. Early on, Graham recommended diversifying investments to reduce risk.

The "thorough analysis" that he insisted upon was explained as "the careful study of available facts with the attempt to draw conclusions therefrom based on established principles and sound logic."[4] And then he went further, describing analysis as a three-step function: (1) descriptive, (2) critical, and (3) selective.

In the descriptive phase, the analyst gathers all the facts outstanding and presents them in an intelligent manner. In the critical phase, the analyst is concerned with the merits of the standards used to communicate information. Ultimately, the analyst is interested in the fair representation of the facts. In the selective phase, the analyst passes judgment on the attractiveness or unattractiveness of the security in question.

For a security to be considered an investment, said Graham, there must be some degree of safety of principal and a satisfactory rate of return. He cautioned that safety is not absolute. Rather, the investment should be considered safe from loss under reasonable conditions. Graham admitted that a most unusual or improbable occurrence can put a safe bond into default.

Satisfactory return—the second necessity—includes not only income but price appreciation. Graham noted that "satisfactory" is a subjective term. He did say that return can be any amount, however low, as long as the investor acts with a degree of intelligence and adheres to the full definition of investment. An individual who conducts a thorough financial analysis based on sound logic, indicating a reasonable rate of return without compromising safety of principal, would be considered, by Graham's definition, an investor, not a speculator.

Had it not been for the bond market's poor performance, Graham's definition of investing might have been overlooked. But when, between 1929 and 1932, the Dow Jones Bond Average declined from 97.70 to 65.78, bonds could no longer be mindlessly labeled pure investments. As with stocks, bonds lost considerable value and many issuers went bankrupt. What was needed, therefore, was a process that could distinguish the investment characteristics of *both* stocks and bonds from their speculative counterparts.

Throughout his career Graham continued to be disturbed by the issues of investment and speculation. Toward the end of his life, he watched with dismay as institutional investors embraced actions that were clearly speculative. Shortly after the 1973–1974 bear market, Graham was invited to attend a conference of money managers hosted by Donaldson, Lufkin and

Jenrette. As Graham sat at the conference roundtable, he was shocked by what was being admitted by his professional peer group. "I could not comprehend," he said, "how the management of money by institutions had degenerated from sound investment to this rat race of trying to get the highest possible return in the shortest period."[5]

Graham's second contribution—after distinguishing between investment and speculation—was a methodology whereby the purchase of common stocks would qualify as an investment. Before *Security Analysis*, little had been accomplished using a quantitative approach to selecting stocks. Prior to 1929, most listed common stocks were railroads. Industrial and utility companies were a small portion of the overall list of stocks, and banks and insurance companies, the favorites of wealthy speculators, were not listed. Companies that arguably had investment value—primarily railroads—traded at a price that was close to their par value. These companies were backed by real capital value.

As the country entered the bull market of the 1920s, the general disposition of all stocks, including industrials, began to improve. Prosperity fueled further investment, most notably in real estate. Despite 1925's short-lived Florida real estate boom, which was followed by the Florida real estate bust of 1926, commercial banks and investment banking firms continued to recommend real estate. Investment in real estate spurred investment activity in general and, ultimately, business activity. This link continued to fan the flames of optimism. As Graham noted, uncontrolled optimism can lead to mania, one of the chief characteristics of which is its inability to recall the lessons of history.

Looking back, Graham identified three forces that he felt were responsible for the stock market crash. First was the manipulation of stocks by the exchanges and investment firms. Every day, brokers were told which stocks to "move" and what to say in order to generate excitement about them. Second was the common practice of lending money for the purpose of buying stocks. Banks freely loaned money to speculators, who anxiously awaited the latest hot tip from Wall Street. Bank lending for securities purchases rose from $1 billion in 1921 to $8.5 billion in 1929. The loans were backed by the value of stocks, so when the crash occurred, everything tumbled down. The third force was the uncontrolled optimism that was driving it all.

Today, securities laws protect individuals from brokerage fraud, and the practice of buying securities on margin is greatly curtailed compared to the 1920s. But the one area that could not be legislated, yet in Graham's mind was just as responsible for the crash, was excessive optimism.

The danger of 1929 was not that speculation tried to masquerade as investing but rather that investing fashioned itself into speculation. Graham noted that historical optimism was rampant. Encouraged by the past, investors projected forward an era of continued growth and prosperity. The buyers of stocks began to lose their sense of proportion about price. Graham said people were paying prices for stocks without any sense of mathematical expectation; stocks were worth any price that the optimistic market quoted. At the height of this insanity, the line between speculation and investment blurred.

When the full impact of the stock market crash was felt, common stocks were once again labeled "speculations." As the Depression began, the whole concept of common stock investing was anathema. However, noted Graham, investment philosophies change with psychological states. After World War II, confidence in common stocks rose once again. When Graham wrote the third edition of *Security Analysis*, between 1949 and 1951, he acknowledged that common stocks had become an instrumental part of an investor's portfolio.

In the 20 years following the 1929 crash, numerous academic studies analyzed the different approaches to common stock investing. Graham himself described three approaches: (1) the cross-section approach, (2) the anticipation approach, and (3) the margin of safety approach.

The cross-section approach would be the equivalent of today's index investing. As Graham explained it, selectivity was exchanged for diversification. An investor would purchase equal amounts of the 30 industrial companies of the Dow Jones Index and benefit equally as well as those selected companies. Graham pointed out that there was no certainty that Wall Street could accomplish results that were better than this index.

The anticipation approach he subdivided into short-term selectivity and the growth stock approach. Using short-term selectivity, investors seek to profit from companies that have the most favorable outlook over the near term—usually, six months to a year. Wall Street expends a great deal of energy forecasting the economic prospects that a company can expect to achieve over the short term, including sales volume, costs, and earnings. The fallacy of this approach, according to Graham, was that sales and earnings are often volatile and the anticipation of near-term economic prospects could easily be discounted in the stock price. Lastly, and more fundamentally, Graham charged that the value of an investment is not what it will earn this month or next, or what next quarter's sales volume will be, but what that investment can expect to return to an investor over a long period of time. Decisions based on short-term data are too often superficial and temporary. Not surprising, because of its emphasis on change and frequent transactions, short-term selectivity is the dominant approach on Wall Street.

Growth stocks, simplistically defined, are companies that grow sales and earnings at rates above the average business. Graham used the National Investors Corporation definition, which identified growth companies as those with earnings that move from cycle to cycle. The difficulties of succeeding with the growth stock approach, explained Graham, centered on investors' ability to identify growth companies and then to ascertain the degree to which the current share price already discounted the growth potential of the company.

Each company has what is called a life cycle of profits. In the early development stage, a company's revenues accelerate and earnings begin to materialize. During the rapid expansion stage, revenues continue to grow, profit margins expand, and there is a sharp increase in earnings. When a company enters the mature growth stage, revenues begin to slow and so do earnings. In the last stage, known as stabilization-decline, revenues drop and profit margins and earnings decline.

Growth investors, according to Graham, face a dilemma. If they select a company that is in the rapid expansion stage, they may find that the success of the company is temporary. Because the company has not endured years of testing, profits may soon evaporate. On the other hand, a company in the mature growth stage may be about to move into the stabilization-decline period, when earnings begin to shrink. The ability to pinpoint where a company is in its life cycle has perplexed financial analysts for decades.

If we assume that an investor has accurately pinpointed a growth company, what price should the investor pay? Obviously, if it is well known that a company is in a period of prosperity, its share price will be relatively high. But how are we to know, Graham asked, whether the price is *too* high? The answer is difficult to determine. Furthermore, even if the price could be accurately determined, the investor immediately faces a new risk: the company may grow more slowly than anticipated. If this occurs, the market likely will price the shares lower and the unlucky investor will have paid too much.

There is a third approach to selecting common stocks; Graham called it the *margin of safety approach*. Investors who are optimistic about a company's future growth and believe that the company will be a suitable addition to their portfolio have two techniques for purchase: (1) purchase shares of the company when the overall market is trading at low prices (generally, this occurs during a bear market or a similar type of correction), or (2) purchase the stock when it trades below its intrinsic value even though the overall market is not substantially cheap. In either technique, said Graham, a margin of safety is present in the purchase price.

The first technique—buying securities only at market lows—leads to some difficulties. It entices the investor to develop some formula that indicates when the market is expensive and when it is cheap. The investor, Graham explained, then becomes hostage to predicting market turns, a process that is far from certain. Also, when the market is fairly valued, investors are unable to profitably purchase common stocks. However, waiting for a market correction before purchasing stocks may become tiring and, in the end, futile.

Graham suggested that an investor's energies would be better applied to the second technique: identifying undervalued securities regardless of the overall market price level. For this strategy to work systematically, Graham admitted, investors need a way to identify undervalued stocks. The goal of the analyst is to develop the ability to recommend stocks that are selling below their calculated value.

The notion of buying undervalued securities regardless of market levels was a novel idea in the 1930s and 1940s. It was Graham's goal to outline such a strategy.

Graham reduced the concept of sound investing to a motto he called the "margin of safety." With this motto he sought to unite all securities—stocks *and* bonds—in a singular approach to investing. If, for example, an analyst reviewed the operating history of a company and discovered that, on average, for the past five years, a company was able to earn annually five times its fixed charges, then the company's bonds, said Graham, possessed a margin of safety. Graham did not expect investors to accurately determine the company's future income. Instead, he figured that if the margin between earnings and fixed charges was large enough, investors would be protected from an unexpected decline in the company's income.

Establishing a margin of safety concept for bonds was not too difficult. The real test was Graham's ability to adapt the concept for common stocks. Graham reasoned that a margin of safety existed for common stocks if the price of the stock was below its intrinsic value.

ESSENTIAL GRAHAM

When a stock is priced well below its intrinsic value, a margin of safety automatically exists.

For the concept to work, analysts needed a technique for determining a company's intrinsic value. Graham's definition of intrinsic value, as it appeared in *Security Analysis,* was "that value which is determined by the facts." These facts included a company's assets, its earnings and dividends, and any future definite prospects.

Graham admitted that the single most important factor in determining a company's value was its future earnings power. Simply stated, a company's intrinsic value could be found by estimating the earnings of the company and multiplying the earnings by an appropriate capitalization factor. This capitalization factor, or multiplier, was influenced by the company's stability of earnings, assets, dividend policy, and financial health.

He added a strong caution: Use of the intrinsic value approach was limited by an analyst's imprecise calculations for a company's economic future. He was concerned that an analyst's projections could be easily negated by a host of potential future factors. Sales volume, pricing, and expenses are difficult to forecast, which makes applying a multiplier that much more complex.

Not to be dissuaded, Graham suggested that the margin of safety could work successfully in three areas. First, it worked well with stable securities such as bonds and preferred stocks. Second, it could be used in comparative analysis. Third, if the spread between the price and the intrinsic value of a company was large enough, the margin of safety concept could be used to select stocks.

Graham asked us to accept that intrinsic value is an elusive concept. It is distinct from the market's quotation price. Originally, intrinsic value was thought to be the same as a company's book value, or the sum of its real assets minus its obligations. This notion led to the early belief that intrinsic value was definite. However, analysts came to know that the value of a company was not only its net real assets but also the value of the earnings that these assets produced. Graham proposed that it was not essential to determine a company's exact intrinsic value; instead, an approximate measure or range of value was acceptable. Even an approximate value, compared against the selling price, would be sufficient to gauge the margin of safety.

Financial analysis is not an exact science, said Graham. To be sure, certain quantitative factors lend themselves to thorough analysis: balance sheets, income statements, earnings and dividends, assets and liabilities. However, some qualitative factors are not easily analyzed but are nonetheless essential ingredients in a company's intrinsic value. Two qualitative factors are customarily addressed: management capability and the nature of the business.

Graham, generally, had misgivings about the emphasis placed on qualitative factors. Opinions about management and the nature of a business are not easily measurable, and that which is difficult to measure, reasoned Graham, could be badly measured. It was not that Graham believed these qualitative factors had no value. Rather, when investors placed too much emphasis on these elusive concepts, the potential for disappointment increased. Optimism over qualitative factors often found its way to a higher multiplier. Graham's experience led him to believe that, to the extent investors moved away from hard assets and toward intangibles, they invited potentially risky ways of thinking.

Make sure of your ground, said Graham. Start with net asset values as the fundamental departure point. If you bought assets, your downside was limited to the liquidation value of those assets. Nobody, reasoned Graham, can bail you out of optimistic growth projections if those projections are unfilled. If a company was perceived to be an attractive business and its superb management was predicting high future earnings, it would no doubt attract a growing number of stock buyers. "So they [investors] will buy it," said Graham, "and in doing so they will bid up the price and hence the price to earnings ratio. As more and more investors become enamored with the promised return, the price lifts free from underlying value and floats freely upward, creating a bubble that expands beautifully until finally it must burst."[6]

If the greatest amount of a company's intrinsic value is measured in the quality of management, the nature of the business, and optimistic growth projections, there is little margin of safety, said Graham. If, on the other hand, a greater amount of a company's intrinsic value is the sum of measurable, quantitative factors, Graham figured that the investor's downside was more limited. Fixed assets are measurable. Dividends are measurable. Current and historical earnings are measurable. Each of these factors can be demonstrated by figures and becomes a source of logic referenced by actual experience.

Graham said that having a good memory was his one burden. The memory of being financially deprived twice in a lifetime led him to embrace an investment approach that stressed downside protection versus upside potential.

There are two rules of investing, said Graham. The first rule is: Don't lose. The second rule is: Don't forget rule number one. This "don't-lose" philosophy steered Graham toward two approaches to selecting common stocks that, when applied, adhered to the margin of safety: (1) buy a company for less than two-thirds of its net asset value, and (2) focus on stocks with low price-to-earnings ratios.

Buying a stock for a price that is less than two-thirds of its net assets fit neatly into Graham's sense of the present and satisfied his desire for some mathematical expectation. Graham gave no weight to a company's plant, property, and equipment. Furthermore, he deducted all of the company's short- and long-term liabilities. What remained was the net current assets. If the stock price was below this per-share value, Graham reasoned, a margin of safety existed and a purchase was warranted. Graham considered this to be a foolproof method of investing. He did clarify that the results were based on the probable outcome of a group of stocks (diversification), not on the basis of individual results. Such stocks were pervasive at bear-market bottoms and more scarce during bull markets.

Acknowledging that waiting for a market correction before making an investment may be unreasonable, Graham set out to design a second approach to buying stocks. He focused on stocks that were down in price and sold at a low price-to-earnings ratio. Additionally, the company must have some net asset value; in other words, the company must owe less than its worth. Throughout his career, Graham worked with several variations of this approach. Shortly before his death, he was revising the fifth edition of *Security Analysis* with Sidney Cottle. At that time, Graham was analyzing the financial results of stocks that were purchased based on: a ten-year low price-to-earnings multiple, a stock price that was equal to half its previous market high, and, of course, a net asset value. Graham tested stocks back to 1961 and found the results very promising.

Many other investors, over the years, have searched for similar shortcuts for determining intrinsic value, and low price-to-earnings ratios—Graham's first technique—have been generally favored. Recently, however, we have learned that making decisions on these ratios alone is not enough to ensure profitable returns. Today, most investors rely on John Burr Williams's classic definition of value, as described in his book, *The Theory of Investment Value:* the value of any investment is the discounted present value of its future cash flow. We will learn more about this dividend discount model in Chapter 4.

For now, we should note that both of Graham's approaches—buying a stock for less than two-thirds of net asset value, and buying stocks with low price-to-earnings multiples—had a common characteristic. The stocks that Graham selected based on these methods were deeply out of favor with the market. Some macro- or microevent caused the market to price these stocks below their value. Graham felt strongly that these stocks, priced "unjustifiably low," were attractive purchases.

Graham's conviction rested on certain assumptions. First, he believed that the market frequently mispriced stocks, usually because of the human emotions of fear and greed. At the height of optimism, greed moved stocks beyond their intrinsic value, creating an overpriced market. At other times, fear moved prices below intrinsic value, creating an undervalued market. His second assumption was based on the statistical phenomenon known as "reversion to the mean," although he did not use that term. More eloquently, he quoted the poet Horace: "Many shall be restored that now are fallen, and many shall fall that now are in honor." However stated, by statistician or poet, Graham believed that an investor could profit from the corrective forces of an inefficient market.

PHILIP FISHER

While Graham was writing *Security Analysis,* Philip Fisher was beginning his career as an investment counselor. After graduating from Stanford's Graduate School of Business Administration, Fisher began work as an analyst at the Anglo London & Paris National Bank in San Francisco. In less than two years, he was made head of the bank's statistical department. From this perch, he witnessed the 1929 stock market crash. Then, after a brief and unproductive career with a local brokerage house, Fisher decided to start his own investment counseling firm. On March 1, 1931, Fisher & Company began soliciting clients.

Starting an investment counseling firm in the early 1930s might have appeared foolhardy, but Fisher figured he had two advantages. First, any investor who had any money left after the crash was probably very unhappy with his or her existing broker. Second, in the midst of the Depression, businesspeople had plenty of time to sit and talk with Fisher.

At Stanford, one of Fisher's business classes had required him to accompany his professor on periodic visits to companies in the San Francisco area. The professor would get the business managers to talk about their operations, and often helped them solve an immediate problem. Driving back to Stanford, Fisher and his professor would recap what they observed about the companies and managers they visited. "That hour each week," Fisher said, "was the most useful training I ever received."[7]

From these experiences, Fisher came to believe that superior profits could be made by (1) investing in companies with above-average potential and (2) aligning oneself with the most capable management. To isolate these exceptional companies, Fisher developed a point system that qualified a company according to the characteristics of its business and its management.

ESSENTIAL FISHER

Investment success depends on finding companies that can sustain above-average growth, in both sales and profits, over a period of several years. Short-term results are deceptive.

The characteristic of a company that most impressed Fisher was its ability to grow sales and profits, over the years, at rates greater than the industry average.[8] To do that, Fisher believed that a company needed to possess "products or services with sufficient market potential to make possible a sizable increase in sales for at least several years."[9] Fisher was not so much concerned with consistent annual increases in sales. Rather, he judged a company's success over a period of several years. He was aware that changes in the business cycle would have a material effect on sales and earnings. However, he believed that two types of companies would, decade by decade, show promise of above-average growth: (1) those that were "fortunate and able" and (2) those that were "fortunate because they are able."

Aluminum Company of America (Alcoa) was an example, he said, of the first type. The company was "able" because the founders of the company were people of great ability. Alcoa's management foresaw the commercial uses for their product and worked aggressively to capitalize the aluminum market to increased sales. The company was also "fortunate," said Fisher, because events outside of management's immediate control were having a positive impact on the company and its market. The swift development of airborne transportation was rapidly increasing sales of aluminum. Because of the aviation industry, Alcoa was benefiting far more than management had originally envisioned.

Du Pont was a good example of a company that was "fortunate because it was able," according to Fisher. If Du Pont had stayed with its original product, blasting powder, the company would have fared as well as most typical mining companies. But because management capitalized on the knowledge it had gained through the manufacturing of gunpowder, Du Pont was able to launch new products—including nylon, cellophane, and Lucite—that created their own markets, ultimately producing billions of dollars in sales for Du Pont.

A company's research and development efforts, noted Fisher, contribute mightily to the sustainability of its above-average growth in sales. Obviously, he explained, neither Du Pont nor Alcoa would have succeeded over the long term without a significant commitment to research and development. Even nontechnical businesses need a dedicated research effort to produce better products and more efficient services.

In addition to research and development, Fisher examined a company's sales organization. According to him, a company could develop outstanding products and services but, unless they were "expertly merchandised," the research and development effort would never translate into revenues. It is the responsibility of the sales organization, Fisher explained, to help customers understand the benefits of a company's products and services. A sales organization, he added, should also monitor its customers' buying habits and be able to spot changes in customers' needs. The sales organization, according to Fisher, becomes the invaluable link between the marketplace and the research and development unit.

However, market potential alone is insufficient. Fisher believed that a company, even though capable of producing above-average sales growth, was an inappropriate investment if it was unable to generate profits for shareholders. "All the sales growth in the world won't produce the right type of investment vehicle if, over the years, profits do not grow correspondingly," he said.[10] Accordingly, Fisher examined a company's profit margins, its dedication to maintaining and improving those margins, and, finally, its cost analysis and accounting controls.

Fisher believed that superior investment returns were never obtained by investing in marginal companies. Those companies often produce adequate profits during expansion periods but see their profits decline rapidly during difficult economic periods. For this reason, Fisher sought companies that were not only the lowest-cost producers of products or services but were dedicated to remaining so. A company with a low breakeven point, or a correspondingly high profit margin, is better able to withstand depressed economic environments. Ultimately, it can drive out weaker competitors, thereby strengthening its own market position.

No company, said Fisher, will be able to sustain its profitability unless it is able to break down the costs of doing business while simultaneously understanding the cost of each step in the manufacturing process. To do so, he explained, a company must instill adequate accounting controls and cost analysis. This cost information, Fisher noted, enables a company to direct its resources to those products or services with the highest economic potential. Furthermore, accounting controls will help identify snags in a company's operations. These snags, or inefficiencies, act as an early-warning device aimed at protecting the company's overall profitability.

Fisher's sensitivity about a company's profitability was linked with another concern: a company's ability to grow in the future without requiring equity financing. If a company is able to grow only by issuing equity, he said, the larger number of shares outstanding will cancel out any benefit that stockholders might realize from the company's growth. A company with high profit margins, explained Fisher, is better able to generate funds internally. These funds can be used to sustain its growth without any dilution of the existing shareholders' ownership via equity financing. In addition, a company that is able to maintain adequate cost controls over its fixed assets and working capital needs is better able to manage its cash needs and avoid equity financing.

ESSENTIAL FISHER

Superior management is the key to superior market performance.

Fisher was aware that superior companies not only possess above-average business characteristics but, equally important, are directed by people with above-average management capabilities. These managers are determined to develop new products and services that will continue to spur sales growth long after current products or services are largely exploited. Many companies, Fisher noted, have adequate growth prospects because their existing lines of products and services will sustain them for several years, but few companies have policies in place to ensure consistent gains for 10 to 20 years. "Management," he said, "must have a viable policy for attaining these ends with all the willingness to subordinate immediate profits for the greater long-range gains that this concept requires."[11] Subordinating immediate profits, he explained, should not be confused with sacrificing immediate profits. An above-average manager has the ability to implement the company's long-range plans while simultaneously focusing on daily operations.

Fisher considered another trait critical: Does the business have a management of unquestionable integrity and honesty? Do the managers behave as if they are trustees for the stockholders, or does it appear as if management is only concerned with its own well-being?

One way to determine their intention, Fisher confided, is to observe how managers communicate with shareholders. All businesses, good and bad, will experience a period of unexpected difficulties. Commonly, when business is good, management talks freely, but when business declines, some managers clam up rather than talking openly about the company's difficulties. How management responds to business difficulties, Fisher noted, tells a lot about the people in charge of the company's future.

For a business to be successful, he argued, management must also develop good working relations with all of its employees. Employees should genuinely feel that their company is a good place to work. Blue-collar employees should feel that they are treated with respect and decency. Executive employees should feel that promotion is based on ability, not favoritism.

Fisher also considered the depth of management. Does the chief executive officer have a talented team, he asked, and is the CEO able to delegate authority to run parts of the business?

Finally, Fisher examined the specific characteristics of a company: its business and management aspects, and how it compares to other businesses in the same industry. In this search,

Fisher tried to uncover clues that might lead him to understand the superiority of a company in relation to its competitors. He argued that reading only the financial reports of a company is not enough to justify an investment. The essential step in prudent investing, he explained, is to uncover as much about a company as possible, from individuals who are familiar with the company. Fisher admitted this was a catch-all inquiry that would yield what he called "scuttlebutt." Today, we might call it the business grapevine. If handled properly, Fisher claimed, scuttlebutt will provide substantial clues that will enable the investor to identify outstanding investments.

Fisher's scuttlebutt investigation led him to interview as many sources as possible. He talked with customers and vendors. He sought out former employees as well as consultants who had worked for the company. He contacted research scientists in universities, government employees, and trade association executives. He also interviewed competitors. Although executives may sometimes hesitate to disclose too much about their own company, Fisher found that they never lack an opinion about their competitors. "It is amazing," he said, "what an accurate picture of the relative points of strength and weaknesses of each company in an industry can be obtained from a representative cross-section of the opinions of those who in one way or another are concerned with any particular company."[12]

Most investors are unwilling to commit the time and energy Fisher felt was necessary for understanding a company. Developing a scuttlebutt network and arranging interviews are time-consuming activities; replicating the scuttlebutt process for each company under consideration can be exhausting. Fisher found a simple way to reduce his workload—he reduced the number of companies he owned. He always said he would rather own a few outstanding companies than a larger number of average businesses. Generally, his portfolios included fewer than ten companies, and three or four companies often represented 75 percent of his entire equity portfolio.

ESSENTIAL FISHER

Owning a few outstanding companies is better than owning a large number of average ones. Among other advantages, it simplifies your research time.

Fisher believed that, to be successful, investors only needed to do a few things well. One was investing only in companies that were within their circle of competence. Fisher said his earlier mistakes were "to project my skill beyond the limits of experience. I began investing outside the industries which I believed I thoroughly understood, in completely different spheres of activity; situations where I did not have comparable background knowledge."[13]

CHARLIE MUNGER

When Warren Buffett began his investment partnership in Omaha in 1956, he had just over $100,000 in capital to work with. One early task, therefore, was to persuade additional investors to sign on. He was making his usual careful and detailed pitch to neighbors Dr. and Mrs. Edwin Davis, when suddenly Dr. Davis interrupted him and abruptly announced they'd give him $100,000. When Buffett asked why, Davis replied, "Because you remind me of Charlie Munger."[14]

Charlie who?

Even though both men grew up in Omaha and had many acquaintances in common, Buffett and Munger did not actually meet until 1959. By that time, Munger had moved to southern California. When he returned to Omaha for a visit when his father died, Dr. Davis decided it was time the two young men met, and he brought them together at a dinner in a local restaurant. It was the beginning of an extraordinary partnership.

Munger, the son of a lawyer and grandson of a federal judge, had established a successful law practice in the Los Angeles area, but his interest in the stock market was already strong. At that first dinner, the two young men found much to talk about, including securities. From then on, they communicated often, with Buffett frequently urging Munger to quit law and concentrate on investing. For a while, Munger did both. In 1962, he formed an investment partnership, much like Buffett's, while still maintaining his law practice. Three very successful years later, he left the law altogether, although to this day he has an office in the firm that bears his name.

Munger's investment partnership in Los Angeles, and Buffett's in Omaha, were similar in approach; both sought to purchase some discount to underlying value. (They also enjoyed similar results; both of them outperformed the Dow Jones Industrial Average by impressive margins.) It is not surprising, then, that they bought some of the same stocks. Munger, like Buffett, began buying shares of Blue Chip Stamps in the late 1960s, and eventually became chairman of its board. When Berkshire and Blue Chip Stamps merged in 1978, he became Berkshire's vice chairman, a position he still holds.

The working relationship between Munger and Buffett was not formalized in an official partnership agreement, but it has evolved over the years into something perhaps even closer and more symbiotic. Even before Munger joined the Berkshire board, the two made many investment decisions together, often conferring daily; gradually, their business affairs became more and more interlinked.

Today, Munger continues as vice chairman of Berkshire Hathaway and serves as chairman of Wesco Financial, which is 80 percent owned by Berkshire and holds many of the same investments as Berkshire. In every way, he functions as Buffett's acknowledged co-managing partner and alter ego. To get a sense of how closely the two are aligned, we have only to count the number of times Buffett reports that "Charlie and I" did this, or decided that, or believe this, or looked into that, or think this—almost as if "Charlie-and-I" were the name of one person.

To their working relationship Munger brought not only financial acumen but the foundation of business law. He also brought an intellectual perspective that is quite different from Buffett's. Munger is passionately interested in many areas of knowledge—science, history, philosophy, psychology, mathematics—and believes that each of those fields holds important concepts that thoughtful people can, and should, apply to all their endeavors, including investment decisions. He calls them "the big ideas," and they are the core of his well-known notion of a latticework of mental models for investors, a concept we noted in Chapter 1.

Together, all these threads—financial knowledge, background in the law, and appreciation of lessons from other disciplines—produced in Munger an investment philosophy somewhat different from Buffett's. Whereas Buffett was still searching for opportunities at bargain prices, Munger believed in paying a fair price for quality companies. He can be very persuasive.

Munger convinced Buffett that paying three times book value for See's Candy was actually a good deal (see Chapter 2 for the full story). That was the beginning of a plate-tectonic shift in Buffett's thinking, and he happily acknowledges that it was Charlie who pushed him in a new direction. Of course, both would quickly add that when you find a quality company that also happens to be available at a discounted price, then you've struck gold—or, in Berkshire's case, the next best thing: Coca-Cola (see Chapter 4).

One reason Buffett and Munger fit so well is that both men possess an uncompromising attitude toward commonsense business principles. Like Buffett, who endured poor returns in the insurance industry and for a time refused to write policies, Charlie, in his function as CEO of Wesco, refused to make loans when confronted with an unruly savings and loan industry. Both exhibit managerial qualities necessary to run high-quality businesses. Berkshire Hathaway's shareholders are blessed in having managing partners who look after their interest and help them make money in all economic environments. With Buffett's policy on mandatory retirement—he does not believe in it—Berkshire's shareholders will continue to benefit—not from one mind, but two—long into the future.

ESSENTIAL MUNGER

Look for companies that generate high cash earnings and require low capital expenditures.

*   *   *

It is far better to pay a fair price for a great company than a great price for a fair company.

A BLENDING OF INFLUENCES

Shortly after Graham's death in 1976, Buffett became the designated steward of Graham's value approach to investing. Indeed, Buffett's name became synonymous with value investing.[15] It is easy to see why. He was the most famous of Graham's dedicated students, and Buffett himself never missed an opportunity to acknowledge the intellectual debt he owed to Graham. Even today, Buffett considers Graham to be the one individual, after his father, who had the most influence on his investment life.[16]

How, then, does Buffett reconcile his intellectual indebtedness to Graham with stock purchases like The Washington Post Company (1973), Capital Cities/ABC (1986), and The Coca-Cola Company (1988)? None of these companies passed

Graham's strict financial test for purchase, yet Buffett made significant investments in all of them.

As early as 1965, Buffett was becoming aware that Graham's strategy of buying cheap stocks was not ideal.[17] Following his mentor's approach of searching for companies that were selling for less than their net working capital, Buffett bought some genuine losers. He came to realize that several companies that he had bought at a cheap price (hence, they met Graham's test for purchase) were cheap because their underlying businesses were suffering.

From the time he made his earliest investment mistakes, Buffett began moving away from Graham's strict teachings. "I evolved," he admitted, "but I didn't go from ape to human or human to ape in a nice even manner."[18] He was beginning to appreciate the qualitative nature of certain companies, compared to the quantitative aspects of others. Still, he searched for bargains, with sometimes horrible results. "My punishment," he confessed, "was an education in the economics of short-line farm implementation manufacturers (Dempster Mill Manufacturing), third-place department stores (Hochschild-Kohn), and New England textile manufacturers (Berkshire Hathaway)."[19] Buffett's evolution was delayed, he admitted, because what Graham taught him was so valuable.

When evaluating stocks, Graham did not think about the specifics of the businesses. Nor did he ponder the capabilities of management. He limited his research investigation to corporate filings and annual reports. If there was a mathematical probability of making money because the share price was less than the assets of the company, Graham purchased the company, regardless of its business or its management. To increase the probability of success, he purchased as many of these statistical equations as possible.

If Graham's teachings were limited to these precepts, Buffett would have little regard for him. But the margin of safety theory that Graham emphasized was so important to Buffett that all other current weaknesses of Graham's methodology can

72

be overlooked. Even today, Buffett continues to embrace Graham's primary idea, the theory of margin of safety. "Forty-two years after reading that," Buffett noted, "I still think those are the three right words."[20] The key lesson that Buffett took from Graham was: Successful investing involves purchasing stocks when their market price is at a significant discount to their underlying business value.

In addition to the margin of safety theory, which became the intellectual framework of Buffett's thinking, Graham helped Buffett appreciate the folly of following stock market fluctuations. Stocks have an investment characteristic and a speculative characteristic, Graham taught, and the speculative characteristics are a consequence of human fear and greed. These emotions, present in most investors, cause stock prices to gyrate far above and, more important, far below a company's intrinsic value, thus presenting a margin of safety. Graham taught Buffett that if he could insulate himself from the emotional whirlwinds of the stock market, he had an opportunity to exploit the irrational behavior of other investors, who purchased stocks based on emotion, not logic.

From Graham, Buffett learned how to think independently. If you reach a logical conclusion based on sound judgment, Graham counseled Buffett, do not be dissuaded just because others disagree. "You are neither right or wrong because the crowd disagrees with you," he wrote. "You are right because your data and reasoning are right."[21]

Phil Fisher, in many ways, was the exact opposite of Ben Graham. Fisher believed that, to make sound decisions, investors needed to become fully informed about a business. That meant investigating all aspects of the company. They had to look beyond the numbers and learn about the business itself, for the type of business it was mattered a great deal. They also needed to study the attributes of the company's management, for management's abilities could affect the value of the underlying business. They were urged to learn as much as they could about the industry in which the company operated, and about its competitors. Every source of information should be exploited. From Fisher, Buffett learned the value of scuttlebutt. Throughout the years, Buffett has developed an extensive network of contacts who assist him in evaluating different businesses.

Finally, Fisher taught Buffett not to overstress diversification. He believed that it was a mistake to teach investors that putting their eggs in several different baskets reduces risk. The danger in purchasing too many stocks, he felt, is that it becomes impossible to watch all the eggs in all the different baskets. Investors run the risk of putting too little in a company they are more familiar with and too much in a company they are unfamiliar with. In his view, buying shares in a company without taking the time to develop a thorough understanding of the business was far riskier than having limited diversification.

The differences between Graham and Fisher are apparent. Graham, the quantitative analyst, emphasized only those factors that could be measured: fixed assets, current earnings, and dividends. His investigative research was limited to corporate filings and annual reports. He spent no time interviewing customers, competitors, or managers.

Fisher's approach was the antithesis of Graham's. Fisher, the qualitative analyst, emphasized factors that he believed increased the value of a company: principally, future prospects and management capability. Whereas Graham was interested in purchasing only cheap stocks, Fisher was interested in purchasing companies that had the potential to increase their intrinsic value over the long term. He would go to great lengths—and even conduct extensive interviews—to uncover bits of information that might improve his selection process.

After Buffett read Phil Fisher's book, *Common Stocks and Uncommon Profits* (1958), he sought out the writer. "When I met him, I was as impressed by the man as by his ideas," Buffett said. "Much like Ben Graham, Fisher was unassuming, generous in spirit and an extraordinary teacher." Graham's and Fisher's investment approaches differ, notes Buffett, but they are "parallel in the investment world."[22] Taking the liberty of rephrasing, I would say that instead of paralleling, in Warren Buffett they dovetail: his investment approach is a combination of a qualitative understanding of the business and its management (as taught by Fisher) and a quantitative understanding of price and value (as taught by Graham).

But there is one other very important person in the picture. That person is Charlie Munger.

Warren Buffett once said, "I'm 15 percent Fisher and 85 percent Benjamin Graham."[23] That remark has been widely quoted, but it is very important to remember that it was made in 1969. In the intervening years, Buffett has made a gradual but definite shift toward Fisher's philosophy of buying a select few good businesses and owning those businesses for several years. My hunch is that if he were to make a similar statement today, the balance would come pretty close to 50/50.

Without question, it was Charlie Munger who was most responsible for moving Buffett toward Fisher's thinking.

In a very real sense, Munger is the active embodiment of Fisher's qualitative theories. From the start, Charlie had a keen appreciation of the value of a better business—and the wisdom of paying a reasonable price for it. See's Candy Shops (see Chapter 2) is a perfect example. It generated huge cash earnings and required very little in annual capital expenditures. Munger knew it was a quality company, but the asking price, at three times book value, violated Graham's rule. Under Munger's insistent encouragement, Berkshire bought it anyway. It marked the beginning of a major shift in Buffett's approach. Through their years together, Charlie has continued to preach the wisdom of paying up for a good business.

In one important respect, however, Munger is also the present-day echo of Ben Graham. Years earlier, Graham had taught Buffett the twofold significance of emotion in investing—the mistakes it triggers for those who make irrational decisions based on it, and the opportunities it thus creates for those who can avoid falling into the same traps. Munger, through his readings in psychology, has continued to develop that theme. He calls it "the psychology of misjudgment," a notion we shall look at more fully in Chapter 7, and through persistent emphasis keeps it an integral part of Berkshire's decision making. It is one of Munger's most important contributions.

Buffett's dedication to Ben Graham, Phil Fisher, and Charlie Munger is understandable. Graham gave Buffett the intellectual basis for investing—the margin of safety—and helped him learn to master his emotions in order to take advantage of market fluctuations. Fisher gave Buffett an updated, workable methodology that enabled him to identify good long-term investments and manage a portfolio over the long term. Munger helped Buffett appreciate the economic returns that come from buying and owning great businesses. The frequent confusion surrounding Buffett's investment actions is easily understood when we acknowledge that Buffett is the synthesis of all three men.

"It is not enough to have good intelligence," Descartes wrote; "the principal thing is to apply it well." Application is what separates Buffett from other investment managers. A number of his peers are highly intelligent, disciplined, and dedicated. Buffett stands above them all because of his formidable ability to integrate the strategies of the three wise men into one cohesive approach.

CHAPTER 4

GUIDELINES FOR BUYING A BUSINESS: TWELVE IMMUTABLE TENETS

Warren Buffett is so thoroughly identified with the stock market that even people who have no interest in the market know his name and reputation. Others—those who read the financial pages of the newspaper only casually—may know him as the head of a company whose own stock sells for upward of $70,000 *per share*. And even the many new investors who enthusiastically devote careful attention to market news think of him primarily as a brilliant stock picker.

Few would deny that the world's most famous and most successful investor is indeed a brilliant stock picker. But that seriously understates the case. His real gift is picking *companies*. I mean this in two senses. First, many casual observers do not realize that Berkshire Hathaway, in addition to its famous stock portfolio, *owns* many companies directly. Second, when considering new stock purchases, Buffett looks at the

underlying business as thoroughly as he would if he were buying the whole company, using a set of basic principles developed over many years.

In fact, Buffett believes, there is no real difference between
buying a business outright and buying shares in a business. In
either case, he follows the same basic strategy: he looks for
companies he understands—businesses that have favorable long-
term prospects, are operated by honest and competent people,
and, importantly, are available at attractive prices.

It has always been Buffett's preference to own a company
directly, for it permits him to influence the most critical issue
in a business: capital allocation. (Berkshire has been moving
more and more in this direction in recent years.) But the disadvantage of not controlling a business, he explains, is offset by
two distinct advantages: the arena for selecting them—the
stock market—(1) is significantly larger and (2) provides more
opportunities for finding bargains.

"When investing," says Buffett, "we view ourselves as business analysts, not as market analysts, not as macroeconomic analysts, and not even as security analysts."[1] When he evaluates a
company, either as a potential acquisition or a possible stock
purchase, Buffett works first and foremost from the perspective
of a businessman. He looks at the business holistically, examin-
ing all quantitative and qualitative aspects of its management,
its financial position, and its purchase price.

By reviewing Buffett's career and all of his purchases, and
by looking for the commonalities, we find a set of twelve basic
principles, or tenets, that guide his decisions. By extracting
these tenets and spreading them out for a closer look, we see
that they naturally group themselves into four categories:

- *Business tenets*—three basic characteristics of the business
  itself.
- *Management tenets*—three important qualities that senior
  managers must display.

- *Financial tenets*—four critical financial decisions that the company must maintain.
- *Market tenets*—two interrelated cost guidelines.

Not all of Buffett's acquisitions will display all twelve tenets, but, taken as a group, these tenets constitute the core of his equity investment approach.

These twelve tenets also serve as the principles by which Buffett runs Berkshire Hathaway. The same qualities he looks

---

Tenets of the Warren Buffett Way

Business Tenets

Is the business simple and understandable?

Does the business have a consistent operating history?

Does the business have favorable long-term prospects?

Management Tenets

Is management rational?

Is management candid with its shareholders?

Does management resist the institutional imperative?

Financial Tenets

Focus on return on equity, not earnings per share.

Calculate "owner earnings."

Look for companies with high profit margins.

For every dollar retained, make sure the company has created at least one dollar of market value.

Market Tenets

What is the value of the business?

Can the business be purchased at a significant discount to its value?

---

for in the businesses he buys, he expects to see when he walks through the front door of his office each day.

▰▰▰ BUSINESS TENETS

For Buffett, stocks are an abstraction.[2] He does not think in terms of market theories, macroeconomic concepts, or sector trends. He makes investment decisions based only on how a business operates. He believes that if people are drawn to an investment because of superficial notions rather than business fundamentals, they are more likely to be scared away at the first sign of trouble and, in all likelihood, will lose money in the process. Instead, Buffett concentrates on learning all he can about the business under consideration. He focuses on three main areas:

Business Tenets

A business must be simple and understandable.

A business must have a consistent operating history.

A business must have favorable long-term prospects.

Simple and Understandable

In Buffett's view, investors' financial success is correlated to the degree to which they understand their investment. This "understanding" is a distinguishing trait that separates investors with a business orientation from most hit-and-run investors—people who merely buy shares of stock.

Over the years, Buffett has owned a vast array of businesses in many different industries. Some of these companies he controlled; in others, he was or is a minority shareholder. But, he is acutely aware of how all these businesses operate. He understands the revenues, expenses, cash flow, labor relations, pricing flexibility, and capital allocation needs of every single one of Berkshire's holdings.

Buffett is able to maintain this high level of knowledge about Berkshire's businesses because he purposely limits his selections to companies that are within his area of financial and intellectual understanding. His logic is compelling. If you own a company (either fully or as a shareholder) in an industry you do not understand, you cannot possibly interpret developments accurately or make wise decisions. "Invest within your circle of competence," Buffett counsels. "It's not how big the circle is that counts, it's how well you define the parameters."[3]

Critics argue that Buffett's self-imposed restrictions exclude him from industries that offer the greatest investment potential, such as technology. His response: Investment success is not a matter of how much you know but how realistically you define what you *don't* know. "An investor needs to do very few things right as long as he or she avoids big mistakes."[4] Producing above-average results, Buffett has learned, often comes from doing rather ordinary things. The key is to do those ordinary things exceptionally well.

Consistent Operating History

Buffett not only avoids the complex, he avoids purchasing companies that are either solving difficult business problems or fundamentally changing direction because their previous plans were unsuccessful. It has been Buffett's experience that the best returns are achieved by companies that have been producing the same product or service for several years. Undergoing major business changes increases the likelihood of committing major business errors.

"Severe change and exceptional returns usually don't mix," Buffett observes.[5] Most individuals, unfortunately, invest as if the opposite were true. In recent years, investors have been attracted to fast-changing industries (technology) and have scrambled to purchase stocks that are in the midst of a corporate reorganization. For some unexplained reason, says Buffett, these

81

investors are so infatuated with the notion of what tomorrow may bring that they ignore today's business reality.

Buffett's experience in operating and investing in businesses has taught him that turnarounds seldom turn. Energy can be more profitably expended by purchasing good businesses at reasonable prices, rather than difficult businesses at cheaper prices. "Charlie [Munger] and I have not learned how to solve difficult business problems," Buffett admits. "What we have learned is to avoid them. To the extent that we have been successful, it is because we concentrated on identifying one-foot hurdles that we could step over rather than because we acquired any ability to clear seven-footers."[6]

Favorable Long-Term Prospects

According to Buffett, the economic world is divided into a small group of franchises and a much larger group of commodity businesses, of which most are not worth purchasing. He defines a franchise as a company providing a product or service that (1) is needed or desired, (2) has no close substitute, and (3) is not regulated. These traits allow a franchise to regularly increase prices without fear of losing market share or unit volume. Often, a franchise can raise its prices even when demand is flat and capacity is not fully utilized. This pricing flexibility, a defining characteristic of franchises, allows them to earn above-average returns on invested capital. Franchises also possess a greater amount of economic goodwill, which enables them to better withstand the effects of inflation.

To fully understand the long-term prospects of a business, first determine whether it is a franchise or a commodity.

Conversely, a commodity business offers a product that is virtually indistinguishable from the products of its competitors. Years ago, basic commodities included oil, gas, chemicals, wheat, copper, lumber, and orange juice. Today, computers, automobiles, airline service, banking, and insurance have become commodity-type products. Despite mammoth advertising budgets, they are unable to achieve meaningful product differentiation.

Commodity businesses, generally, are low-returning businesses and "prime candidates for profit trouble."[7] Their product is basically no different from anyone else's, so they can compete only on the basis of price—which, of course, cuts into their profit margins severely. The most dependable way to make a commodity business profitable is to be the low-cost provider. The only other time commodity businesses turn a profit is during periods of tight supply—a factor that can be extremely difficult to predict. A key to determining the long-term profitability of a commodity business, Buffett notes, is the ratio of "supply-tight to supply-ample years." However, this ratio is often fractional. The most recent supply-tight period in Berkshire's textile division, Buffett quips, lasted the "better part of a morning."

Continuing his examination of long-term prospects, after analyzing a company's economic characteristics, Buffett next judges its competitive strengths and weaknesses. "What I like," he confides, "is economic strength in an area where I understand it and where I think it will last."[8]

Economic strengths are most often found in franchises. One strength is the potential to freely raise prices and earn high rates on invested capital. Another is the ability to survive economic mishaps and still endure. It is comforting, says Buffett, to be in a business where mistakes can be made and above-average returns can still be achieved. "Franchises," he tells us, "can tolerate mismanagement. Inept managers may diminish a franchise's profitability, but they cannot inflict mortal damage."[9]

A major weakness with franchises is that their value is per-ishable. Success will inevitably attract other entrepreneurs. Competition will ensue. Substitute products will be intro-duced, and the differentiation between products will narrow. During this competitive period, a franchise slowly deteriorates into what Buffett calls a "weak franchise" and then further into a "strong business." Eventually, the once-promising franchise may be reduced to a commodity business.

When that happens, the value and importance of good man-agement increase exponentially. A franchise can survive inept management; a commodity business cannot.

MANAGEMENT TENETS

The highest compliment Buffett can pay a manager is to say that the manager unfailingly behaves and thinks like an owner of the company. Managers who behave like owners tend to (1) not lose sight of the company's prime objective—increasing shareholder value—and (2) make rational decisions that further that goal. Buffett also greatly admires managers who take seriously their responsibility to report fully and genuinely to shareholders, and who have the courage to resist what he has termed the "institu-tional imperative"—blindly following industry peers.

When he considers a business acquisition, Buffett looks hard at the quality of management. He tells us that the com-panies Berkshire purchases must be operated by honest and competent people, managers for whom he can feel admiration and trust. In particular, he looks for three traits:

Management Tenets

Management should be rational.

Management should be candid with the shareholders.

Management should resist the institutional imperative.

Rationality

 The most important management act is allocation of the company's capital. It ranks first because, over time, allocation of capital determines shareholder value. Deciding what to do with the company's earnings—reinvest in the business, or return money to shareholders—is, in Buffett's mind, an exercise in logic and rationality. "Rationality is the quality that Buffett thinks distinguishes his style with which he runs Berkshire— and the quality he often finds lacking in other corporations," observed Carol Loomis of *Fortune*.[10]

The question of where to allocate earnings is linked to where a company is in its life cycle. As a company moves through the stages of its economic life cycle—defined as: (1) development, (2) rapid growth, (3) maturity, and (4) decline—its growth rates, sales, earnings, and cash flows change dramatically. During the development stage, a company loses money as it tests and introduces products and establishes markets. During the second stage, rapid growth, the company is profitable but is growing so fast that it cannot support the growth; often, it has to retain all of its earnings *and* borrow money or issue equity to finance this growth.

In the third stage, maturity, a company's growth rate slows; it begins to generate more cash than it needs for development and operating costs. In the last stage, decline, the company suffers reductions in sales and earnings but continues to generate excess cash. In phases 3 and 4, but particularly in phase 3, the question arises: How should those earnings be allocated?

If the extra cash, reinvested internally, can produce an above-average return on equity—a return that is higher than the cost of capital—then the company should retain all of its earnings and reinvest them.[11] That is the only logical course. Retaining earnings in order to reinvest in the company at *less* than the average cost of capital is completely irrational—and is also quite common.

A company that provides average or below-average investment returns but generates cash in excess of its needs has three options:

1. It can ignore the problem and continue to reinvest at below-average rates.
2. It can buy growth.
3. It can return the money to shareholders.

It is at this crossroad that Buffett keenly focuses on management's behavior. Will management behave rationally or irrationally?

The biggest test of management's rationality is the decision on how to allocate extra cash.

Generally, managers who continue to reinvest despite below-average returns believe that the situation is temporary. They are convinced that, with managerial prowess, they can improve their company's profitability, and shareholders become mesmerized with management's forecast of improvements. If a company continually ignores this scenario, cash will become an increasingly idle resource and the stock price will decline. A company with poor economic returns, a lot of cash, and a low stock price will attract corporate raiders, which often is the beginning of the end of the current management's tenure. To protect themselves, executives frequently choose the second option: They purchase growth by acquiring another company.

Announcing an acquisition plan has the effect of exciting shareholders and dissuading corporate raiders. However, Buffett is skeptical of companies that need to buy growth because (1) it often comes at an overvalued price, and (2) a company that must integrate and manage a new business is apt to make mistakes that could be costly to shareholders.

In Buffett's mind, the only reasonable and responsible course for companies that have a growing pile of cash that cannot be reinvested at above-average rates is to return that money to the shareholders. Two methods are available: raise the dividend, or buy back shares.

With cash in hand from their dividends, shareholders have the opportunity to look elsewhere for higher returns. On the surface, this seems a good deal; many people view increased dividends as a sign of companies' doing well. Buffett believes that this is so only if investors can get more for their cash than the company could generate if it retained the earnings and reinvested in the company.

Over the years, Berkshire Hathaway has earned very high returns from its capital and has retained all of its earnings. With such high returns, shareholders would have been ill served if they were paid a dividend. Not surprisingly, Berkshire does not pay a dividend. And that's just fine with the shareholders. In 1985, Buffett asked shareholders which of three dividend options they preferred: (1) continue to reinvest all earnings and pay no cash dividend; (2) pay out modest dividends (5 to 15 percent of operating earnings); (3) pay out dividends at a rate typical of American industry (40 to 50 percent of earnings). A very large majority of those who responded—88 percent—preferred to continue the existing policy. The ultimate test of owners' faith is revealed when they allow management to reinvest 100 percent of earnings. Berkshire's owners' faith in Buffett is high.

If the real value of dividends is sometimes misunderstood, the second mechanism for returning earnings to the shareholders—stock repurchase—is even more so. The benefit to the owners is, in many respects, less direct, less tangible, and less immediate.

When management repurchases stock, Buffett feels that the reward is twofold. If the stock is selling below its intrinsic value, then purchasing shares makes good business sense. If a company's stock price is $50 and its intrinsic value is $100, then, with each purchase of stock, management is acquiring $2 of intrinsic value for every $1 spent. Transactions of this nature can be very profitable for the remaining shareholders.

Furthermore, says Buffett, when executives actively buy the company's stock in the market, they are demonstrating that they have the best interests of their owners at hand rather than a careless need to expand the corporate structure. That kind of stance sends good signals to the market and attracts other investors who are looking for a well-managed company that increases its shareholders' wealth. Frequently, shareholders are rewarded twice; once from the initial open-market purchase and subsequently as investor interest has a positive effect on price.

Candor

Buffett holds in high regard managers who report their companies' financial performance fully and genuinely, admit mistakes as readily as they announce successes, and are in all ways candid with shareholders. In particular, he respects managers who are able to communicate the performance of their company without hiding behind Generally Accepted Accounting Principles (GAAP).

Financial accounting standards only require disclosure of business information classified by industry segment. Some managers exploit this minimum requirement and lump together all of the company's businesses into one industry segment, making it difficult for owners to understand the dynamics of their separate business interests. "What needs to be reported," Buffett insists, "is data—whether GAAP, non-GAAP, or extra GAAP—that helps the financially literate readers answer three key questions: (1) Approximately how much is this company worth? (2) What is the likelihood that it can meet its future obligations? and (3) How good a job are its managers doing, given the hand they have been dealt?"[12]

Berkshire Hathaway's own annual reports are a good example. They of course meet GAAP obligations but go much further. Buffett includes the separate earnings of each of Berkshire's businesses and any other additional information that he feels owners would deem valuable when judging a company's economic performance. Buffett admires CEOs who are able to report to their shareholders in the same candid fashion.

He also admires those with the courage to discuss failure openly. He believes that managers who confess mistakes publicly are more likely to correct them. According to Buffett, most annual reports are a sham. Over time, every company makes mistakes, both large and inconsequential. Too many managers, he believes, report with excess optimism rather than honest explanation, serving perhaps their own interests in the short term but no one's interests in the long run.

Buffett credits Charlie Munger with helping him understand the value of studying one's mistakes rather than concentrating only on success. In his annual reports to Berkshire Hathaway shareholders, Buffett is very open about Berkshire's economic and management performance, both good and bad. Through the years, he has admitted the difficulties that Berkshire encountered in both the textile and insurance businesses, and his own management failures in regard to these businesses. In the 1989 Berkshire Hathaway Annual Report, he started a formal practice of listing his mistakes as: "Mistakes of the First Twenty-Five Years (A Condensed Version)." Two years later, the title was changed to "Mistake du Jour." Here, Buffett confessed not only mistakes made but opportunities lost because he failed to act appropriately.

Critics have argued that Buffett's practice of publicly admitting his mistakes is made easier because, as the owner of such a large share of Berkshire's common stock, he never has to worry about being fired. This is true. But it does not diminish the fundamental value of Buffett's belief that candor benefits the manager at least as much as it benefits the shareholder. "The CEO who misleads others in public," he says, "may eventually mislead himself in private."[13]

The Institutional Imperative

If management stands to gain wisdom and credibility by facing mistakes, why do so many annual reports trumpet only successes? And if allocation of capital is so simple and logical, why is capital so poorly allocated? The answer, Buffett has learned, is an unseen force he calls "the institutional imperative"—the lemming-like tendency of corporate management to imitate the behavior of other managers, no matter how silly or irrational it may be.

It was, Buffett confesses, the most surprising discovery of his business career. At school, he was taught that experienced managers of companies were honest and intelligent, and automatically made rational business decisions. Once out in the business world, he learned instead that "rationality frequently wilts when the institutional imperative comes into play."[14]

According to Buffett, the institutional imperative is responsible for several serious, but distressingly common, conditions: "(1) [the organization] resists any change in its current direction; (2) just as work expands to fill available time, corporate projects or acquisitions will materialize to soak up available funds; (3) any business craving of the leader, however foolish, will quickly be supported by detailed rate-of-return and strategic studies prepared by his troops; and (4) the behavior of peer companies, whether they are expanding, acquiring, setting executive compensation or whatever, will be mindlessly imitated."[15]

Buffett learned this lesson early. Jack Ringwalt, head of National Indemnity, which Berkshire acquired in 1967, helped Buffett discover the destructive power of the imperative. While the majority of insurance companies were writing insurance policies on terms guaranteed to produce inadequate returns—

or worse, a loss—Ringwalt stepped away from the market and refused to write new policies. (The full story has been told in Chapter 2.) Buffett recognized the wisdom of Ringwalt's decisions and followed suit. Today, Berkshire's insurance companies still operate on this principle.

What is behind the institutional imperative that drives so many businesses? Human nature. Most managers are unwilling to look foolish and expose their company to an embarrassing quarterly loss when other "lemming" companies are still able to produce quarterly gains, even though they assuredly are heading into the sea. Shifting direction is never easy. It is often easier to follow other companies down the path leading to failure than to alter the direction of the company.

Admittedly, in this regard Buffett and Munger enjoy the same protected position as in their freedom to be candid about bad news: They don't have to worry about getting fired, and this frees them to make unconventional decisions. Still, a manager with strong communication skills should be able to persuade owners to accept a short-term loss in earnings and a change in the direction of their company if that strategy will yield superior results over time. Inability to resist the institutional imperative, Buffett has learned, often has less to do with the owners of the company than with the willingness of its managers to accept fundamental change.

Even when managers accept the notion that their company must radically change or face the possibility of shutting down, carrying out this plan is too difficult for most managers to accomplish. Instead, many succumb to the temptation to buy a new company rather than face the financial facts of the current problem.

Why would they do this? Buffett isolates three factors as being most influential in management's behavior:

1. Most managers cannot control their lust for activity. Such hyperactivity often finds its outlet in business takeovers.

2. Most managers are constantly comparing their business's sales, earnings, and executive compensation to other companies within and beyond their industry. These comparisons invariably invite corporate hyperactivity.

3. Most managers have an exaggerated sense of their own management capabilities.

Another common problem is poor allocation skills. As Buffett points out, CEOs often rise to their position by excelling in other areas of the company, including administration, engineering, marketing, or production. Because they have little experience in allocating capital, most CEOs instead turn to their staff members, consultants, or investment bankers, and the institutional imperative begins to enter the decision-making process. If the CEO craves a potential acquisition that requires a 15 percent return on investment to justify the purchase, it is amazing, Buffett points out, how smoothly the troops report back that the business can actually achieve 15.1 percent.

The final justification for the institutional imperative is mindless imitation. "If companies A, B, and C are all doing the same thing," reasons the CEO of company D, "it must be all right for our company to behave the same way."

It is not venality or stupidity, Buffett believes, that positions these companies to fail. Rather, the institutional dynamics of the imperative make it difficult to resist doomed behavior. Speaking before a group of Notre Dame students, Buffett displayed a list of 37 failed investment banking firms. All of them, he explained, failed even though the volume of the New York Stock Exchange had multiplied fifteenfold. These firms were headed by hard-working individuals with very high IQs, all of whom had an intense desire to succeed. Buffett paused; his eyes scanned the room. "You think about that," he said sternly. "How could they get a result like that? I'll tell you how," he said. "Mindless imitation of their peers."[16]

Buffett has been fortunate to work with some of the brightest managers in corporate America, including Tom Murphy at

Capital Cities/ABC, Roberto Goizueta and Donald Keough at Coca-Cola, and Carl Reichardt at Wells Fargo. However, he knows there is a point where even the brightest and most capable manager cannot rescue a difficult business. "If you put those same guys to work in a buggy whip company," Buffett says, "it wouldn't have made much difference."[17] The buggy whip company would still have gone bankrupt.

Can We Really Put a Value on Management?

Buffett would be the first to admit that evaluating managers along these dimensions—rationality, candor, and independent thinking—is more difficult than measuring financial performance, for the simple reason that human beings are more complex than numbers.

Indeed, many analysts believe that because measuring human activity is vague and imprecise, we simply cannot value management with any degree of confidence, and therefore the exercise is futile. Without a decimal point, they seem to suggest, there is nothing to measure. Others hold the view that the value of management is fully reflected in the company's performance statistics—including sales, profit margins, and return on equity—and no other measuring stick is necessary.

Both of these opinions have some validity, but neither is, in my view, strong enough to outweigh the original premise. The reason for taking the time to evaluate management is that it yields early warning signs of eventual financial performance. If you look closely at the words and actions of a management team, you will find clues that will help you measure the value of the team's work long before it shows up in the company's financial reports or in the stock pages of a daily newspaper. Doing so will take some digging, and that may be enough to discourage the weak of heart or the lazy. That is their loss and your gain.

For gathering the necessary information, Buffett offers a few tips. Review annual reports from a few years back, paying special attention to what management said then about strategies for the future. Then compare those plans to today's results: how fully were the plans realized? Also compare strategies of a few years ago to this year's strategies and ideas: how has the thinking changed? Buffett also suggests that it can be very valuable to compare annual reports of the company you are interested in with reports from similar companies in the same industry. It is not always easy to find exact duplicates, but even relative performance comparisons can yield insights.

Expand your reading horizons. Be alert for articles in newspapers and financial magazines about the company you are interested in and about its industry in general. Read what the company's executives have to say, and what others say about them. If you notice that the chairman recently made a speech or presentation, get a copy from the investor relations department and study it carefully. Make use of the company's Web pages for up-to-the-minute information. In every way you can think of, raise your antennae. The more you develop the habit of staying alert for information, the easier the process will become.

One note of caution, however: Do not fall into the trap of overweighting this information just because you worked hard to collect it. Keep it within the broader perspective. No matter how impressive management is, Buffett will not invest in people alone. "When a management with a reputation for brilliance tackles a business with a reputation for poor fundamental economics," he writes, "it is the reputation of the business that stays intact."[18]

FINANCIAL TENETS

The financial tenets by which Buffett values both managerial excellence and economic performance are all grounded in some typically Buffettlike principles. For one thing, he does not take yearly results too seriously. Instead, he focuses on four- or five-year averages. Often, he notes, profitable business returns might not coincide with the time it takes for our planet to circle the sun. He also has little patience with accounting sleight-of-hand that produces impressive year-end numbers but little real value. Instead, he is guided by a few timeless financial principles:

Financial Tenets

Focus on return on equity, not earnings per share.

Calculate "owner earnings" to get a true reflection of value.

Look for companies with high profit margins.

For every dollar retained, has the company created at least a dollar of market value?

Return on Equity

Customarily, analysts measure annual company performance by looking at earnings per share. Did they increase over last year? Are they high enough to brag about? For his part, Buffett considers earnings per share a smokescreen. Most companies retain a portion of their previous year's earnings as a way of increasing their equity base, so he sees no reason to get excited about record earnings per share. There is nothing spectacular about a company that increases earnings per share by 10 percent, if at the same time, it is growing its equity base by 10 percent. That's no different, he explains, from putting money in a savings account and letting the interest accumulate and compound.

The test of economic performance, he believes, is whether a company achieves a high earnings rate on equity capital ("without undue leverage, accounting gimmickry, etc."), not whether it has consistent gains in earnings per share.[19] To measure a company's annual performance, Buffett prefers return on equity—the ratio of operating earnings to shareholders' equity.

To use this ratio, though, we need to make several adjustments. First, all marketable securities should be valued at cost and not at market value, because values in the stock market as a whole can greatly influence the returns on shareholders' equity in a particular company. For example, if the stock market rose dramatically in one year, thereby increasing the net worth of a company, a truly outstanding operating performance would be diminished when compared to a larger denominator. Conversely, falling prices reduce shareholders' equity, which means that mediocre operating results appear much better than they really are.

Second, we must also control the effects that unusual items may have on the numerator of this ratio. Buffett excludes all capital gains and losses as well as any extraordinary items that may increase or decrease operating earnings. He is seeking to isolate the specific annual performance of a business. He wants to know how well management accomplishes its task of generating a return on the operations of the business, given the capital it employs. That, he says, is the single best measure of management's economic performance.

Buffett also believes that a business should achieve good returns on equity while employing little or no debt. We know that companies can increase their return on equity by increasing their debt-to-equity ratio. Buffett is aware of this, but the idea of adding a couple of points to Berkshire Hathaway's return on equity simply by taking on more debt does not impress him. "Good business or investment decisions," he says, "will produce quite satisfactory economic results with no aid from leverage."[20] Furthermore, highly leveraged companies are vulnerable during economic slowdowns. He would rather err on the side of financial quality than risk the welfare of Berkshire's owners by increasing the risk that is associated with debt.

Despite his conservative stance, Buffett is not phobic when it comes to borrowing money. In fact, he prefers to borrow money in anticipation of using it farther down the road, rather than borrowing the money after a need is announced. It would be ideal, he notes, if the timing of business acquisitions profitably coincided with the availability of funds. However, experience has shown that just the opposite occurs. Cheap money has the tendency to force prices of assets higher. Tight money and higher interest rates raise liability costs and often force the price of assets downward. Just when the best prices are available for purchasing businesses, the cost of money (higher interest rates) is likely to diminish the attractiveness of the opportunity. For this reason, says Buffett, companies should manage their assets and liabilities independently of each other.

This philosophy—borrow now in hopes of finding a good business opportunity later—will penalize near-term earnings. For this reason, Buffett acts only when he is reasonably confident that the return of this future business will more than offset the expense of the debt. Because the availability of attractive business opportunities is limited, Buffett wants Berkshire to be prepared. "If you want to shoot rare, fast-moving elephants," he advises, "you should always carry a gun."[21]

Buffett does not give us any suggestions as to what debt levels are appropriate or inappropriate for a business. Different companies, depending on their cash flows, can manage different levels of debt. Buffett does tell us that a good business should be able to earn a good return on equity without the aid of leverage. Companies that can earn good returns on equity only by employing significant debt should be viewed suspiciously.

"Owner Earnings"

Investors, Buffett warns, should be aware that accounting earnings per share are the *starting point* for determining the economic value of a business, not the *ending point*. "The first point to understand," he says, "is that not all earnings are created equal."[22] Companies with high assets to profits, he points out, tend to report ersatz earnings. Because inflation extracts a toll on asset-heavy businesses, the earnings of these businesses take on a miragelike quality. Hence, accounting earnings are useful to the analyst only if they approximate the expected cash flow of the company.

But even cash flow, Buffett warns, is not a perfect tool for measuring value; often, cash flow misleads investors. Cash flow is an appropriate way to measure businesses that have large investments in the beginning and smaller outlays later on, such as real estate, gas fields, and cable companies. On the other hand, companies that require ongoing capital expenditures (manufacturers, for example) are not accurately valued using only cash flow.

A company's cash flow is customarily defined as net income after taxes plus depreciation, depletion, amortization, and other noncash charges. The problem with this definition, explains Buffett, is that it leaves out a critical economic fact: capital expenditures. How much of the year's earnings must the company use for new equipment, plant upgrades, and other improvements needed to maintain its economic position and unit volume? According to Buffett, approximately 95 percent of America's businesses require capital expenditures that are roughly equal to their depreciation rates. You can defer capital expenditures for a year or so, he says, but if, over a long period, you don't make the necessary improvements, your business will surely decline. These capital expenditures are as much an expense to a company as are labor and utility costs.

The popularity of cash flow numbers heightened during the leverage buyout period of the 1980s, because the exorbitant prices paid for businesses were justified by companies' cash flow. Buffett believes that cash flow numbers "are frequently used by marketers of business and securities in attempts to justify the unjustifiable and thereby sell what should be unsalable. When earnings look inadequate to service debt of a junk bond or justify a foolish stock price, how convenient it becomes to focus on cash flow."[23] But you cannot focus on cash flow, Buffett cautions, unless you are willing to subtract the necessary capital expenditures.

Instead of cash flow, Buffett prefers to use what he calls "owner earnings"—a company's net income plus depreciation, depletion, and amortization, less the amount of capital expenditures and any additional working capital that might be needed.

It is not a mathematically precise measure, Buffett admits, for the simple reason that calculating future capital expenditures often requires rough estimates. Still, quoting Keynes, he says, "I would rather be vaguely right than precisely wrong."

Profit Margins

Like Philip Fisher, Buffett is aware that great businesses make lousy investments if management cannot convert sales into profits. In his experience, managers of high-cost operations tend to find ways to continually add to overhead, whereas managers of low-cost operations are always finding ways to cut expenses.

Buffett has little patience for managers who allow costs to escalate. Frequently, these same managers have to initiate a restructuring program to bring down costs and align them with sales. Each time a company announces a cost-cutting program, he knows this company has not figured out what expenses can do to a company's owners. "The really good manager," Buffett says, "does not wake up in the morning and say, 'This is the day I'm going to cut costs,' any more than he wakes up and decides to practice breathing."[24]

Buffett has singled out the accomplishments of Carl Reichardt and Paul Hazen at Wells Fargo, and Tom Murphy and Dan Burke at Capital Cities/ABC for their relentless attack on unnecessary expenses. They "abhor having a bigger head count than is needed," he says, and both managerial teams "attack costs as vigorously when profits are at record levels as when they are under pressure."[25] Buffett himself can be tough when it comes to costs and unnecessary expenses. He is very sensitive about Berkshire's profit margins. He understands the right size staff for any business operation, and he believes that for every dollar of sales there is an appropriate level of expenses.

Berkshire Hathaway is a unique corporation. The corporate staff at Kiewit Plaza would have difficulty fielding a softball team. Berkshire Hathaway does not have a legal department nor a public/investor relations department. There are no strategic planning departments staffed with MBA-trained workers plotting mergers and acquisitions. Berkshire does not employ limo drivers or messengers. The company's after-tax overhead corporate expense runs less than 1 percent of operating earnings. Compare this, says Buffett, to other companies with similar earnings but 10 percent corporate expenses; shareholders lose 9 percent of the value of their holdings simply because of corporate overhead.

The One-Dollar Premise

We know that the stock market will track business value reasonably well over long periods, although, in any one year, prices can gyrate widely for reasons other than value. The same is true for retained earnings, Buffett explains. If a company uses retained earnings unproductively over an extended period, the market, eventually and quite justifiably, will price its shares disappointingly. Conversely, if a company has been able to achieve above-average returns on augmented capital, that success will be reflected in increased stock price.

Buffett believes that if he has selected a company that has favorable long-term economic prospects and is run by able shareholder-oriented managers, the proof will be reflected in the increased market value of the company. He uses a quick test: the increased market value should, at the very least, match the amount of retained earnings dollar for dollar. If the value exceeds the retained earnings, so much the better. All in all, explains Buffett, "within this gigantic auction arena, it is our job

100

to select a business with economic characteristics allowing each dollar of retained earnings to be translated into at least a dollar of market value."[26]

MARKET TENETS

All the principles embodied in the tenets described so far lead to one decision point: buying or not buying shares in a company. At that point, any investor must weigh two factors: Is this company a good value? And is this a good time to buy it—that is, is the price favorable?

Price is established by the stock market. Value is determined by the analyst/investor, after weighing all the known information about a company's business, management, and financial traits. Price and value are not necessarily equal. If the stock market were truly efficient, prices would instantaneously adjust to all available information. We know this does not occur. The prices of securities move above and below company values for numerous reasons, not all of them logical.

Theoretically, the actions of an investor are determined by the differences between price and value. If the price is lower than the per-share value, a rational investor will decide to buy. If the price is higher than the per-share value, any reasonable investor will pass.

As the company moves through its economic life cycle, the analyst will periodically reassess the company's value in relation to market price, and will buy, sell, or hold shares accordingly.

In sum, then, two timeless principles are the key components of rational investing:

Market Tenets

Determine the value of the business.

Purchase the business at a significant discount to its value.

Determine the Value of the Business

Through the years, financial analysts have used many formulas for calculating the intrinsic value of a company. Some are fond of various shorthand methods: low price-to-earnings ratios, low price to book values, and high dividend yields. But the best system, according to Buffett, was determined more than 60 years ago by John Burr Williams in *The Theory of Investment Value.* Paraphrasing Williams's theory, Buffett tells us the value of a business is the total of the net cash flows (owner earnings) expected to occur over the life of the business, discounted by an appropriate interest rate.[27] He considers it simply the most appropriate yardstick with which to measure a basket of all different investment types: government bonds, corporate bonds, common stocks, apartment buildings, oil wells, and farms.

The mathematical exercise, Buffett tells us, is very similar to valuing a bond. The bond market each day adds up the future coupons of a bond and discounts those coupons at the prevailing interest rate. That procedure determines the value of the bond. To determine the value of a business, an analyst estimates the "coupons" that the business will generate for a period into the future and then discounts all of these coupons back to the present. "So valued," Buffett says, "all businesses, from manufacturers of buggy whips to operators of cellular telephones, become economic equals."[28]

To summarize: Calculating the current value of a business means, first, estimating the total earnings that will likely occur over the life of the business, and then discounting that total backward to today. (Keep in mind that, for "earnings," Buffett uses owner earnings—net cash flow adjusted for capital expenditures.) To estimate the total future earnings, we would apply all we had learned about the company's business characteristics, its financial health, and the quality of its managers, using the analysis principles described thus far in this chapter. For the second part of the formula, we need only decide what the discount rate should be; more on that in a moment.

T*o determine what a company is worth today,*
estimate the total of its future cash earnings, and
then discount that total by the appropriate rate.

Buffett is firm on one point: He looks for companies with future earnings that are as predictable, and as certain, as the earnings of bonds. If the company has operated with consistent earnings power *and* if the business is simple and understandable, Buffett believes he can determine its future earnings with a high degree of certainty. If he is unable to project with confidence what the future cash flows of a business will be, he will not attempt to value the company.

This is the distinction of Buffett's approach. Although he admits that Microsoft is a dynamic company and he highly regards Bill Gates as a manager, Buffett confesses he hasn't a clue how to estimate the future cash earnings of this company. This is what he means by "the circle of competence"; he does not know the technology industry well enough to project the long-term earnings potential of any company within it.

This brings us to the second element in the formula: What is the appropriate discount rate? Buffett's answer is simple: The rate that would be considered risk-free. For many years, he used the rate then current for long-term government bonds. Because the certainty that the U.S. government will pay its coupon over the next 30 years is virtually 100 percent, we can say that this is a risk-free rate. When interest rates are low, Buffett adjusts the discount rate upward. When bond yields dipped below 7 percent, Buffett upped his discount rate to 10 percent. If interest rates work themselves higher over time, he has successfully matched his discount rate to the long-term rate. If they do not, he has increased his margin of safety by three additional points.

Some academicians argue that no company, regardless of its strengths, can ensure future cash earnings with the same

103

certainty as a bond. Therefore, they insist, a more appropriate discount factor would be the risk-free rate of return *plus* an equity risk premium, added to reflect the uncertainty of the company's future cash flows. Buffett does not add a risk premium. Instead, he relies on the margin of safety that comes from buying at a substantial discount in the first place, and on his single-minded focus on companies with consistent and predictable earnings. "I put a heavy weight on certainty," Buffett says. "If you do that, the whole idea of a risk factor doesn't make any sense to me."[29]

Buy at Attractive Prices

Focus on businesses that are understandable, have enduring economics, and are run by shareholder-oriented managers. All those tenets are important, Buffett says, but by themselves will not guarantee investment success. For that, he must first buy at a sensible price, and then the company must perform to his business expectations. The second activity is not always easy to control, but the first is. If the price isn't satisfactory, he passes.

Buffett's basic goal is to identify businesses that earn above-average returns, and then to purchase these businesses at prices below their indicated value. Graham taught Buffett the importance of buying a stock only when the difference between its price and its value represents a margin of safety. Today, this is still his guiding principle, even though, as we have seen, his partner Charlie Munger has encouraged him toward occasionally paying more for outstanding companies.

The margin of safety principle assists Buffett in two ways. First, it protects him from downside price risk. If he calculates that the value of a business is only slightly higher than its per-share price, he will not buy the stock; he reasons that if the company's intrinsic value were to dip even slightly, the stock price would eventually drop too—perhaps below the amount he paid for it. But if the margin between price and value is large enough, the risk of declining value is less. If Buffett is able to purchase a company at 75 percent of its intrinsic value (a 25 percent discount) and the value subsequently declines by 10 percent, his original purchase price will still yield an adequate return.

AN ESSENTIAL BUFFETT STRATEGY

Find companies with above-average returns, and buy their stock when it is priced below its intrinsic value.

The margin of safety also provides opportunities for extraordinary stock returns. If Buffett correctly identifies a company with above-average economic returns, the value of its stock over the long term will steadily march upward. If a company consistently earns 15 percent on equity, its share price will appreciate more each year than that of a company that earns 10 percent on equity. Additionally, if Buffett, by using the margin of safety, is able to buy this outstanding business at a significant discount to its intrinsic value, Berkshire will earn an extra bonus when the market corrects the price of the business. "The market, like the Lord, helps those who help themselves," says Buffett. "But unlike the Lord, the market does not forgive those who know not what they do."[30]

Over the years, Warren Buffett has made several celebrated stock purchases using the twelve fundamental tenets presented in this chapter. Starting with American Express (described in Chapter 2), the *Washington Post,* Capital Cities/ABC, and the early purchases of GEICO shares, he has managed to put his principles into action with astonishing success. None of them, however, was more spectacular than the 1988–1989 purchase of Coca-Cola. Because it serves to illustrate Buffett's methods like no other, we will look at this transaction in some detail.

THE COCA-COLA COMPANY

Coca-Cola is the world's largest manufacturer, marketer, and distributor of carbonated soft drink concentrates and syrups. The company's soft drink product, first sold in the United States in 1886, is now sold in nearly 200 countries worldwide.

Buffett's relationship with Coca-Cola dates back to his childhood, when he started buying six Cokes for a quarter from his grandfather's grocery store and reselling them in his neighborhood for a nickel each. For the next 50 years, Buffett admits, he observed the phenomenal growth of Coca-Cola but purchased textile mills, department stores, and windmill and farm equipment manufacturers. Even in 1986, when he formally announced that Cherry Coke would become the official soft drink of Berkshire Hathaway's annual meetings, Buffett had still not purchased a single share of Coca-Cola. Two years later, in the summer of 1988, Buffett began buying stock in Coca-Cola.

Tenet: Simple and Understandable

The business of Coca-Cola is relatively simple. The company purchases commodity inputs and combines them to manufacture a concentrate that is sold to bottlers. The bottlers then combine the concentrate with other ingredients and sell the finished product to retail outlets, including mini-marts, supermarkets, and vending machines. The company also provides soft-drink syrups to fountain retailers, who sell soft drinks to consumers in cups and glasses.

The company's name-brand products include Coca-Cola, Diet Coke, Sprite, Mr. PiBB, Mello Yello, Ramblin' Root Beer,

Fanta soft drinks, Tab, and Fresca. Its beverages also include Hi-C fruit drinks, Minute Maid juices, Powerade, Nestea, and Nordic Mist. The company owns 40 percent of Coca-Cola Enterprises, the largest bottler in the United States, and 37 percent of Coca-Cola Amatil, an Australian bottler that has interests not only in Australia but in New Zealand and Eastern Europe.

The strength of Coca-Cola is not only its name-brand products but also its unmatched worldwide distribution system. Today, international sales of Coca-Cola products account for 62 percent of the company's net sales and 68 percent of its profits. In addition to Coca-Cola Amatil, the company has equity interests in bottlers located in Mexico, South America, Southeast Asia, Taiwan, Hong Kong, and China.

Tenet: A Consistent Operating History

No other company today can match Coca-Cola's consistent operating history. The business was started in the 1880s with sales of a beverage product. Today, 120 years later, Coca-Cola is selling the same beverage. Even though the company periodically invested in unrelated businesses, its core beverage business has remained largely unchanged.

The only significant differences today would be the company's size and its geographical reach. One hundred years ago, the company employed ten traveling salesmen to cover the entire United States. At that point, the company was selling 116,492 gallons of syrup a year, for annual sales of $148,000.[31] Fifty years later, in 1938, the company was selling 207 million cases of soft drinks annually (having converted sales from gallons to cases). That same year, an article in *Fortune* magazine noted: "It would be hard to name any company comparable to Coca-Cola and selling, as Coca-Cola does, an unchanged product that can point to a ten-year record anything like Coca-Cola's."[32]

Today, more than 60 years after that article was published, Coca-Cola is still selling syrup. The only difference is the increase in quantity. By the year 2000, the company was selling over 16.5 billion cases of soft drink in more than 200 countries, and generating $20 billion a year in sales.

Tenet: Favorable Long-Term Prospects

Shortly after Berkshire's 1989 public announcement that it owned 6.3 percent of The Coca-Cola Company, Buffett was interviewed by Melissa Turner, a business writer for the *Atlanta Constitution*. She asked Buffett a question he has been asked often: Why hadn't he bought shares in the company sooner? By way of answer, Buffett related what he was thinking at the time he finally made the decision.

"Let's say you were going away for ten years," he explained, "and you wanted to make one investment and you know everything that you know now, and you couldn't change it while you're gone. What would you think about?" Of course the business would have to be simple and understandable. Of course the company would have to have demonstrated a great deal of business consistency over the years. And of course the long-term prospects would have to be favorable. "If I came up with anything in terms of certainty, where I knew the market was going to continue to grow, where I knew the leader was going to continue to be the leader—I mean worldwide—and where I knew there would be big unit growth, I just don't know anything like Coke," Buffett concluded. "I'd be relatively sure that when I came back they would be doing a hell of a lot more business than they do now."[33]

But what took him so long? Coca-Cola's business attributes, as described by Buffett, have existed for several decades. And why purchase at that particular time? What caught his eye, he confesses, were the changes occurring at Coca-Cola during the

1980s, under the leadership of Roberto Goizueta and Donald Keough. Those two men made all the difference.

The 1970s were dismal years for Coca-Cola. The decade was marred by disputes with bottlers, accusations of mistreatment of migrant workers at the company's Minute Maid groves, environmentalists' claim that Coke's "one way" containers contributed to the country's growing pollution problem, and the Federal Trade Commission's charge that the company's exclusive franchise system violated the Sherman Anti-Trust Act. Coca-Cola's international business was reeling as well. The Arab boycott of Coke, begun when the company issued an Israeli franchise, dismantled years of investment. Japan, where the company's earnings were growing the fastest, was a battlefield of corporate mistakes. Coke's 26-ounce take-home bottles were exploding—literally—on store shelves. In addition, Japanese consumers angrily objected to the company's use of artificial coal-tar coloring in Fanta Grape. When the company developed a new version using real grape skins, the contents fermented and the grape soda was tossed into Tokyo Bay.

During the 1970s, Coca-Cola was a fragmented and reactive company rather than an innovator setting the pace within the beverage industry. Paul Austin was appointed chairman of the company in 1971, after serving as president since 1962. Despite its problems, the company continued to generate millions of dollars in earnings. But instead of reinvesting in Coca-Cola's own beverage market, Austin diversified the company with investments in water projects and shrimp farms, despite their slim profit margins. He also purchased a winery. Shareholders bitterly opposed this investment, arguing that Coca-Cola should not be associated with alcohol. To deflect criticism, Austin directed unprecedented amounts of money for advertising campaigns.

Meanwhile, Coca-Cola earned 20 percent on equity. However, pretax margins were slipping (see Figure 4.1). The market value of the company at the end of the bear market of 1974 was

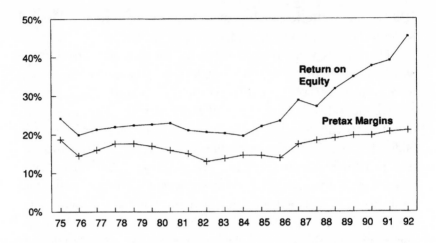

Figure 4.1   The Coca-Cola Company: Return on equity and pretax margins.

$3.1 billion (see Figure 4.2). Six years later, the value had increased to $4.1 billion. In other words, from 1974 to 1980, the company's market value rose an average annual rate of 5.6 percent, vastly underperforming the Standard & Poor's 500 Index. For every dollar the company retained in those six years, it created only $1.02 of market value.

Coca-Cola's corporate woes were exacerbated by Austin's behavior.[34] He was intimidating and unapproachable, and his wife, Jeane, was a disruptive influence within the company. She redecorated corporate headquarters with modern art, shunning the company's classic Norman Rockwell paintings. She even ordered a corporate jet to help her facilitate the search for works of art. But it was her last order that contributed to her husband's downfall.

In May 1980, Mrs. Austin ordered the company's park closed to employee luncheons. Their food droppings, she complained, attracted pigeons on the well-manicured lawns. Employee morale hit an all-time low. Robert Woodruff, the company's 91-year-old patriarch, who had led Coca-Cola from

110

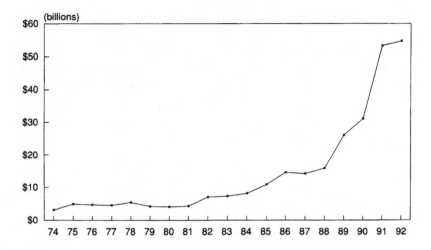

Figure 4.2 The Coca-Cola Company: Market value.

1923 until 1955 and was still chairman of the board's finance committee, had heard enough. He demanded Austin's resignation and replaced him with Roberto Goizueta.

Goizueta, raised in Cuba, was Coca-Cola's first foreign chief executive officer. He was as outgoing as Austin was reticent. One of his first acts was to bring together Coca-Cola's top 50 managers for a meeting in Palm Springs, California. "Tell me what we're doing wrong," he said. "I want to know it all, and once it's settled, I want 100 percent loyalty. If anyone is not happy, we will make you a good settlement and say goodbye."[35] From this meeting evolved the company's "Strategy for the 1980s," a 900-word pamphlet outlining the corporate goals for Coca-Cola.

Goizueta encouraged his managers to take intelligent risks. He wanted Coca-Cola to initiate action rather than to be reactive. He began cutting costs, and he demanded that any business that Coca-Cola owned must optimize its return on assets. These actions translated, immediately, into increasing profit margins.

Tenet: High Profit Margins

In 1980, Coca-Cola's pretax profit margins were a low 12.9 percent. Margins had been falling for five straight years and were substantially below the company's 1973 margins of 18 percent. In Goizueta's first year, pretax margins rose to 13.7 percent; by 1988, when Buffett bought his Coca-Cola shares, margins had climbed to a record 19 percent.

Tenet: Return on Equity

In "Strategy for the 1980s," Goizueta pointed out that the company would divest any business that no longer generated acceptable returns on equity. Any new business venture must have sufficient real growth potential to justify an investment. Coca-Cola was no longer interested in battling for share in a stagnant market. "Increasing earnings per share and effecting increased return on equity are still the name of the game," Goizueta announced.[36] His words were followed by actions. Coca-Cola's wine business was sold to Seagram's in 1983.

Although the company earned a respectable 20 percent return on equity during the 1970s, Goizueta was not impressed. He demanded better returns, and the company obliged. By 1988, Coca-Cola's return on equity had increased to 31.8 percent.

By any measurement, Goizueta's Coca-Cola was doubling and tripling the financial accomplishments of Austin's Coca-Cola. The results could be seen in the market value of the company. In 1980, Coca-Cola had a market value of $4.1 billion. By the end of 1987, even after the stock market crash in October, the market value had risen to $14.1 billion (see Figure 4.2). In seven years, Coca-Cola's market value rose an average annual rate of 19.3 percent. For every dollar Coca-Cola retained during this period, it gained $4.66 in market value.

Tenet: Candid Management

Goizueta's strategy for the 1980s pointedly included shareholders. "We shall, during the next decade, remain totally committed to our shareholders and to the protection and enhancement of their investment," he wrote.[37] "In order to give our shareholders an above-average total return on their investment," he explained, "we must choose businesses that generate returns in excess of inflation."

Goizueta not only had to grow the business, which required capital investment; he also was obliged to increase shareholder value. To do so, Coca-Cola, by increasing profit margins and return on equity, was able to pay increasing dividends while simultaneously reducing the dividend payout ratio. Dividends to shareholders, in the 1980s, were increasing 10 percent per year and the payout ratio was declining from 65 percent to 40 percent. This enabled Coca-Cola to reinvest a greater percentage of the company's earnings to help sustain its growth rate while not shortchanging shareholders.

Each year, in its annual report, Coca-Cola begins the financial review and management's discussion by stating: "Management's primary objective is to maximize shareholder value over time." The company's business strategy emphasizes maximizing long-term cash flows. To do so, the company focuses on investing in the high-return soft drink business, increasing returns on existing businesses, and optimizing the cost of capital. If successful, the evidence will be growth in cash flow, increased return on equity, and an increased total return to shareholders.

Tenet: Rational Management

The growth in net cash flow has allowed Coca-Cola to increase its dividend to shareholders and to repurchase its shares in the open market. In 1984, the company authorized its first-ever buyback, announcing it would repurchase 6 million shares of stock. Since then, the company has repurchased more than 1 billion shares. This represents 32 percent of the shares outstanding as of January 1, 1984, at an average price per share of $12.46. In other words, the company spent approximately $12.4 billion to buy in shares that today would have a market value of approximately $60 billion.

Tenet: "Owner Earnings"

In 1973, "owner earnings" (net income plus depreciation minus capital expenditures) were $152 million (see Figure 4.3). By 1980, owner earnings were $262 million, an 8 percent annual compounded growth rate. From 1981 through 1988, owner earnings grew from $262 million to $828 million, a 17.8 percent average annual compounded growth rate.

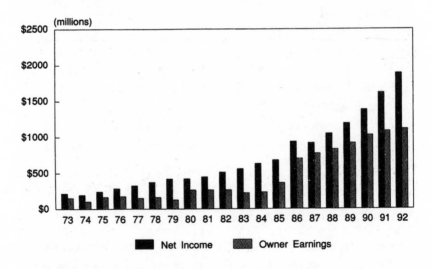

Figure 4.3   The Coca-Cola Company: Net income and "owner earnings."

The growth in owner earnings is reflected in the share price of Coca-Cola. This is particularly obvious if we look at ten-year periods. From 1973 to 1982, the total return of Coca-Cola grew at an average annual rate of 6.3 percent. From 1983 to 1992, the average annual rate was 31.1 percent.

Tenet: Resist the Institutional Imperative

When Goizueta took over Coca-Cola, one of his first moves was to jettison the unrelated businesses that the previous CEO, Paul Austin, had developed, and return the company to its core business: selling syrup. It was a clear demonstration of Coca-Cola's ability to resist the institutional imperative.

Reducing the company to a single-product business was undeniably a bold move. What made Goizueta's strategy even more remarkable was his willingness to take this action at a time when others in the industry were doing the exact opposite. Several leading beverage companies were investing their profits in other unrelated businesses. Anheuser-Busch used the profits from its beer business to invest in theme parks. Brown-Forman, a producer and distributor of wine and spirits, invested its profits in china, crystal, silver, and luggage businesses, all of which had much lower returns. Seagram Company, Ltd., a global spirits and wine business, bought Universal Studios. Pepsi, Coca-Cola's chief beverage rival, bought snack businesses (Frito-Lay) and restaurants, including Taco-Bell, Kentucky Fried Chicken, and Pizza Hut. Only recently (April 1999) has Pepsi spun off its restaurant business into TRICON Global Restaurants.

It is important to note that not only did Goizueta's action focus the company's attention on its largest and most important product, but it worked to reallocate the company's resources into its most profitable business. Because the economic returns of selling syrup far outweighed the economic returns of the other businesses, the company was now reinvesting its profits in its highest-return business.

Tenet: Determine the Value

Key analysis to intrinsic value calculation

When Buffett first purchased Coca-Cola in 1988, people asked: "Where is the value in Coke?" The company's price was 15 times earnings and 12 times cash flow—a 30 percent and 50 percent premium to the market average. Buffett paid five times book value for a company with a 6.6 percent earning yield. He was willing to do that because of Coke's extraordinary level of economic goodwill. The company was earning 31 percent return on equity while employing relatively little in capital investment. Buffett has explained that price tells us nothing about value. The value of Coca-Cola, he says, like that of any other company, is determined by the total owner earnings expected to occur over the life of the business, discounted at an appropriate interest rate.

In 1988, owner earnings of Coca-Cola equaled $828 million (see Table 4.1). The 30-year U.S. Treasury Bond (the risk-free rate) at that time traded near a 9 percent yield. Coca-Cola's 1988 owner earnings, discounted by 9 percent, would produce an intrinsic value of $9.2 billion. When Buffett purchased Coca-Cola, the market value was $14.8 billion, suggesting that Buffett might have overpaid for the company. But $9.2 billion represents the discounted value of Coca-Cola's then-current owner earnings. If buyers were willing to pay a price for Coca-Cola that was 60 percent higher than $9.2 billion, it must have been because they perceived part of the value of Coca-Cola to be its future growth opportunities.

When a company is able to grow owner earnings without the need for additional capital, it is appropriate to discount owner earnings by the difference between the risk-free rate of return and the expected growth of owner earnings. Analyzing Coca-Cola, we find that owner earnings from 1981 through

Table 4.1 The Coca-Cola Company—"Owner Earnings" Analysis
(figures in $ millions)

	Annual Sales	Annual Income	Depreciation	Capital Expenditures	Owner Earnings
73	2145	215	59.1	121.3	152.8
74	2522	196	59.5	150.1	105.4
75	2872	239	67.7	143.3	163.4
76	3032	285	71.7	182.2	174.5
77	3559	326	85.4	260.9	150.5
78	4337	374	95.0	306.0	163.0
79	4961	420	117.0	409.3	127.7
80	5912	422	138.0	298.0	262.0
81	5889	447	144.9	329.6	262.3
82	6249	512	150.7	400.3	262.4
83	6829	558	156.0	492.0	222.0
84	7364	629	170.0	565.0	234.0
85	7904	678	335.0	652.0	361.0
86	8669	934	430.0	665.0	699.0
87	7658	916	153.0	300.0	769.0
88	8338	1045	170.0	387.0	828.0
89	8966	1193	184.0	462.0	915.0
90	10236	1382	236.0	593.0	1025.0
91	11572	1618	254.0	792.0	1080.0
92	13074	1884	310.0	1083.0	1111.0
Compounded Annual Growth Rates					
1973–1980	15.6%	10.1%	12.9%	13.7%	8.0%
1981–1988	5.1%	12.9%	2.3%	2.3%	17.8%
1988–1992	11.9%	15.9%	16.2%	29.3%	7.6%

1988 grew at a 17.8 percent annual rate—faster than the risk-free rate of return. When this occurs, analysts use a two-stage discount model. It permits them to calculate future earnings when a company has extraordinary growth for a limited number of years and then has a period of constant growth at a slower rate.

We can use this two-stage process to calculate the 1988 present value of the company's future cash flows. In 1988, Coca-Cola's owner earnings were $828 million. If we assume that Coca-Cola would be able to grow owner earnings at 15 percent per year for the next 10 years (a reasonable assumption, since that rate is lower than the company's previous seven-year average), by year 10, owner earnings will equal $3.349 billion. Let's further assume that, starting in year 11, growth rate will slow to 5 percent a year. Using a discount rate of 9 percent (the long-term bond rate at the time), we can back-calculate the intrinsic value of Coca-Cola in 1988: $48.377 billion (see Table 4.2).[38]

We can repeat this exercise using different growth rate assumptions. If we assume that Coca-Cola can grow owner earnings at 12 percent for 10 years, followed by 5 percent growth, the present value of the company, discounted at 9 percent, would be $38.163 billion. At 10 percent growth for 10 years and 5 percent thereafter, the value of Coca-Cola would be $32.497 billion. And if we assume only 5 percent throughout, the company would still be worth at least $20.7 billion [$828 million divided by (9 percent − 5 percent)].

Tenet: Buy at Attractive Prices

In June 1988, the price of Coca-Cola was approximately $10 per share (split-adjusted). Over the next ten months, Buffett acquired 93,400,000 shares, for a total investment of $1.023 billion. His average cost per share was $10.96. At the end of 1989, Coca-Cola represented 35 percent of Berkshire's common stock portfolio.

From the time that Goizueta took control of Coca-Cola in 1980, the company's stock price had increased every year. In the five years before Buffett purchased his first shares, the average annual gain in share price was 18 percent. The company's fortunes were so good that Buffett was unable to purchase any shares at distressed prices. Still, he charged ahead. Price, he reminds us, has nothing to do with value.

The stock market's value of Coca-Cola in 1988 and 1989, during Buffett's purchase period, averaged $15.1 billion. But by Buffett's estimation, remember, the intrinsic value of the

Table 4.2 The Coca-Cola Company Discounted Owners Cash Flow Using a Two-Stage "Dividend" Discount Model (first stage is ten years)

	Year									
	1	2	3	4	5	6	7	8	9	10
Prior year cash flow	$828	$ 952	$1,095	$1,259	$ 1,448	$1,665	$1,915	$2,202	$2,532	$2,912
Growth rate (add)	15%	15%	15%	15%	15%	15%	15%	15%	15%	15%
Cash flow	$952	$1,095	$1,259	$1,448	$ 1,665	$1,915	$2,202	$2,532	$2,912	$3,349
Discount factor (multiply)	0.9174	0.8417	0.7722	0.7084	0.6499	0.5963	0.5470	0.5019	0.4604	0.4224
Discounted value per annum	$873	$ 922	$ 972	$1,026	$ 1,082	$1,142	$1,204	$1,271	$1,341	$1,415
Sum of present value of cash flows					$11,248					

Residual Value

Cash flow in year 10	$ 3,349
Growth rate (g) (add)	5%
Cash flow in year 11	$ 3,516
Capitalization rate ($k - g$)	4%
Value at end of year 10	$87,900
Discount factor at end of year 10 (multiply)	0.4224
Present Value of Residual	37,129
Market Value of Company	$48,377

Notes: Assumed first-stage growth rate = 15.0%; assumed second-stage growth rate = 5.0%; discount rate = 9.0%. Dollar amounts are in millions.

119

company was anywhere from $20.7 billion (assuming 5 percent growth in owner earnings) to $32.4 billion (assuming 10 percent growth), or $38.1 billion (assuming 12 percent growth), or $48.3 billion (assuming 15 percent growth). Buffett's margin of safety—the discount to intrinsic value—could be as low as a conservative 27 percent or as high as 70 percent.

Tenet: The One-Dollar Premise

Since Buffett began buying its shares, the price performance of Coca-Cola has been extraordinary. A $100 investment in its common stock on December 31, 1989, with dividends reinvested, grew in pretax value to $681 10 years later—an average annual compound return of 21 percent. Since 1989, the market value of Coca-Cola has risen from $25.8 billion to $143.9 billion. Between December 31, 1989, and December 31, 1999, the company produced $26.9 billion in profits, paid out $10.5 billion in dividends to shareholders, and retained $16.4 billion for reinvestment. For every dollar the company has retained, it has created $7.20 in market value. At year-end 1999, Berkshire's original $1.023 billion investment in Coca-Cola was worth $11.6 billion.

Coca-Cola is the only production and distribution business capable of bringing refreshments to every part of the world. In the United States, Coca-Cola serves 425 eight-ounce servings per person every year. Compare this to China, where each person consumes seven servings a year. The potential for growth is clear. Through increased per-capita consumption of Coca-Cola's beverages in Eastern Europe, the former Soviet Union, India, Africa, and the Far East, the company will reach its goal of growing sales at an above-average rate.

The best business to own, says Buffett, is one that, over a period of time, can employ large amounts of capital at very high rates of return. This description fits Coca-Cola. It is the most widely recognized and esteemed name brand in the world. It is easy to understand why Buffett considers Coca-Cola the world's most valuable franchise.

THE INTELLIGENT INVESTOR

The most distinguishing trait of Buffett's investment philosophy is the clear understanding that, by owning shares of stocks, he owns businesses, not pieces of paper. The idea of buying stocks without understanding the company's operating functions—its products and services, labor relations, raw materials expenses, plant and equipment, capital reinvestment requirements, inventories, receivables, and needs for working capital—is unconscionable, says Buffett. This mentality reflects the attitude of a business owner as opposed to a stock owner, and is the only mentality an investor should have. In the summation of *The Intelligent Investor,* Benjamin Graham wrote: "Investing is most intelligent when it is most businesslike." Those are, says Buffett, "the nine most important words ever written about investing."

A person who holds stocks has the choice to become the owner of a business or the bearer of tradable securities. Owners of common stocks who perceive that they merely own a piece of paper are far removed from the company's financial statements. They behave as if the market's ever-changing price is a more accurate reflection of their stock's value than the business's balance sheet and income statement. They draw or discard stocks like playing cards. For Buffett, the activities of a common-stock holder and a business owner are intimately connected. Both should look at ownership of a business in the same way. "I am a better investor because I am a businessman," Buffett says, "and a better businessman because I am an investor."[39]

Buffett is often asked what types of companies he will purchase in the future. First, he says, "I will avoid commodity businesses and managers that I have little confidence in." What he will purchase is the type of company that he understands—one that possesses good economics and is run by trustworthy managers. "A good business is not always a good purchase," he concludes, "although it is a good place to look for one."[40]

CHAPTER 5

FOCUS INVESTING: THEORY AND MECHANICS

Up to this point, we have studied Warren Buffett's approach to choosing the stocks he invests in, an approach built on timeless principles codified into 12 tenets. We have seen how those principles were applied in the well-known purchase of Coca-Cola. And we have taken the time to understand how insights from others helped shape his philosophy about investing.

But, as every investor knows, deciding which stocks to buy is only half the story. The other half is the ongoing process of managing the portfolio: knowing which stocks to hold, and for how long; deciding if, when, and how to cash out some investments and move into others; and learning how to cope with the emotional roller coaster that inevitably accompanies such decisions.

It is no surprise that here, too, the leadership of Warren Buffett will show us the way.

Hollywood has given us a visual cliché of what money managers look like: talking into two phones at once, frantically taking notes while trying to keep an eye on a bank of computer screens that blink and blip endlessly, and pained expressions whenever one of those computer blinks shows a minuscule drop in a stock price.

Warren Buffett is far from that kind of frenzy. He moves with the calm that comes of great confidence. He has no need to watch a dozen computer screens at once; the minute-by-minute changes in the market are of no interest to him. Warren Buffett doesn't think in minutes, or days, or months, but years. He doesn't need to keep up with hundreds of companies, because his investments are focused in a select few. He refers to himself as a "focus investor"—"We just focus on a few outstanding companies."[1] This approach—let's call it *focus investing*—greatly simplifies the task of portfolio management.

Focus investing is a remarkably simple idea, and yet, like most simple ideas, it rests on a complex foundation of interlocking concepts. In this chapter and the next, we will look more closely at each of these underlying concepts and at the effects they produce. To say this in different terms, the present chapter describes the "why" and the "how" of focus investing; the following chapter describes the "what happens next." The goal of these two chapters is to give you a new way of thinking about investment decisions and managing investment portfolios. Fair warning: In all likelihood, this new way is the opposite of what you have always been told about investing in the stock market.

Status Quo: A Choice of Two

The current state of portfolio management appears to be locked into a tug-of-war between two competing strategies: (1) active portfolio management and (2) index investing.

Active portfolio managers are constantly at work buying and selling a great number of common stocks. Their job is to try to keep their clients satisfied, and that means consistently out-performing the market so that, on any given day, if a client applies the obvious measuring stick—"How is my portfolio doing, compared to the market overall?"—the answer is positive and the client leaves her money in the fund. To stay on top, active managers try to predict what will happen with stocks in the coming six months and continually churn the portfolio, hoping to take advantage of their own predictions. On average, common-stock mutual funds own more than 100 stocks and generate 80 percent turnover ratios.

Index investing, on the other hand, is a buy-and-hold, passive approach. It involves assembling, and then holding, a broadly diversified portfolio of common stocks deliberately designed to mimic the behavior of a specific benchmark index, such as the Standard & Poor's 500.

Compared to active management, index investing is somewhat new and far less common. Ever since the 1980s, when index funds fully came into their own as a legitimate alternative strategy, proponents of both approaches have waged combat to determine which one will ultimately yield the higher investment return.

Active portfolio managers argue that, by virtue of their superior stock-picking skills, they can do better than any index. Index strategists, for their part, have recent history on their side. In a study that tracked results in a 20-year period (1977 through 1997), the percentage of equity mutual funds that have been able to beat the Standard & Poor's 500 Index dropped dramatically, from 50 percent in the early years to barely 25 percent in the last four years. Since 1997, the news is even worse. As of November 1998, 90 percent of actively managed funds were underperforming the market (averaging 14 percent *lower* than the S&P 500), which means that only 10 percent were doing better.[2]

Active portfolio management, as commonly practiced today, stands a very small chance of outperforming index investing. Because they frenetically buy and sell hundreds of stocks each year, institutional money managers have, in a sense, become the market. Their basic theory is: Buy today whatever we predict can be sold soon at a profit, regardless of what stock it is. The fatal flaw in that logic is that, given the complex nature of the financial universe, predictions are impossible. Further complicating this shaky theoretical foundation is the effect of the inherent costs that go with this high level of activity, costs that diminish the net returns to investors. When we factor in these costs, it becomes apparent that the active money management business has created its own downfall.

Indexing, because it does not trigger equivalent expenses, is better than actively managed portfolios in many respects. But even the best index fund, operating at its peak, will net only the returns of the overall market. Index investors can do no worse than the market—and no better.

From an investor's point of view, the underlying attraction of both strategies is the same: to minimize risk through diversification. By holding a large number of stocks representing many industries and many sectors of the market, investors hope to build in a warm blanket of protection against the horrific loss that could occur if they had all their money in one arena and that arena suffered some disaster. In a normal period, so the thinking goes, some stocks in a diversified fund will go down, others will go up, so let's keep our fingers crossed that the latter will compensate for the former. The more stocks the portfolio contains, active managers believe, the better our chances. Ten is better than one, and 100 is better than 10.

An index fund, by definition, affords this kind of diversification, if the index it mirrors is also diversified. (Most indexes are.) So does the traditional stock mutual fund, which has upward of 100 stocks constantly in motion.

We have all heard this mantra of diversification for so long, we have become intellectually numb to its inevitable consequence: mediocre results. Both active and index funds do offer diversification, but, in general, neither strategy will give you exceptional returns.

Intelligent investors must ask themselves: Am I satisfied with "average?" Can I do better?

A New Choice

What does Warren Buffett say about this ongoing debate? Given these two particular choices, indexing versus active strategy, he would unhesitatingly pick indexing. So would investors who have a very low tolerance for risk, and people who know very little about the economics of a business but still want to participate in the long-term benefits of investing in common stocks. "By periodically investing in an index fund," Buffett says in his inimitable style, "the know-nothing investor can actually outperform most investment professionals."[3]

Buffett, however, would be quick to point out that there is a third alternative, a very different kind of active portfolio strategy that significantly increases the odds of beating the index. That alternative is *focus investing*.

FOCUS INVESTING: THE BIG PICTURE

Reduced to its essence, focus investing means this: Choose a few stocks that are likely to produce above-average returns over the long haul, concentrate the bulk of your investments in those stocks, and have the fortitude to hold steady during any short-term market gyrations.

Let's break the process into separate elements, and look at each one.

"Find Outstanding Companies"

Over the years, Warren Buffett has developed a way of choosing the companies that, in his view, are worthy places to put his money. His way rests on a notion of great common sense: If the company itself is doing well and is managed by smart people, eventually its inherent value will be reflected in its stock price. Buffett thus devotes most of his attention not to tracking share price but to analyzing the economics of the underlying business and assessing its management.

The analytical process that Buffett uses involves checking each opportunity against a set of investment tenets, or fundamental principles. These tenets, described in Chapter 4, can be thought of as a kind of tool belt. Each individual tenet is one analytical tool, and, in the aggregate, they provide a method for isolating the companies with the best chance for high economic returns.

The Warren Buffett tenets, if followed closely, lead inevitably to good companies that make sense for a focus portfolio. The companies chosen will have a long history of superior performance and a stable management, and that stability points toward a high probability that they will perform in the future as they have in the past. That is the heart of focus investing: concentrating your investments in companies with the highest probability of above-average performance.

Probability theory, which comes to us from the field of mathematics, is one of the underlying concepts that make up the rationale for focus investing. We shall learn more about it later in this chapter.

"Less Is More"

Remember Buffett's advice to a "know-nothing" investor, to stay with index funds? What is more interesting for our purposes is what he said next: "If you are a know-something investor, able to understand business economics and to find five to ten sensibly priced companies that possess important long-term competitive advantages, conventional diversification [broadly based active portfolios] makes no sense for you."[4]

What's wrong with conventional diversification? For one thing, it greatly increases the chances that you will buy something you don't know enough about. "Know-something" investors, applying the Buffett tenets, would do better to focus their attention on just a few companies—5 to 10, Buffett suggests. For the average investor, a legitimate case can be made for investing in 10 to 20 companies.

More critical than determining the exact number is understanding the general concept behind it. Focus investing falls apart if it is applied to a large portfolio containing dozens of stocks.

THE FOCUS INVESTOR'S GOLDEN RULES

1. *Concentrate your investments in outstanding companies run by strong management.*
2. *Limit yourself to the number of companies you can truly understand. Ten is a good number; more than 20 is asking for trouble.*
3. *Pick the very best of your good companies, and put the bulk of your investment there.*
4. *Think long term—5 to 10 years, minimum.*
5. *Volatility happens. Carry on.*

As we know from Chapter 3, Buffett's thinking was profoundly influenced by Philip Fisher, and we clearly see Fisher's hand in this area. Fisher was known for his focus portfolios; he always said he preferred owning a small number of outstanding companies that he understood well, rather than a large number

129

of average companies, many of which he understood poorly. As we have seen, Fisher generally limited his portfolios to fewer than ten companies, of which three or four often represented 75 percent of the total investment.

Ken Fisher, the son of Phil Fisher, is also a successful money manager. He summarizes his father's philosophy this way: "My dad's investment approach is based on an unusual but insightful notion that less is more."[5]

"Put Big Bets on High-Probability Events"

Fisher's influence on Buffett can also be seen in his belief that the only reasonable course, when you encounter a strong opportunity, is to make a large investment. Today, Warren Buffett echoes that thinking: "With each investment you make, you should have the courage and the conviction to place at least ten percent of your net worth in that stock."[6]

You can see why Buffett says the ideal portfolio should contain no more than ten stocks, if each is to receive 10 percent. Yet, focus investing is not a simple matter of finding ten good stocks and dividing an investment pool equally among them. Even though all the stocks in a focus portfolio are high-probability events, some will inevitably be higher than others, and they should be allocated a greater proportion of the investment.

Blackjack players understand this strategy intuitively; when the odds are strongly in their favor, they put down a big bet. Investors and gamblers draw from the same science: mathematics. Along with probability theory, mathematics provides another piece of the focus investing rationale; the Kelly Optimization Model, which is described in detail later in this chapter. The Kelly formula uses probability to calculate optimization—in this case, optimal investment proportion.

Think back for a moment to Buffett's decision to buy American Express for the limited partnership, described in Chapter 2. When threat of scandal caused the company's share price to drop by almost half, Buffett invested a whopping 40 percent of the partnership's assets in this one company. He was convinced that, in spite of the controversy, the company was solid and eventually the stock price would return to its proper level; in the meantime, he recognized a terrific opportunity. But was it worth almost half of his total assets? It was a big bet that paid off handsomely: two years later, he sold the much-appreciated shares for a nifty profit of $20 million.

"Be Patient"

Focus investing is the antithesis of a broadly diversified high-turnover approach. Although focus investing stands the best chance, among all active strategies, of outperforming an index return over time, it does require investors to patiently hold their portfolio when it appears that other strategies are marching ahead. In shorter periods, we realize that changes in interest rates, inflation, or the near-term expectation for a company's earnings can affect share prices. But as the time horizon lengthens, the trend line economics of the underlying business will increasingly dominate its share price.

How long is that ideal time line? There is no hard and fast rule (although Buffett would probably say that anything less than five years is a fool's theory). The goal is not zero turnover; that's foolish in the opposite direction, for it would prevent you from taking advantage of something better when it comes along. I suggest that, as a general rule of thumb, we should be thinking of a turnover rate between 10 and 20 percent. A 10 percent turnover ratio suggests that an investor holds the stock for ten years; a 20 percent ratio implies a five-year period.

"Don't Panic over Price Changes"

Focus investing pursues *above*-average results, and, as we will see in the next chapter, there is strong evidence, both in academic research and actual case histories, that the pursuit is successful. There can be no doubt, however, that the ride is bumpy, for price volatility is a necessary by-product of the focus approach. Focus investors tolerate the bumpiness because they know that, in the long run, the underlying economics of the companies will more than compensate for any short-term price fluctuations.

Buffett is a master bump-ignorer. So is his partner, Charlie Munger, who came to the fundamental concept of focus investing through a slightly different route. "Back in the 1960s," he explained, "I actually took a compound interest rate table, and I made various assumptions about what kind of edge I might have in reference to the behavior of common stocks generally." (OID)[7] He worked through several scenarios to determine the number of stocks he would need in the portfolio of his investment partnership and what kind of volatility he could expect.

"I knew from being a poker player that you have to bet heavily when you've got huge odds in your favor," Charlie said. He concluded that as long as he could handle the price volatility, owning as few as three stocks would be plenty. "I knew I could handle the bumps psychologically, because I was raised by people who believe in handling bumps." (OID)[8]

Maybe you also come from a long line of people who can handle bumps. But even if you were not born so lucky, you can acquire some of their traits. You need to consciously decide to change how you think and behave. Acquiring new habits and thought patterns does not happen overnight, but gradually teaching yourself not to panic or act rashly in response to the vagaries of the market is certainly doable.

DO THE MATH

We start the process of focus investing by picking out a handful of high-performing companies, using the investment tenets introduced in Chapter 4. No one would deny that doing such intensive research takes time, but it is also true that it takes no unusual or esoteric skill. To do that research well, you must know how to read and how to think—skills you already possess. But then, about midway through the process, you need to know something about a couple of areas of mathematics, some of which might be new to you: probability theory and optimization theory.

Probability Theory

It is a vast oversimplification, but not an overstatement, to say that the stock market is an uncertain universe. In this universe are hundreds, or even thousands, of single forces that combine to set prices, all of which forces are constantly in motion, any one of which can have a drastic impact, and none of which is predictable to an absolute certainty. The task for investors, then, is to narrow the field by identifying and removing that which is the most unknown, and then focusing on the least unknown. That task is an exercise in probability.

When we are unsure about a situation but still want to express our opinion, we often preface our remarks by saying: "The chances are," or "Probably," or "It's not very likely. . . ." When we go one step further and attempt to quantify those general expressions, we then are dealing with probabilities. Probabilities are the mathematical language of uncertainty.

What is the probability of a cat's giving birth to a bird? Zero. What is the probability the sun will rise tomorrow? That event, which is considered certain, is given a probability of 1. All events that are neither certain nor impossible have a probability that is a fraction somewhere between 0 and 1.0. Determining the fraction is what probability theory is all about.

In 1654, Blaise Pascal and Pierre de Fermat exchanged a series of letters that formed the basis of what today is probability theory. Pascal, a child prodigy gifted in both mathematics and philosophy, had been challenged by Chevalier de Méré, a philosopher and gambler, to solve the riddle that had stumped many mathematicians: How should two card players divide the stakes of a game if they had to leave before the game was completed? Pascal approached Fermat, a mathematical genius in his own right, about de Méré's challenge.

"The 1654 correspondence between Pascal and Fermat on this subject," says Peter Bernstein in *Against the Gods,* his wonderfully written treatise on risk, "signaled an epochal event in the history of mathematics and the theory of probability."[9] Although they attacked the problem differently (Fermat used algebra whereas Pascal turned to geometry), they were able to construct a system to determine the probability of several possible outcomes. Indeed, Pascal's triangle of numbers solves many problems, including the probability that your favorite baseball team will win the World Series after losing the first game.

The work by Pascal and Fermat marks the beginning of the theory of decision making. Decision theory is the process of deciding what to do when you are uncertain what will happen. "Making that decision," writes Bernstein, "is the essential first step in any effort to manage risk."[10]

Although Pascal and Fermat are both credited with developing probability theory, another mathematician, Thomas Bayes, wrote the piece that laid the groundwork for putting probability theory to practical action.

Born in England in 1701, exactly 100 years after Fermat and 78 years after Pascal, Bayes lived an unremarkable life. He was a member of the Royal Society, but published nothing in mathematics during his lifetime. After his death, his paper entitled "Essays Towards Solving A Problem In The Doctrine Of Chances" appeared. At the time, no one thought much of it. However, according to Peter Bernstein, Bayes's essay was a "strikingly original piece of work that immortalized Bayes among statisticians, economists, and other social scientists."[11] It provides a way for investors to make use of the mathematical theory of probability.

Bayesian analysis gives us a logical way to consider a set of outcomes of which all are possible but only one will actually occur. It is conceptually a simple procedure. We begin by assigning a probability to each of the outcomes, on the basis of whatever evidence is then available. If additional evidence becomes available, the initial probability is revised to reflect the new information. Bayes's theorem gives us a mathematical procedure for updating our original beliefs, thus changing our relevant odds.

How does it work? Let's imagine that you and a friend have spent the afternoon playing your favorite board game, and now, at the end of the game, you are chatting about this and that. Something your friend says leads you to make a friendly wager: that with one roll of the die from the game, you will get a 6. Straight odds are one in six, a 16 percent probability. But then suppose your friend rolls the die, quickly covers it with her hand, and takes a peek. "I can tell you this much," she says; "it's an even number." Now you have new information and your odds change dramatically to one in three, a 33 percent probability. While you are considering whether to change your bet, your friend teasingly adds: "And it's not a 4." With this additional bit of information, your odds have changed again, to one in two, a 50 percent probability.

With this very simple example, you have performed a Bayesian analysis. Each new piece of information affected the original probability, and that is a Bayesian inference.

Bayesian analysis is an attempt to incorporate all available information into a process for making inferences, or decisions, about the underlying state of nature. Colleges and universities use Bayes's theorem to help their students study decision making. In the classroom, the Bayesian approach is more popularly called the decision tree theory; each branch of the tree represents new information that, in turn, changes the odds in making decisions. "At Harvard Business School," explains Charlie Munger, "the great quantitative thing that bonds the first-year class together is what they call decision tree theory. All they do is take high school algebra and apply it to real life problems. The students love it. They're amazed to find that high school algebra works in life." (OID)[12]

The Subjective Interpretation of Probability

As Charlie points out, basic algebra is extremely useful in calculating probabilities. But to put probability theory to practical use in investing, we need to look a bit deeper at how the numbers are calculated. In particular, we need to pay attention to the notion of frequency.

What does it mean to say that the probability of guessing heads on a single coin toss is 1/2? Or that the probability that an odd number will appear on a single throw of a die is 1/2? If a box is filled with 70 red marbles and 30 blue marbles, what does it mean that the probability is 3/10 that a blue marble will be picked? In all these examples, the probability of the event is what is referred to as a *frequency interpretation,* and it is based on the law of averages.

If an uncertain event is repeated countless times, the frequency of the event's occurrence is reflected in the probability of the event. For example, if we toss a coin 100,000 times, the number of events that are expected to be heads is 50,000. Note that I did not say it *would be* equal to 50,000. The law of large numbers says the relative frequency and the probability need be equal only for an infinite number of repetitions. Theoretically, we know that, in a fair toss of a coin, the chance of getting heads is 1/2 but we will never be able to say the chance is equal until an infinite number of tosses has passed.

In any problem that deals with uncertainty, we will, quite obviously, never be able to make a definitive statement. However, if the problem is well defined, we should be able to list all the possible outcomes. If an uncertain event is repeated often enough, the frequency of the outcomes should reflect the probability of

136

the different possible outcomes. The difficulty arises when we are concerned with an event that happens only once.

How do we estimate the probability of passing tomorrow's science test or the probability of the Green Bay Packers winning the Super Bowl? The problem we face is that each of these events is unique. We can look back at all the statistics on the Green Bay games, but we don't have enough exact matchups with the exact personnel who played each other repeatedly under identical circumstances. We can recall previous science exams to get an idea of how well we test, but all tests are not identical and our knowledge is not constant.

Without repeated tests that would produce a frequency distribution, how can we calculate probability? We cannot. Instead, we must rely on a *subjective* interpretation of probabilities. We do it all the time. We might say that the odds of the Packers' winning the big prize are two to one, or the possibility of passing that hard test is one in ten. These are probabilistic statements; they describe our "degree of belief" about the event. When it isn't possible to do enough repetitions of a certain event to get an interpretation of probability based on frequency, we have to rely on our own good sense.

You can immediately see that many subjective interpretations of those two events would lead you in the wrong direction. In subjective probability, the burden is on you to analyze your assumptions. Stop and think them through. Are you assuming a one-in-ten chance of doing well on the science test because the material is more difficult and you haven't adequately prepared, or because of false modesty? Is your lifelong loyalty to the Packers blinding you to the superior strength of the other team?

According to the textbooks on Bayesian analysis, if you believe that your assumptions are reasonable, it is "perfectly acceptable" to make your subjective probability of a certain event equal to a frequency probability.[13] What you have to do is sift out the unreasonable and illogical and retain the reasonable. It is helpful to think about subjective probabilities as nothing more than extensions of the frequency probability method. In fact, in many cases, subjective probabilities are value added because this approach allows you to take operational issues into account rather than depend on long-run statistical regularity.

Whether or not investors recognize it, virtually all the decisions they make are exercises in probability. For them to succeed, it is critical that their probability statement combines the historical record with the most recent data available. And that is Bayesian analysis in action.

Probabilities, Buffett Style

"Take the probability of loss times the amount of possible loss from the probability of gain times the amount of possible gain. That is what we're trying to do," says Buffett. "It's imperfect, but that's what it is all about."[14]

A useful example to clarify the link between investing and probability theory is the practice of risk arbitrage. Pure arbitrage is nothing more than profiting from the discrepancy in the price of a security quoted in two different markets. For example, commodities and currencies are quoted in several different markets around the world. If two separate markets quote a different price on the same commodity, you could buy in one market, sell in another market, and pocket the difference.

Risk arbitrage, which is the form more commonly practiced today, involves announced corporate mergers or acquisitions. (Some speculators practice risk arbitrage on unannounced corporate events, but this is an area that Buffett avoids and so shall we.) In a speech to a group of Stanford students, Buffett shared his views on risk arbitrage. "My job," he said, "is to assess the probability of the events [announced mergers] actually transpiring and the gain/loss ratio." (OID)[15]

Let's preface Buffett's next remarks to the Stanford students with this scenario. Suppose the Abbott Company began the trading day at $18 per share. Then, in midmorning, it is announced that sometime this year, perhaps in six months, Abbott will be sold to the Costello Company for $30 per share. Immediately, the share price of Abbott races to $27, where it settles in and begins to trade back and forth.

Buffett sees the announced merger and must make a decision. First of all, he tries to assess the degree of certainty. Some corporate deals don't materialize. The board of directors could unexpectedly resist the idea of a merger or the Federal Trade Commission might voice an objection. No one ever knows with certainty whether a risk arbitrage deal will close, and that is where the risk comes in.

Buffett's decision process is an exercise in subjective probability. He explained: "If I think an event has a 90 percent chance of occurring and there is 3 points on the upside, and there is a 10 percent chance that it will fall through and there's 9 points on the downside, then that's $.90 off of $2.70, leaving $1.80 mathematical expectation." (OID)[16]

Next, said Buffett, you have to figure in the time span involved and then relate the return of the investment to other investments available to you. If you bought one share of Abbott Company at $27, there is, according to Buffett's mathematics, a potential 6.6 percent return ($1.80/$27). If the deal is expected to close in six months, the annualized return on the investment would be 13.2 percent. Buffett would then compare the return from this risk arbitrage with other returns available to him.

Buffett freely acknowledges that risk arbitrage carries the potential for loss. "We're perfectly willing to lose money on a given transaction," he said, "arbitrage being one example, but we're not willing to enter into any transaction in which we think the probability of a number of mutually independent events of a similar type has an expectancy of loss. We hope," he added, "that we're entering into transactions where our calculations of those probabilities have validity." (OID)[17]

We can see quite clearly that Buffett's risk arbitrage estimates are subjective probabilities. There is no frequency distribution in risk arbitrage. Every deal is different. Every circumstance requires different estimations. Even so, there is value to approaching the risk arbitrage deal with some rational mathematical calculation.

The process is no different when you invest in common stocks. To illustrate this, let's look at one well-known Berkshire Hathaway common stock purchase—Wells Fargo.

Investing in Wells Fargo

In October 1990, Berkshire Hathaway purchased 5 million shares of Wells Fargo & Company, investing $289 million in the company at an average price of $57.88 per share.[18] With this purchase, Berkshire owned 10 percent of the shares outstanding and became the largest shareholder of the bank.

It was a very controversial move. Earlier in the year, the share price had traded as high as $86, then dropped sharply as investors abandoned California banks in droves. At the time, the West Coast was in the throes of a severe recession, and some observers speculated that banks, with their loan portfolios chock-full of commercial and residential mortgages, were in trouble. Wells Fargo, with the most commercial real estate of any California bank, was thought to be particularly vulnerable.

Buffett was well aware what was being said, but he came to a different conclusion about Wells Fargo. Did he know something these other investment professionals did not? Not really. He just analyzed the situation differently. Let's walk through the thinking process with him, for it gives us a clear example of how Buffett uses probabilities.

A risky investment is not so risky when gain, weighted for probabilities, considerably exceeds loss, comparably weighted.

140

"Ownership of a bank is far from riskless," said Buffett.[19] However, "if you believe that your gain, weighted for probabilities, considerably exceeds your loss, comparably weighted, you may consciously purchase a risky investment."[20] In analyzing the Wells Fargo situation, Buffett spread out multiple scenarios and assigned various probabilities to them. In his mind, the risk of owning Wells Fargo centered around three possibilities:

"California banks face the specific risk of a major earthquake, which might wreak havoc on borrowers that in turn destroy the banks lending to them. A second risk is systemic: the possibility of a business contraction or financial panic so severe it would endanger almost every highly leveraged institution, no matter how intelligently run. The market's major fear of the moment is that West Coast real estate values will tumble because of overbuilding and deliver huge losses to banks that have financed the expansion."[21]

Now, Buffett said, none of these scenarios can be ruled out. However, he concluded, based on best evidence, that the probability of an earthquake or a severe financial panic was low. (Buffett gives us no figures, but a "low" probability might be something less than 10 percent.)

Then he turned his attention to the probability of the third scenario. First, Buffett reasoned that a meaningful drop in real estate values should not cause major problems for a well-managed bank like Wells Fargo. "Consider some mathematics," he explained to Berkshire Hathaway shareholders in the annual report. "Wells Fargo currently earns well over $1 billion pretax annually after expensing more than $300 million for loan losses. If 10 percent of all $48 billion of the bank's loans—not just its real estate loans—were hit by problems in 1991, and these produced losses (including forgone interest) averaging 30 percent of principal, the company would roughly break even." Now consider that a 10 percent loss in a bank's portfolio would certainly qualify as severe business contraction, which Buffett had already rated a "low" probability. But even if that were to occur, the bank would still break even. Buffett continued, "A year like that—which we consider only a low-level possibility, not a likelihood—would not distress us."[22]

In the multiple scenarios that Buffett mentally laid out, the probability of any major long-lasting damage to Wells Fargo was, at best, low. Still, the market priced Wells Fargo's shares down by 50 percent. In Buffett's mind, the odds of making money by purchasing shares of Wells Fargo were now in the order of 2:1, with no corresponding increase in the probabilities of being wrong.

The Kelly Optimization Model

Each time you step foot inside a casino, the probability of coming out a winner is pretty low. You shouldn't be surprised; after all, we all know the house has the best odds. But one game, if played correctly, gives you a legitimate chance to beat the house: blackjack. In a worldwide best seller called *Beat the Dealer: A Winning Strategy for the Game of Twenty-One,* Edward O. Thorp, a mathematician by training, outlined a process for outsmarting a casino.[23]

Thorp's strategy was based on a simple concept. When the deck is rich with 10s, face cards, and aces, the player—let's say it's you—has a statistical advantage over the dealer. If you assign a −1 for the high cards and a +1 for the low cards, it's quite easy to keep track of the cards dealt; just keep a running tally in your head, adding or subtracting as each card shows. When the count turns positive, you know there are more high cards yet to be played. Smart players save their biggest bets for when the card count reaches a high relative number.

Buried deep inside Thorp's book was a notation on the Kelly betting model.[24] Kelly, in turn, took his inspiration from Claude Shannon, the inventor of information theory.

A mathematician with Bell Laboratories in the 1940s, Shannon spent a good part of his career trying to find the most optimal way to transmit information over copper lines without having the information become garbled by random molecular noise. In 1948, in an article called "A Mathematical Theory of Communication," he described what he had discovered.[25] Included in the article was the mathematical formula for the optimal amount of information that, considering the possibilities of success, can be pushed through the copper wire.

A few years later, J.L. Kelly, another mathematician, read Shannon's article and realized that the formula could just as easily work in gambling—another human endeavor that would be enhanced by knowing the possibilities of success. In 1956, in a paper entitled "A New Interpretation of Information Rate," Kelly pointed out that Shannon's various transmission rates and the possible outcomes of a chance event are essentially the same thing—probabilities—and the same formula could optimize both.[26]

The Kelly Optimization Model, often called the optimal growth strategy, is based on the concept that if you know the probability of success, you bet the fraction of your bankroll that maximizes the growth rate. It is expressed as a formula:

$$2p - 1 = x$$

where 2 times the probability of winning (p) minus 1 equals the percentage of the total that should be bet (x). For example, if the probability of beating the house is 55 percent, you should bet 10 percent of your bankroll to achieve maximum growth of your winnings. If the probability is 70 percent, bet 40 percent. And if you know the odds of winning are 100 percent, the model would say: Bet it all.

The stock market, of course, is far more complex than the game of blackjack. In the game, there is a finite number of cards and therefore a limited number of possible outcomes. The market, with many hundreds of common stocks and millions of investors, has an almost unlimited number of outcomes. Using the Kelly approach requires constant recalculations and adjustments throughout the investment process. Nonetheless, the underlying concept—mathematically linking degree of probability to investment size—carries important lessons.

I believe the Kelly model is an attractive tool for focus investors. However, it will benefit only those who use it responsibly. There are risks to employing the Kelly approach, and investors would be wise to understand its three limitations:

1. Anyone who intends to invest, using the Kelly model or not, should have a long-term horizon. Even if a blackjack player has a sound model that can beat the house, it does not always hold that success will be revealed in the first few hands dealt. The same is true for investing. How many times have investors seen that they have selected the right company but the market has taken its own sweet time in rewarding the selection?

2. Be wary of using leverage. The danger of borrowing to invest in the stock market (with a margin account) has been trumpeted loudly by both Ben Graham and Warren Buffett. The unexpected call on your capital can occur at the most unfortunate time in the game. If you use the Kelly model in a margin account, a stock market decline can force you to remove your high-probability bets.

3. The biggest danger in playing high-probability games is the risk of overbetting. If you judge an event has a 70 percent probability of success when in fact it is only a 55 percent event, you run the risk of "gambler's ruin." The way to minimize that risk is to underbet by using what is known as a *half-Kelly* or *fractional-Kelly* model. For example, if the Kelly model would tell you to bet 10 percent of your capital, you might choose to invest only 5 percent (a half-Kelly) instead. The fractional Kelly provides a margin of safety in portfolio management; that, together with the margin of safety we apply to selecting individual stocks, provides a double layer of protection.

Because the risk of overbetting far outweighs the penalties of underbetting, I believe that all investors, especially those who are just beginning to use a focus investment strategy, should use fractional Kelly bets. Unfortunately, minimizing

144

your bets also minimizes your potential gain. However, because the relationship in the Kelly model is parabolic, the penalty for underbetting is not severe. A half-Kelly, which reduces the amount you bet by 50 percent, reduces the potential growth rate by only 25 percent.

To Succeed with the Kelly Model

1. *Learn to think in probabilities.*
2. *Stay in the game long enough to achieve its rewards.*
3. *Avoid using leverage, with its unfortunate consequence.*
4. *Demand a margin of safety with each bet you make.*

It's All About Odds

In 1994, Charlie Munger accepted an invitation from Dr. Guilford Babcock to address the student investment seminar at the University of Southern California's business school. His remarks that day, reprinted in *Outstanding Investor Digest,* have become something of a classic among investors, and the entire transcript is well worth careful study. Charlie touched on many topics that day. He also explained, as only he can, what he thinks about probabilities and optimization.

"The model I like—to sort of simplify the notion of what goes on in a market for common stocks—is the parimutuel system at the racetrack," he said. "If you stop to think about it, a parimutuel system is a market. Everybody goes there and bets, and the odds are changed based on what's bet. That's what happens in the stock market.

"Any damn fool can see that a horse carrying a light weight with a wonderful win rate and good position et cetera is way more likely to win than a horse with a terrible record and extra weight and so on and so on. But if you look at the odds, the bad horse pays 100 to 1, whereas the good horse pays 3 to 2. Then it's not clear which is statistically the best bet. The prices have changed in such a way that it's very hard to beat the system." (OID)[27]

Charlie's racetrack analogy is perfect for investors. Too often, investors are attracted to a long shot that pays incredible odds but, for any one of countless reasons, never finishes the race. Or sometimes they pick the sure thing without ever considering the payoff. It appears to me that the most sensible way to approach horse racing, or the stock market, is to wait until the good horse comes to the post with inviting odds.

Andrew Beyer, columnist for the *Washington Post* and author of several books on thoroughbred racing, has spent many years watching racegoers bet and has seen far too many lose money through impetuosity. At the track, as elsewhere, the casino mentality—the itch to get into the action: to put down the money, toss the dice, pull the lever, do *something*—compels people to bet foolishly, without taking the time to think through what they are doing.

Beyer, who understands this psychological urge to get into the game, advises players to accommodate it by dividing their strategy between action bets and prime bets. Prime bets are reserved for serious players when two conditions occur: (1) confidence in the horse's ability to win is high, and (2) payoff odds are greater than they should be. Prime bets call for serious money. Action bets, as the name implies, are reserved for the long shots and hunches that satisfy the psychological need to play. They are smaller bets and are never allowed to become a large part of the players' betting pool.

When a horseplayer starts blurring the distinction between prime bets and action bets, says Beyer, he or she is "taking a step that will inevitably lead toward helter-skelter betting with no proper balance between . . . strong and weak selections."[28]

Probability Theory and the Market

Now, let us move away from the racetrack and put all this theory together into the reality of the stock market. The chain of thinking is the same.

1. *Calculate probabilities.* This is the probability you are concerned with: What are the chances that this stock I am considering will, over time, achieve an economic return greater than the market?

Using frequency if it is available, and subjective interpretation if it is not, make your best estimate. Do the most thorough job you can of collecting and analyzing information about the company, and convert your analysis to a percentage number. That number represents how obvious it is to you that the company is a winner.

2. *Adjust for new information.* Knowing that you are going to wait until the odds turn in your favor, pay scrupulous attention in the meantime to whatever the company does. Has management begun to act irresponsibly? Have the financial decisions begun to change? Has something happened to change the competitive landscape in which the business operates? If so, the probabilities will likely change.

3. *Decide how much to invest.* Of all the money you have available for investing in the market, what proportion should go to this particular purchase? Start with the Kelly formula, then adjust it downward, perhaps by half.

4. *Wait for best odds.* The odds of success tip in your favor when you have a margin of safety; the more uncertain the situation, the greater the margin you need. In the stock market, that safety margin is provided by a discounted price. When the company you like is selling at a price that is below its intrinsic value, that is your signal to act.

Thinking about probabilities may be new to you, but it is not impossible. If you are able to teach yourself to think about stocks this way, you are well on your way to being able to profit from your own lessons. An opportunity such as Coca-Cola in the late 1980s (an outstanding business priced substantially below intrinsic value) doesn't happen often. But when it does occur, those who understand probabilities will recognize it and will know what to do. As Charlie Munger puts it, "The wise [investors] bet heavily when the world offers them that opportunity. They bet big when they have the odds. And the rest of the time, they don't. It's just that simple." (OID)[29]

MODERN PORTFOLIO THEORY

Warren Buffett's faith in the fundamental ideas of focus investing puts him at odds with many other financial gurus and with a package of concepts that is collectively known as modern portfolio theory. Because you will hear so much about modern portfolio theory as you continue to learn about investing, I believe it is important to cover some of its most important elements. As we do so, we will give Buffett an opportunity to weigh in on each.

Portfolio Management through Diversification

In March 1952, about the time recent college graduate Warren Buffett went to work for his father's brokerage firm, there appeared in the *Journal of Finance* an article entitled "Portfolio Selection," by a University of Chicago graduate student named

Harry Markowitz. It was not long—only 14 pages—and, by the standards of academic journals, it was unremarkable: only four pages of text (the rest of the pages were consumed by graphs and mathematical equations) and only three citations. Yet that brief article is credited with launching modern finance.[30]

From Markowitz's standpoint, it didn't take volumes to explain what he believed was a rather simple notion: return and risk are inextricably linked. As an economist, he believed it was possible to quantify the relationship between the two, to a statistically valid degree, and thus determine the degree of risk that would be required for various levels of return. In his paper, he presented the calculations that supported his conclusion: No investor can achieve above-average gains without assuming above-average risk.

"I was struck with the notion that you should be interested in risk as well as return," Markowitz later remarked.[31] Today, this statement appears amazingly self-evident in light of what we have learned about investing, but it was a revolutionary concept in the 1950s. Until that time, investors gave very little thought to managing a portfolio or to the concept of risk. Portfolios were constructed haphazardly. If a manager thought a stock was going to go up in price, it was simply added to the portfolio. No other thinking was required.

That puzzled Markowitz. Surely it was foolish, he reasoned, to believe that you can generate high returns without exposing yourself to some kind of risk. To help clarify his thoughts, Markowitz devised what he called the *efficient frontier*.

"Being an economist," he explained, "I drew a trade-off graph with the expected return on one axis and risk on the other axis."[32] The efficient frontier is simply a line drawn from the bottom left to the top right. Each point on that line represents an intersection between potential reward and its corresponding level of risk. The most efficient portfolio is the one that gives the highest return for a given level of portfolio risk. An inefficient portfolio is one that exposes the investor to a level of risk without a corresponding level of return. The goal

149

for investment managers, said Markowitz, is to match portfolios to an investor's level of risk tolerance while limiting or avoiding inefficient portfolios.

In 1959, Markowitz published his first book, *Portfolio Selection: Efficient Diversification of Investment,* based on his PhD dissertation. In it he described more thoroughly his ideas about risk. "I used standard deviation as a measure of risk," Markowitz explains. Variance (deviation) can be thought of as the distance from average; according to Markowitz, the greater the distance from the average, the greater the risk.

We might think the riskiness of a portfolio, defined by Markowitz, is simply the weighted average variance of all the individual stocks in the portfolio. But this misses a crucial point. Although variance may provide a gauge to the riskiness of an individual stock, the average of two variances (or 100 variances) will tell you very little about the riskiness of a two-stock (or a 100-stock) portfolio. What Markowitz did was find a way to determine the riskiness of the entire portfolio. Many believe it is his greatest contribution.

He called it covariance, based on the already established formula for the variance of the weighted sum. Covariance measures the direction of a group of stocks. We say that two stocks exhibit high covariance when their prices, for whatever reason, tend to move together. Conversely, low covariance describes two stocks that move in opposite directions. In Markowitz's thinking, the risk of a portfolio is not the variance of the individual stocks but the covariance of the holdings. The more they move in the same direction, the greater is the chance that economic shifts will drive them all down at the same time. By the same token, a portfolio composed of risky stocks might actually be a conservative selection if the individual stock prices move differently. Either way, Markowitz said, diversification is the key.

According to Markowitz, the appropriate action for an investor is to first identify the level of risk that can be comfortably handled, and then construct an efficient diversified portfolio of low-covariance stocks.

Markowitz's book, like his original paper seven years earlier, was, for all practical purposes, soundly ignored by investment professionals.

A Mathematical Definition of Risk

Then, about ten years after Markowitz's groundbreaking paper first appeared, a young PhD student named Bill Sharpe approached Markowitz, who was then working on linear programming at the RAND Institute. Sharpe was in need of a dissertation topic, and one of his professors at UCLA had suggested he track down Markowitz. Obliging the young Sharpe, Markowitz told him of his work in portfolio theory and the need for estimating countless covariances. Sharpe listened intently, then returned to UCLA.

The next year, in 1963, Sharpe's dissertation was published: "A Simplified Model of Portfolio Analysis." While fully acknowledging his reliance on Markowitz's ideas, Sharpe suggested a simpler method that would avoid the countless covariant calculations required by Markowitz.

It was Sharpe's contention that all securities bear a common relationship with some underlying base factor. That factor could be a stock market index, the gross national product (GNP), or some other price index, as long as it was the single most important influence on the behavior of the security. Using Sharpe's theory, an analyst would need only to measure the relationship of the security to the dominant base factor. It greatly simplified Markowitz's approach.

Let's look at common stocks. According to Sharpe, the base factor for stock prices, the single greatest influence on their behavior, was the stock market itself. (Also important but less influential were industry groups and unique characteristics about the stock itself.) If the price of an individual stock is more volatile than the market as a whole, then that stock will make the portfolio more variable and therefore more risky.

151

Conversely, if the stock price is less volatile than the market, then adding this stock will make the portfolio less variable and less volatile. Now the volatility of the portfolio could be determined easily by the simple weighted average volatility of the individual securities.

Sharpe's volatility measure was given a name: beta factor. Beta is described as the degree of correlation between two separate price movements: the market as a whole and the individual stock. Stocks that rise and fall in value exactly in line with the market are assigned a beta of 1.0. If a stock rises and falls twice as far as the market, its beta is 2.0; if a stock's move is only 80 percent of the market's move, the beta is 0.8. Using just this information, we can ascertain the weighted average beta of the portfolio. The conclusion is that any portfolio with a beta greater than 1.0 will be more risky than the market, and a portfolio beta less than 1.0 will be less risky.

A year after publishing his dissertation on portfolio theory, Sharpe introduced a far-reaching concept called the Capital Asset Pricing Model (CAPM). It was a direct extension of his single-factor model for composing efficient portfolios. According to CAPM, stocks carry two distinct risks. One risk is simply the risk of being in the market, which Sharpe called "systemic risk." Systemic risk is "beta" and it cannot be diversified away. The second type, called "unsystemic risk," is the risk specific to a company's economic position. Unlike systemic risk, unsystemic risk *can* be diversified away by simply adding different stocks to the portfolio.

Peter Bernstein, the noted writer and researcher, and the founding editor of *The Journal of Portfolio Management,* has spent considerable time with Sharpe and has studied his work in depth. Bernstein believes that Sharpe's research points out one "inescapable conclusion": "The efficient portfolio is the stock market itself. No other portfolio with equal risk can offer a higher expected return; no other portfolio with equal expected return will be less risky."[33] In other words, the Capital Asset

Pricing Model says the market portfolio lies perfectly on Markowitz's efficient frontier.

In the space of one decade, two academicians had defined two important elements of what we would later call modern portfolio theory: Markowitz with his idea that the proper reward/risk balance depends on diversification, and Sharpe with his definition of risk. A third piece—the efficient market theory—came from a young assistant professor of finance at the University of Chicago, Eugene Fama.

Efficient Market Theory

Although several other distinguished researchers have written on efficient markets, including MIT economist Paul Samuelson, Eugene Fama is most credited with developing a comprehensive theory of the behavior of the stock market.

Fama began studying the changes in stock prices in the early 1960s. An intense reader, he absorbed all the written work on stock market behavior then available, but it appears he was especially influenced by the French mathematician Benoit Mandelbrot. Mandelbrot, who developed fractal geometry, argued that because stock prices fluctuated so irregularly, they would never oblige any fundamental or statistical research; furthermore, the pattern of irregular price movements was bound to intensify, causing unexpectedly large and intense shifts.

Fama's PhD dissertation, "The Behavior of Stock Prices," was published in *Journal of Business* in 1963 and later excerpted in *Financial Analysts Journal* and *Institutional Investor*. Fama, a relatively young newcomer, had definitely caught the attention of the finance community.

Fama's message was very clear: Stock prices are not predictable, because the market is too efficient. In an efficient market, as information becomes available, a great many smart people (Fama called them "rational profit maximizers") aggressively apply that information in a way that causes prices to adjust instantaneously, before anyone can profit. Predictions about the future therefore have no place in an efficient market, because the share prices adjust too quickly.

Fama does admit that it is impossible to test empirically the idea of an efficient market. The alternative, he figured, was to identify trading systems or traders who could outperform the stock market. If such a group existed, the market was obviously not efficient. But if no one could demonstrate an ability to beat the market, then we could assume that prices reflect all available information and hence the market is efficient.

The intertwined threads of modern portfolio theory were of consuming interest to the theorists and researchers who developed them, but, throughout the 1950s and 1960s, Wall Street paid little attention. Peter Bernstein has suggested a reason: during this time, portfolio management was "uncharted territory." However, by 1974, this all changed.

The bear market of 1973–1974 was, in the opinion of most analysts, the second worst financial disaster in our history. In its devastating impact on the country at large, it was exceeded only by the 1929 crash. Rather than one dramatic and awful day, it was a slow, tortuous process of unrelenting losses that lasted for two uninterrupted years. The broader markets declined by over 60 percent. Fixed-income holders who owned lower-coupon bonds saw their investment shrink. Interest rates and inflation soared to double digits. Oil and gasoline prices skyrocketed. Mortgage rates were so high that very few could afford to buy a new home. It was a dark, brutal time.

So severe was the financial damage that investment managers began to question their own approach. The self-inflicted financial wounds caused by decades of careless speculation were simply too deep. Looking for answers, most of the investment professionals gradually turned—some of them with great reluctance—to a body of academic study that had been largely ignored for two decades.

"The market disaster of 1974 convinced me that there had to be a better way to manage investment portfolios," Bernstein said. "Even if I could have convinced myself to turn my back on the theoretical structure that the academics were erecting, there was too much of it coming from major universities for me to accept the view of my colleagues that it was 'a lot of baloney.' "[34]

Thus, for the first time in history, our financial destiny rested not within Wall Street or Washington, DC, and not even in the hands of business owners. Rather, the financial landscape going forward would be defined by a group of university professors on whose doors the finance professionals had finally come knocking. From their ivory towers, they now became the new high priests of modern finance.

Buffett and Modern Portfolio Theory

Meanwhile, even as he concentrated his energies on the Berkshire Hathaway business, Warren Buffett was keeping a keen eye on the market. Whereas most investment professionals saw 1973–1974 as a period of debilitating losses, Buffett, the disciple of Ben Graham, saw only opportunity. And he knew when to act.

Consider, for example, what happened with *The Washington Post*.

"We bought The Washington Post Company at a valuation of $80 million back in 1974," Buffett later recalled in a lecture at Stanford Law School. "If you'd asked any one of 100 analysts how much the company was worth when we were buying it, no one would have argued about the fact it was worth $400 million. Now under the whole theory of beta and modern portfolio theory, we would have been doing something riskier buying stock for $40 million than we were buying it for $80 million, even though it's worth $400 million—because it would have had more volatility. With that, they've lost me." (OID)[35]

The purchase of the *Post* was a clear signal that Buffett was embarking on a course that would put him at odds with most other investment professionals. He also made clear what he thought of the three main ingredients of modern portfolio theory: risk, diversification, and an efficient market.

Buffett's View of Risk

In modern portfolio theory, risk is defined by the volatility of the share price. But, throughout his career, Buffett has always perceived a drop in share prices as an opportunity to make additional money. In his mind, then, a dip in price actually *reduces* risk. He points out, "For owners of a business—and that's the way we think of shareholders—the academics' definition of risk is far off the mark, so much so that it produces absurdities."[36]

Buffett has a different definition of risk: the possibility of harm or injury. And that is a factor of the "intrinsic value risk" of the business, not the price behavior of the stock.[37] The real risk, Buffett says, is whether after-tax returns from an investment "will give him [an investor] at least as much purchasing power as he had to begin with, plus a modest rate of interest on that initial stake."[38] In Buffett's view, harm or injury comes from misjudging the future profits of the business, plus the uncontrollable, unpredictable effect of taxes and inflation.

ON RISK

*R*isk does not reside in price changes, but in miscalculations of intrinsic value.

Furthermore, risk, for Buffett, is inextricably linked to an investor's time horizon. If you buy a stock today, he explains, with the intention of selling it tomorrow, then you have entered into a risky transaction. The odds of predicting whether share prices will be up or down in a short period are the same as the odds of predicting the toss of a coin; you will lose half of the time. However, says Buffett, if you extend your time horizon out to several years, the probability of its being a risky transaction declines meaningfully—assuming, of course, that you have made a sensible purchase. "If you asked me to assess the risk of buying Coca-Cola this morning and selling it tomorrow morning," Buffett says, "I'd say that that's a very risky transaction." (OID)[39] But in Buffett's way of thinking, buying Coca-Cola this morning and holding it for ten years puts the risk at zero.

Buffett's View of Diversification

Buffett's view on risk drives his diversification strategy. Here too, his thinking is the polar opposite of modern portfolio theory. According to that theory, remember, the primary benefit of a broadly diversified portfolio is to mitigate the price volatility of the individual stocks. But if you are unconcerned with price volatility, as Buffett is, then you will also see portfolio diversification in a different light.

"The strategy we've adopted precludes our following standard diversification dogma," says Buffett. "Many pundits would therefore say the strategy must be riskier than that employed by more conventional investors. We believe that a policy of portfolio concentration may well decrease risk if it raises, as it should, both the intensity with which an investor thinks about a business and the comfort level he must feel with its economic characteristics before buying into it."[40] That is, by purposely focusing on just a few select companies, you are better able to study them closely and understand their intrinsic value. The more knowledge you have about your company, the less risk you are likely taking.

"Diversification serves as protection against ignorance," explains Buffett. "If you want to make sure that nothing bad happens to you relative to the market, you should own everything. There is nothing wrong with that. It's a perfectly sound approach for somebody who doesn't know how to analyze businesses." (OID)[41]

Buffett's View of the Efficient Market Theory

If the efficient market theory is correct, there is no possibility except random chance that any person or group could outperform the market, and certainly no chance that the same one person or group could consistently do so. Yet Buffett's performance record for the past 30 years is prima facie evidence that it *is* possible. So what does that say about the efficient market theory?

Buffett's problem with the efficient market theory rests on one central point: It makes no provision for investors who analyze all the available information and gain a competitive advantage by doing so. "Observing correctly that the market was frequently efficient, they went on to conclude incorrectly that it was *always* efficient. The difference between these propositions is night and day."[42]

Nonetheless, efficient market theory (EMT) is still religiously taught in business schools, a fact that gives Warren Buffett no end of satisfaction. "Naturally the disservice done students and gullible investment professionals who have swallowed EMT has been an extraordinary service to us and other followers of Graham," Buffett wryly observed. "In any sort of a contest—financial, mental, or physical—it's an enormous advantage to have opponents who have been taught it's useless to even try. From a selfish standpoint, we should probably endow chairs to ensure the perpetual teaching of EMT."[43]

In many ways, modern portfolio theory protects investors who have limited knowledge and understanding of how to value a business. But that protection comes with a price. According to Buffett, "Modern portfolio theory tells you how to be average. But I think almost anybody can figure out how to do average in the fifth grade." (OID)[44]

Anyone who chooses to embrace the focus investing philosophy used with such success by Warren Buffett must first disengage from the constructs of modern portfolio theory. Ordinarily, it would be easy to reject a model that is largely considered ineffectual. After all, there is nothing prideful or rewarding about being average. But modern portfolio theory has developed a long history and a deep culture; it is full of neat formulas and Nobel Prize winners. We should not expect its defenders to leave the field quietly.

Fortunately, we do not have to take on the task of dismantling modern portfolio theory. Unfolding events will take care of that. If we follow Buffett's advice, the success we earn will eventually work to overthrow the less-than-effective model.

Although modern portfolio theory has its share of intellectual heavyweights, do not lose sight of the fact that the lineage of focus investing includes some of history's greatest investors: John Maynard Keynes, Phil Fisher, Warren Buffett, Charlie Munger, Lou Simpson, and Bill Ruane.

Some of them, of course, you already know. We shall meet the others in the next chapter.

CHAPTER 6

MANAGING YOUR PORTFOLIO: THE CHALLENGE OF FOCUS INVESTING

In the preceding chapter, my goal was to lay out the argument for adopting the focus investing approach that Warren Buffett uses with such great success. I would be doing you less than full service if I did not also make it plain that one unavoidable consequence of this approach is *heightened volatility*. When your portfolio is focused on just a few companies, a price change in any one of them is all the more noticeable and has greater overall impact.

The ability to withstand that volatility without undue second-guessing is crucial to your peace of mind, and, ultimately, to your financial success. Coming to terms with it is partly a matter of understanding the emotional side effects of investing, an area we shall explore in the next chapter. You will also, I believe, find some comfort in the experiences of others who have followed this path and realized outstanding results. And that is the subject of this chapter.

In 1934, during the height of the Great Depression, a re-markable book with the unremarkable title of *Security Analysis* was published. Its coauthors, Benjamin Graham and David Dodd, had been working on it for five years. Their writing time had been interrupted by teaching at Columbia and helping clients cope with the aftereffects of the 1929 crash. Graham later said the delay was providential, for it allowed him to in-clude "wisdom acquired at the cost of much suffering."[1]

Security Analysis is universally acclaimed a classic; it is still in print after five editions and 67 years. It is impossible to over-state the book's influence on the modern world of investing, or the enormous contributions of Ben Graham to the profession.

Fifty years after its original publication, the Columbia Uni-versity Business School sponsored a seminar marking the an-niversary of this seminal text by two of its illustrious faculty. Warren Buffett, one of the school's best-known alumni and the most famous modern-day proponent of Graham's value ap-proach, was invited to address the gathering. His speech, titled "The Superinvestors of Graham-and-Doddsville," has become, in its own way, as much a classic as the book it honored.[2]

Most of those in the audience that day in 1984—university professors, researchers, and other academicians, along with many investment professionals—still held firmly to modern portfolio theory and the validity of the efficient market. Buf-fett, as we know, just as firmly disagreed, and in his speech he quietly demolished the platform on which rested the efficient market theory.

He began by recapping the central argument of modern portfolio theory—that the stock market is efficient, all stocks are priced correctly, and therefore anyone who beats the market year after year is simply lucky. Maybe so, he said, but I know some folks who have done it, and their success can't be ex-plained away as simply random chance.

And he proceeded to lay out the evidence. All the examples he presented that day were of people who had managed to beat the market consistently over time, and who had done so not because of luck but because they all followed principles learned from the same source: Ben Graham. They all reside, he said, in the "intellectual village" of Graham-and-Doddsville.

Although they may make specific decisions differently, Buffett explained, they are linked by a common approach that seeks to take advantage of discrepancies between market price and intrinsic value. "Needless to say, our Graham and Dodd investors do not discuss beta, the capital asset pricing model or covariance of returns," Buffett said. "These are not subjects of any interest to them. In fact, most of them would have trouble defining those terms."

In a published article based on his 1984 speech, Buffett included tables that presented the impressive performance results of the residents of Graham-and-Doddsville.[3] Nearly two decades later, I thought it might be interesting to take an updated look at a few people who exemplify the approach defined by Graham and who also share Buffett's belief in the value of a focused portfolio with a smaller number of stocks. I think of them as the Superinvestors of Buffettville: Charlie Munger, Bill Ruane, Lou Simpson, and, of course, Buffett himself. From their performance records there is much we can learn. But before we start this investigation, let us begin with the very first focus investor.

JOHN MAYNARD KEYNES

Most people recognize John Maynard Keynes for his contributions to economic theory. In addition to being a great macroeconomic thinker, Keynes was also a legendary investor. Proof of his investment prowess can be found in the performance record of the Chest Fund at King's College in Cambridge, England.

Before 1920, King's College investments were restricted to fixed-income securities. However, when Keynes was appointed the Second Bursar in late 1919, he persuaded the trustees to begin a separate fund that would contain only common stocks, currency, and commodity futures. This separate account became the Chest Fund. From 1927, when he was named First Bursar, until his death in 1945, Keynes had sole responsibility for this account. In all that time, he kept its holdings focused on just a few companies. In 1934, the same year that *Security Analysis* was published, Keynes wrote to a colleague, explaining his reasoning.

"It is a mistake to think one limits one's risks by spreading too much between enterprises about which one knows little and has no reason for special confidence. . . . One's knowledge and experience are definitely limited and there are seldom more than two or three enterprises at any given time in which I personally feel myself entitled to put full confidence."[4]

That letter may be the first piece ever written about focus investing.

Four years later, Keynes prepared a full policy report for the Chest Fund, outlining his investment principles:

"**1.** A careful selection of a few investments having regard to their cheapness in relation to their probable actual and potential *intrinsic* [emphasis his] value over a period of years ahead and in relation to alternative investments at the time;

"**2.** A steadfast holding of these fairly large units through thick and thin, perhaps for several years, until either they have fulfilled their promise or it is evident that they were purchased on a mistake;

"**3.** A *balanced* [emphasis his] investment position, i.e, a variety of risks in spite of individual holdings being large, and if possible opposed risks."[5]

Although he did not use the term, I believe it is clear, from reading Keynes's investment policy, that he was a focus investor. He purposely limited his stocks to a select few and relied on fundamental analysis to estimate the value of his picks relative to their price. He liked to keep portfolio turnover at a very low rate. He recognized the importance of diversifying his risks. And he aimed to "oppose risk" by introducing a variety of economic positions concentrated in high-quality, predictable businesses.

How well did Keynes perform? A quick study of Table 6.1 shows his stock selection and portfolio management skills were outstanding. During his 18-year stewardship, the Chest Fund achieved an average annual return of 13.2 percent, at a time when the overall U.K. market return remained basically flat.

Table 6.1   John Maynard Keynes

	Annual Percentage Change	
Year	Chest Fund (%)	U.K. Market (%)
1928	0.0	0.1
1929	0.8	6.6
1930	−32.4	−20.3
1931	−24.6	−25.0
1932	44.8	−5.8
1933	35.1	21.5
1934	33.1	−0.7
1935	44.3	5.3
1936	56.0	10.2
1937	8.5	−0.5
1938	−40.1	−16.1
1939	12.9	−7.2
1940	−15.6	−12.9
1941	33.5	12.5
1942	−0.9	0.8
1943	53.9	15.6
1944	14.5	5.4
1945	14.6	0.8
Average Return	13.2	−0.5
Standard Deviation	29.2	12.4
Minimum	−40.1	−25.0
Maximum	56.0	21.5

Considering that the time period included both the Great Depression and World War II, we would have to say that Keynes's performance was extraordinary.

Even so, the Chest Fund endured some painful periods. In three separate years (1930, 1938, and 1940), its value dropped significantly more than the overall U.K. market. Reviewing Keynes's performance record in 1983, two modern analysts commented, "From the large swings in the Fund's fortune, it is obvious that the Fund must have been more volatile than the market."[6] Indeed, if we measure the standard deviation of the Chest Fund, we find it was almost two and a half times more volatile than the general market. Without a doubt, investors in the fund occasionally had a bumpy ride but, in the end, outscored the market by a significantly large margin.

Lest you think Keynes, with his macroeconomic background, possessed market timing skills, take further note of his investment policy.

"We have not proved able to take much advantage of a general systematic movement out of and into ordinary shares as a whole at different phases of the trade cycle," he wrote. "As a result of these experiences I am clear that the idea of wholesale shifts is for various reasons impracticable and indeed undesirable. Most of those who attempt to sell [do so] too late and buy too late, and do both too often, incurring heavy expenses and developing too unsettled and speculative a state of mind, which, if it is widespread has besides the grave social disadvantage of aggravating the scale of the fluctuations."[7]

High turnover produces heavy expenses, fuels a speculative state of mind, and makes the overall market fluctuation worse. True then, true now.

CHARLES MUNGER PARTNERSHIP

Although Berkshire Hathaway's investment performance is usually tied to its chairman, we should never forget that vice chairman Charlie Munger is an outstanding investor himself. Shareholders who have attended Berkshire's annual meeting or read Charlie's thoughts in *Outstanding Investor Digest* realize what a fine intellect he has.

"I ran into him in about 1960," said Buffett, "and I told him law was fine as a hobby but he could do better."[8] As you may recall from Chapter 2, Munger at the time had a thriving law practice in Los Angeles, but gradually shifted his energies to a new investment partnership bearing his name. The results of his talents can be found in Table 6.2.

"His portfolio was concentrated in very few securities and, therefore, his record was much more volatile," Buffett explained, "but it was based on the same discount-from-value approach." In making investment decisions for his partnership,

Table 6.2 Charles Munger Partnership

	Annual Percentage Change	
Year	Overall Partnership (%)	Dow Jones Industrial Average (%)
1962	30.1	−7.6
1963	71.7	20.6
1964	49.7	18.7
1965	8.4	14.2
1966	12.4	−15.8
1967	56.2	19.0
1968	40.4	7.7
1969	28.3	−11.6
1970	−0.1	8.7
1971	25.4	9.8
1972	8.3	18.2
1973	−31.9	−13.1
1974	−31.5	−23.1
1975	73.2	44.4
Average Return	24.3	6.4
Standard Deviation	33.0	18.5
Minimum	−31.9	−23.1
Maximum	73.2	44.4

Charlie followed the Graham methodology and would only look at companies that were selling below their intrinsic value. "He was willing to accept greater peaks and valleys in performance, and he happens to be a fellow whose psyche goes toward concentration."[9]

Notice that Buffett does not use the word *risk* in describing Charlie's performance. Using the conventional definition of risk (price volatility), we would have to say that, over its 13-year history, Charlie's partnership was extremely risky. Its standard deviation was almost twice that of the market. But beating the average annual return of the market by 18 points over those same 13 years was an achievement not of a risk taker but of an astute investor.

SEQUOIA FUND

Buffett first met Bill Ruane in 1951, when both were attending Ben Graham's Security Analysis class at Columbia. The two classmates stayed in contact, and Buffett watched Ruane's investment performance over the years with admiration. When Buffett closed his investment partnership in 1969, he asked Ruane if he would be willing to handle the funds of some of the partners. That, as we have seen, was the beginning of the Sequoia Fund.

Both men knew it was a difficult time to set up a mutual fund, but Ruane plunged ahead. The stock market was splitting into a two-tier market. Most of the hot money was gyrating toward the so-called Nifty Fifty (the big-name companies like IBM and Xerox), leaving the value stocks far behind. Although, as Buffett pointed out, comparative performance for value investors was difficult in the beginning, "I am happy to say that my partners, to an amazing degree, not only stayed with him but added money, with happy results."[10]

Sequoia Fund was a true pioneer, the first mutual fund run on the principles of focus investing. The public record of Sequoia's holdings demonstrates clearly that Bill Ruane and Rick

Cuniff, his partner in Ruane, Cuniff & Company, managed a tightly focused, low-turnover portfolio. On average, well over 90 percent of the fund was invested in a group of six to ten companies. Even so, the economic diversity of the portfolio was, and continues to be, broad. Ruane has often pointed out that even though Sequoia is a focused portfolio, it has owned a variety of businesses engaged in commercial banking, pharmaceuticals, and automobile and property casualty insurance.

Bill Ruane's point of view is in many ways unique among money managers. Generally speaking, most investment management begins with some preconceived notion about portfolio management and then fills in the portfolio with various stocks. At Ruane, Cuniff & Company, the partners begin with the idea of selecting the best possible stocks; then they let the portfolio form around those selections.

Selecting the best possible stocks, of course, requires a high level of research, and here again Ruane, Cuniff & Company stands apart from the rest of the industry. The firm has built a reputation as one of the brightest shops in money management. The principals eschew Wall Street's broker-fed research reports. Instead, they rely on their own intensive company investigations. "We don't go in much for titles at our firm," Ruane once said, "[but] if we did, my business card would read Bill Ruane, Research Analyst."

Such thinking is unusual on Wall Street, he explains. "Typically, people start out their careers in an 'analyst' function but aspire to get promoted to the more prestigious 'portfolio manager' designation, which is considered to be a distinct and higher function. To the contrary, we have always believed that if you are a long-term investor, the analyst function is paramount and the portfolio management follows naturally."[11]

How well has this unique approach served their shareholders? Table 6.3 outlines the investment performance of Sequoia Fund from 1971 through 1999. During this period, Sequoia earned an average annual return of 18.9 percent, compared to the 15.2 percent of the Standard & Poor's 500 Index.

Table 6.3   Sequoia Fund, Inc.

| | Annual Percentage Change | |
Year	Sequoia Fund	S&P 500 Index
1971	13.5	14.3
1972	3.7	18.9
1973	−24.0	−14.8
1974	−15.7	−26.4
1975	60.5	37.2
1976	72.3	23.6
1977	19.9	−7.4
1978	23.9	6.4
1979	12.1	18.2
1980	12.6	32.3
1981	21.5	−5.0
1982	31.2	21.4
1983	27.3	22.4
1984	18.5	6.1
1985	28.0	31.6
1986	13.3	18.6
1987	7.4	5.2
1988	11.1	16.5
1989	27.9	31.6
1990	−3.8	−3.1
1991	40.0	30.3
1992	9.4	7.6
1993	10.8	10.0
1994	3.3	1.4
1995	41.4	37.5
1996	21.7	22.9
1997	42.3	33.4
1998	35.3	28.6
1999	−16.5	21.0
Average Return	18.9	15.2
Standard Deviation	21.2	16.1
Minimum	−24.0	−26.4
Maximum	72.3	37.5

Like other focus portfolios, Sequoia achieved this above-average return with a slightly bumpier ride. The standard deviation of the market during this period (which, you remember, is one way to express volatility) was 16.1 percent, compared to Sequoia's 21.2 percent. Some might call that a higher risk, but knowing the care and diligence Ruane, Cuniff & Company takes in selecting stocks, the conventional definition of risk does not apply here.

LOU SIMPSON

About the time Warren Buffett began acquiring the stock of GEICO insurance company in the late 1970s, he also made an acquisition that would have a direct benefit on GEICO's financial health. His name was Lou Simpson.

Simpson, who earned a master's degree in economics from Princeton, worked for both Stein Roe & Farnham and Western Asset Management before Buffett lured him to GEICO in 1979. He is now CEO. Recalling his job interview, Buffett remembers that Lou had "the ideal temperament for investing."[12] Lou, he said, was an independent thinker who was confident of his own research and "who derived no particular pleasure from operating with or against the crowd."

Lou is a voracious reader who ignores Wall Street research. Instead, he pores over annual reports. His common-stock selection process is similar to Buffett's. He purchases only high-return businesses that are run by able management and are available at reasonable prices. Lou has something else in common with Buffett. He focuses his portfolio on only a few stocks. GEICO's billion-dollar equity portfolio customarily owns fewer than ten stocks.

Between 1980 and 1996, GEICO's portfolio achieved an average annual return of 24.7 percent, compared to the market's return of 17.8 percent (see Table 6.4). "These are not only terrific figures," says Buffett, "but, fully as important, they have

171

Table 6.4   Lou Simpson, GEICO

Year	GEICO Equities (%)	S&P 500 (%)
	Annual Percentage Change	
1980	23.7	32.3
1981	5.4	−5.0
1982	45.8	21.4
1983	36.0	22.4
1984	21.8	6.1
1985	45.8	31.6
1986	38.7	18.6
1987	−10.0	5.1
1988	30.0	16.6
1989	36.1	31.7
1990	−9.1	−3.1
1991	57.1	30.5
1992	10.7	7.6
1993	5.1	10.1
1994	13.3	1.3
1995	39.7	37.6
1996	29.2	37.6
Average Return	24.7	17.8
Standard Deviation	19.5	14.3
Minimum	−10.0	−5.0
Maximum	57.1	37.6

been achieved in the right way. Lou has consistently invested in undervalued common stocks that, individually, were unlikely to present him with a permanent loss and that, collectively, were close to risk-free."[13]

Here again we see Buffett's sense of risk: It has nothing to do with volatility, but rather with the certainty that the individual stocks will, over time, produce a profit.

Simpson's performance and investment style fit neatly inside Buffett's way of thinking. "Lou takes the same conservative concentrated approach to investments that we do at Berkshire and it is an enormous plus for us to have him on board," says Buffett. "There are very few people who I will let run money and businesses that we have control over, but we are delighted in the case of Lou. His presence on the scene assures us that Berkshire would have an extraordinary professional immediately available to handle its investments if something were to happen to Charlie and me."[14]

Buffett, Munger, Ruane, Simpson. It is clear that the Superinvestors of Buffettville have a common intellectual approach to investing. They are united in their belief that the way to reduce risk is to buy stocks only when the margin of safety (that is, the favorable discrepancy between the intrinsic value of the company and today's market price) is high. They also believe that concentrating their portfolio around a limited number of these high-probability events not only reduces risk, but helps to generate returns far above the market rate of return.

Still, when we point out these successful focus investors, many people remain skeptical. They wonder: Are all these people successful because of their close professional relationship? As it turns out, all these stock pickers picked different stocks. Buffett didn't own what Munger owned, and Munger didn't own what Ruane owned; Ruane didn't own what Simpson owned, and nobody owned what Keynes owned.

Well, that may be true, say the skeptics, but you've offered only five examples of focus investors, and five observations are not enough to draw a statistically meaningful conclusion. In an industry that has thousands of portfolio managers, five successes could simply be random chance.

Fair enough. To eliminate any notion that the five Superinvestors of Buffettville are nothing more than statistical aberrations, we need to examine a wider field. Unfortunately, we do not have a large number of focus investors to study. Without more cases, how do we proceed? By going inside a statistical laboratory and designing a universe of 12,000 portfolios.

▪▬▬▬ THREE THOUSAND FOCUS INVESTORS

Using the Compustat database of common stock returns, we isolated 1,200 companies that displayed measurable data—including revenues, earnings, and return on equity—from 1979 through 1986.[15] We then asked the computer to randomly assemble, from these 1,200 companies, 12,000 portfolios of various sizes:

1. 3,000 portfolios containing 250 stocks.
2. 3,000 portfolios containing 100 stocks.
3. 3,000 portfolios containing 50 stocks.
4. 3,000 portfolios containing 15 stocks.

Next, we calculated the average annual rate of return of each portfolio in each group over two different time periods: 10 years (1987–1996) and 18 years (1979–1996). (The 10-year distribution is shown in Figure 6.1.) Then we compared the returns of the four portfolio groups to the overall stock market (defined as the Standard & Poor's 500 Index) for the same time periods.

From all this, one key finding emerged: In every case, when we reduce the number of stocks in a portfolio, we begin to increase the probability of generating returns that are higher than the market's rate of return.

Let's look a little deeper, using the ten-year time frame (Figure 6.1). All four portfolio groups had an average yearly return of around 13.8 percent; the S&P average for the same period was somewhat higher: 15.2 percent. Keep in mind that the S&P 500 is a weighted index dominated by the largest companies, and the time period under consideration is one in which large-capitalization stocks did particularly well. In our study, the portfolios are equally weighted and include not only large capitalization stocks but small and midsize companies as well. So we can say that the four groups of "laboratory"

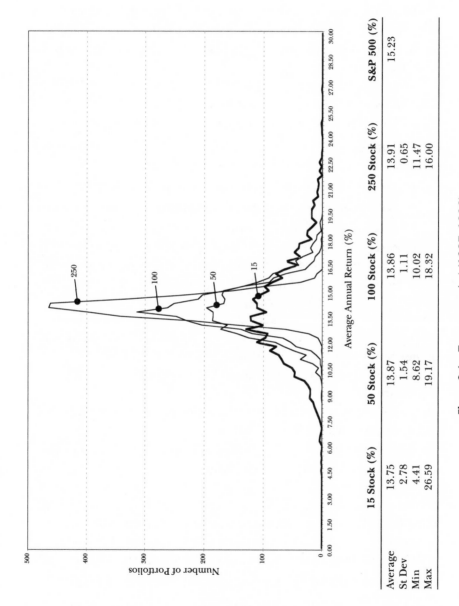

Figure 6.1 Ten-year period (1987–1996).

	15 Stock (%)	50 Stock (%)	100 Stock (%)	250 Stock (%)	S&P 500 (%)
Average	13.75	13.87	13.86	13.91	15.23
St Dev	2.78	1.54	1.11	0.65	
Min	4.41	8.62	10.02	11.47	
Max	26.59	19.17	18.32	16.00	

portfolios are performing on an approximate par with the general market.

Where this starts to get interesting, though, is when we look at the minimum/maximum numbers—the worst performing and the best performing portfolios in each group. Here's what we find:

- Among the portfolios containing 250 stocks, the best return was 16.0 percent and the worst was 11.4 percent.
- Among the 100-stock portfolios, the best return was 18.3 percent and the worst was 10.0 percent.
- Among the 50-stock portfolios, the best return was 19.1 percent and the worst was 8.6 percent.
- Among the 15-stock portfolios, the best return was 26.6 percent and the worst was 6.7 percent. These are the focus portfolios in the study, and the only group with best returns substantially higher than the S&P.

The same relative trends held when we considered the 18-year periods. Here, too, the small portfolios showed much higher highs and lower lows than the large portfolios.

This leads us to two inescapable conclusions:

1. You have a much higher chance of doing better than the market with a focus portfolio.
2. You also have a much higher chance of doing worse than the market with a focus portfolio.

To reinforce the first conclusion for the skeptics, we found some remarkable statistics when we sorted the ten-year data:

Out of 3,000 15-stock portfolios, 808 beat the market.
Out of 3,000 50-stock portfolios, 549 beat the market.
Out of 3,000 100-stock portfolios, 337 beat the market.
Out of 3,000 250-stock portfolios, 63 beat the market.

I submit this as convincing evidence that the probabilities go up as the size of the portfolio goes down. With a 15-stock portfolio, you have a 1-in-4 chance of outperforming the market. With a 250-stock portfolio, you have a 1-in-50 chance.[16]

Another important consideration: In our study, we did not factor in the effect of trading expenses; obviously, where the turnover rate is higher, so are the costs. If these realized expenses had been included in our graphs, the annualized returns would have shifted to the left, making it even harder to beat a market rate of return.

As to the second conclusion, it simply reinforces the critical importance of intelligent stock selection. It is no coincidence that the Superinvestors of Buffettville are also superior stock pickers. If you have not picked the right companies, your underperformance will be striking. However, we can suggest that the outsized returns earned by the Superinvestors are made possible by their willingness to focus their portfolios on their best ideas.

A BETTER WAY TO MEASURE PERFORMANCE

In that famous speech about Graham-and-Doddsville, Warren Buffett said many important things, none more profound than this: "When the price of a stock can be influenced by a 'herd' on Wall Street with prices set at the margin by the most emotional person, or the greediest person, or the most depressed person, it is hard to argue that the market always prices rationally. In fact, market prices are frequently nonsensical."[17]

It is profound because of where it leads us. If we accept the idea that prices are not always rational, then we are freed from the shortsightedness of using them as the sole basis for decisions. If we accept the idea that share price is not everything, we can broaden our horizon to focus on what counts: the thoughtful research and analysis of the underlying businesses. Of course we always want to be aware of prices, so we can recognize when they dip below value, but we need no longer be strangled by this one-dimensional measure that can so seriously lead us in the wrong direction.

Making this shift will not be easy. Our entire industry—money managers, institutional investors, and all manner of individual investors—is price-myopic. If the price of a particular stock is going up, we assume good things are happening; if the price starts to go down, we assume something bad is happening, and we act accordingly.

It's a poor mental habit, and it is exacerbated by another: evaluating price performance over very short periods of time. Not only are we depending on the wrong thing (price), Buffett would say, we're looking at it too often and we're too quick to jump when we don't like what we see.

This double-barreled foolishness—this price-based, short-term mentality—is a flawed way of thinking, and it shows up at every level in our business. It is what prompts some people to check stock quotes every day, and to call their broker so often that they have the phone number on speed-dial. It is why institutional investors, with responsibility for billions of dollars, are ready to buy or sell at the snap of a finger. It is the reason managers of mutual funds churn the stocks in the fund's portfolio at dizzying rates: They think it is their job to do so.

Amazingly, those same money managers are the first to urge their clients to remain calm when things start to look shaky. They send out reassuring letters lauding the virtue of staying the course. So why don't they practice what they preach?

It is especially easy to observe this contradiction in the handling of mutual funds because their actions are so thoroughly documented and scrutinized by the financial press. Because so much information is available, and because mutual funds are so familiar and so well understood, I believe we can learn a great deal about the folly of a price-based measure by looking at how it works in mutual funds.

The Double Standard in Mutual Funds

Writing in *Fortune* late in 1997, Joseph Nocera pointed out the obvious inconsistencies between what mutual fund managers recommend shareholders do—namely, "buy and hold"—and what managers actually do with their own portfolio—namely, buy-sell, buy-sell, buy-sell. Reinforcing his own observations of this double standard, Nocera quoted Morningstar's Don Phillips: "There is a huge disconnect between what the fund industry does and what it tells investors to do."[18]

The obvious question becomes: If investors are counseled to wisely buy and hold, why do managers frenetically buy and sell stocks each year? The answer, says Nocera, "is that the internal dynamics of the fund industry make it almost impossible for fund managers to look beyond short term."[19] Why? Because the business of mutual funds has turned into a senseless short-term game of who has best performance, measured totally by price.

Today, there is substantial pressure on portfolio managers to generate eye-catching short-term performance numbers. These numbers attract a lot of attention. Every three months, leading publications such as *The Wall Street Journal* and *Barron's* publish quarterly performance rankings of mutual funds. The funds that have done best in the past three months move to the top of the list, are praised by financial commentators on television and in newspapers, rush to put out self-congratulatory advertising and promotion, and attract a flurry of new deposits. Investors, who have been waiting to see which fund manager has the "hot hand," pounce on these rankings. Indeed, quarterly performance rankings are increasingly used to separate the gifted managers from those who are mediocre.

This fixation on short-term price performance, while acutely obvious in mutual funds, is not limited to them; it dominates thinking throughout our industry. We are no longer in an environment where managers are measured over the long term. Even people who function as their own manager, as many of you may do, are infected by the unhealthy nuances of this environment. In many ways, we have become enslaved to a marketing machine that all but guarantees underperformance.

Caught in a vicious circle, there appears to be no way out. But of course, as we have learned, there is a way to improve investment performance. What we must do now is find a better way to *measure* performance. The cruel irony is that the strategy most likely to provide above-average returns over time appears incompatible with how we judge performance—a mutual fund manager's or our own.

The Tortoise and the Hare

In 1986, V. Eugene Shahan, a Columbia University Business School alumnus and portfolio manager at U.S. Trust, wrote a follow-up article to Buffett's "The Superinvestors of Graham-and-Doddsville." In his piece (titled "Are Short-Term Performance and Value Investing Mutually Exclusive?"), Shahan took on the same question that we are now asking: How appropriate is it to measure a money manager's skill on the basis of short-term performance?

He noted that, with the exception of Buffett himself, many of the people Buffett described as "Superinvestors"—undeniably skilled, undeniably successful—faced periods of short-term underperformance. In a money-management version of the tortoise and the hare, Shahan commented: "It may be another of life's ironies that investors principally concerned with short-term performance may very well achieve it, but at the expense of long-term results. The outstanding records of the Superinvestors of Graham-and-Doddsville were compiled with apparent indifference to short-term performance."[20] In today's mutual fund performance derby, he points out, many of the Superinvestors of Graham-and-Doddsville would have been overlooked.

The same is also true of the Superinvestors of Buffettville. Table 6.5 shows that they would have struggled through several

Table 6.5 The Superinvestors of Buffettville

	Number of Years of Performance	Number of Years of Underperformance	Number of Consecutive Years of Underperformance	Underperformance Years as a Percent of All Years
Keynes	18	6	3	33
Munger	14	5	3	36
Ruane	29	11	4	37
Simpson	17	4	1	24

difficult periods. Only Buffett went through the performance derby unscathed.

John Maynard Keynes, who managed the Chest Fund for 18 years, underperformed the market one-third of the time. Indeed, he underperformed the market the first three years he managed the fund, which put him behind the market by 18 percentage points.

The story is similar at Sequoia Fund. Over the marking period, Sequoia underperformed 37 percent of the time. Like Keynes, Ruane also had difficulty coming of age. "Over the years," he has said, "we have periodically qualified to be the Kings of Underperformance. We had the blurred vision to start the Sequoia Fund in mid-1970 and suffered the Chinese water-torture of underperforming the S&P four straight years." By the end of 1974, Sequoia was a whopping 36 percentage points behind the market. "We hid under the desk, didn't answer the phones and wondered if the storm would ever clear."[21] But of course the storm did clear. By the end of 1978, Sequoia had gained 220 percent, versus 60 percent for the Standard & Poor's 500 Index.

Even Charlie Munger couldn't escape the inevitable bumps of focus investing. Over 14 years, Charlie underperformed 36 percent of the time. Like other focus investors, he had a string of bad luck. From 1972 through 1974, Munger fell behind the market by 37 percentage points. Over 17 years, Lou Simpson underperformed in 4 years, or 24 percent of the time. His worst relative performance, which occurred in a one-year period, put him 15 percentage points behind the market.

Incidentally, we see the same trends when we analyze the behavior of our laboratory focus portfolios. (See Table 6.6.) Of the 3,000 portfolios holding 15 stocks, 808 beat the market during the ten-year period from 1987 to 1996. Yet, of those 808 winners, an astonishing 95 percent endured some prolonged period of underperformance—three, four, five, or even six years out of ten.

What do you think would happen to Keynes, Munger, Simpson, and Ruane if they were rookie managers starting their careers in today's environment, which can see only the value of one year's performance? They would probably be canned, to their clients' profound loss.

Yet, following the argument that the focus strategy does sometimes mean enduring several weak years, we run into a very real problem. How can we tell, using just price performance as our measure, whether we are looking at a very bright manager who is having a poor year (or even a poor three years) but will

Table 6.6   Focus (15-Stock) Portfolios—10-Year Data (1987–1996)

Number of Years Outperform/Underperform S&P 500	Number of Portfolios	Percentage Total (%)
10—0	0	0.00
9—1	1	0.12
8—2	20	2.48
7—3	128	15.84
6—4	272	33.66
5—5	261	32.30
4—6	105	13.00
3—7	21	2.60
2—8	0	0.00
1—9	0	0.00
0—10	0	0.00

do well over the long haul, or one who is starting a long string of bad years? We can't.

Not that we haven't tried.

Academics and researchers have invested considerable energy in trying to determine which money managers, and which strategies, have the best chance of beating the market over time. In the past few years, the prestigious *Journal of Finance* has published several articles based on studies by prominent university professors, all asking the same basic question: Is there a pattern to mutual fund performance? Together, these professors all bring considerable intellectual weight and data analysis to the problem, but their findings fail to produce a perfect answer.

Four of these studies dealt with what academics term "persistence"—the tendency of investors to choose funds with the best recent records because they believe a fund manager's track record is an indication of future performance. This creates a kind of self-fulfilling momentum; this year's money follows the top fund from the past few years. When this momentum is measured in one-year units (picking next year's winner by buying last year's winner), we describe this as the "hot hands" phenomenon. It is all a matter of trying to predict which funds will do well in the near future by observing what they did in the near past. Can it be done? That was what these studies attempted to find out.

In two separate studies, Mark Carhart of the University of Southern California School of Business Administration and Burton Malkiel of Princeton were unable to find any meaningful correlation between persistence and future performance.[22] In the third study, three professors from the John F. Kennedy School of Government at Harvard (Darryll Hendricks, Jayendu Patel, and Richard Zeckhauser) looked at fifteen years' data and concluded that there appears to be no guarantee that buying this year's "hot hand" manager would ensure owning next year's "hot hand" fund.[23] Finally, Stephen Brown, at the Leonard Stern School of Business at New York University, and William Goetzmann, at Yale's School of Management, concluded that

183

persistence is largely a matter of commonalities in strategy. In other words, among any group of hot hands, we would probably find several managers following the same strategy.[24]

Working separately, these academics came to the same conclusion: There appears to be no significant available evidence that will help investors locate next year's top performers. Bouncing from one hot fund to the next, when "hot" is defined by price performance, does nothing to aid investors in building their net worth.

We can well imagine what Warren Buffett might make of these academic studies. For him, the moral of the story is clear: We have to drop our insistence on price as the only measuring stick, and we have to break ourselves of the counterproductive habit of making short-term judgments.

But if price is not the best measuring stick, what are we to use instead? "Nothing" is not a good answer. Even buy-and-hold strategists don't recommend keeping your eyes shut. We just have to find another benchmark for measuring performance. Fortunately, there is one, and it is the cornerstone to how Buffett judges his performance and the performance of his operating units at Berkshire Hathaway.

A New Benchmark for Performance

Warren Buffett once said he "wouldn't care if the stock market closed for a year or two. After all it closes every Saturday and Sunday and that hasn't bothered me yet."[25] It is true that "an active trading market is useful, since it periodically presents us with mouth-watering opportunities," said Buffett. "But by no means is it essential."[26]

To fully appreciate this statement, you need to think carefully about what Buffett said next. "A prolonged suspension of trading in securities we hold would not bother us any more than does the lack of daily quotations for World Book or Fechheimer [two Berkshire Hathaway subsidiaries]. Eventually

184

our economic fate will be determined by the economic fate of the business we own, whether our ownership is partial [in the form of shares of stock] or total."[27]

If you owned a business and there was no daily quote to measure its performance, how would you determine your progress? Likely you would measure the growth in earnings, or perhaps the improvement in operating margins, or a reduction in capital expenditures. You simply would let the economics of the business dictate whether you were increasing or decreasing the value of your business. In Buffett's mind, the litmus test for measuring the performance of a publicly traded company is no different. "Charlie and I let our marketable equities tell us by their operating results—not by their daily, or even yearly, price quotations—whether our investments are successful," he explains. "The market may ignore business success for a while, but it eventually will confirm it."[28]

But can we count on the market to reward us for picking the right economic companies? Can we draw a significantly strong correlation between the operating earnings of a company and its future share price? The answer appears to be *yes*, if we are given the appropriate time horizon.

The relationship between market value and business value strengthens with time. Those who can see the latter before the former catches up are in a good position to profit from their astuteness.

When we set out to determine how closely price and earnings are connected, using our laboratory group of 1,200 companies, we learned that the longer the time period, the stronger the correlation:

- With stocks held for three years, the degree of correlation ranged from .131 to .360. (A correlation of .360 means that 36 percent of the variance in price was explained by the variance in earnings.)

- With stocks held for five years, the correlation ranged from .374 to .599.

- In a ten-year holding period, the correlation increased to a range of .593 to .695.

- For the entire 18-year period, the correlation between earnings and share price is .688—a significantly meaningful relationship.

This bears out Buffett's thesis that a strong business will eventually command a strong price, given enough time. He cautions, though, that the translation of earnings into share price is both "uneven" and "unpredictable." Although the relationship between earnings and price strengthens over time, it is not always prescient. "While market values track business values quite well over long periods," Buffett notes, "in any given year the relationship can gyrate capriciously."[29] Sixty-five years ago, Ben Graham gave us the same lesson: "In the short run the market is a voting machine but in the long run it is a weighing machine."[30]

It is clear that Buffett is in no hurry to have the market affirm what he already believes is true. "The speed at which a business's success is recognized, furthermore, is not that important as long as the company's intrinsic value is increasing at a satisfactory rate," he says. "In fact, delayed recognition can be an advantage: It may give us the chance to buy more of a good thing at a bargain price."[31]

Look-Through Earnings

To help shareholders appreciate the value of Berkshire Hathaway's large common stock investments, Buffett coined the term "look-through" earnings. Berkshire's look-through earnings are made up of the operating earnings of its consolidated businesses (its subsidiaries), the retained earnings of its large common stock investments, and an allowance for the tax that Berkshire would have had to pay if the retained earnings were actually paid out.

The notion of look-through earnings was originally devised for Berkshire's shareholders, but it also represents an important lesson for focus investors who seek a way to understand the value of their portfolio when, as will happen from time to time, share prices disengage from underlying economics. "The goal of each investor," says Buffett, "should be to create a portfolio (in effect, a 'company') that will deliver him or her the highest possible look-through earnings a decade or so from now."[32]

According to Buffett, since 1965 (the year Buffett took control of Berkshire Hathaway), the company's look-through earnings have grown at almost the identical rate of the market value of its securities. However, the two have not always moved in lockstep. On many occasions, earnings moved ahead of prices; at other times, prices moved far ahead of earnings. What is important to remember is that the relationship works over time. "An approach of this kind," counsels Buffett, "will force the investor to think about long-term business prospects rather than short-term market prospects, a perspective likely to improve results."[33]

Buffett's Measuring Stick

When Buffett considers adding an investment, he first looks at what he already owns to see whether the new purchase is any better. What Berkshire owns today is an economic measuring stick used to compare possible acquisitions. "What Buffett is saying is something very useful to practically any investor," Charlie Munger stresses. "For an ordinary individual, the best thing you already have should be your measuring stick." What

happens next is one of the most critical but widely overlooked se-
crets to increasing the value of a portfolio. "If the new thing you
are considering purchasing is not better than what you already
know is available," says Charlie, "then it hasn't met your threshold. This screens out 99 percent of what you see." (OID)[34]

> *When debating whether to buy a new stock, ask
> yourself: How does it compare to the very best of
> your* current *holdings?*

You already have at your disposal, with what you now own,
an economic benchmark—a measuring stick. You can define
your own personal economic benchmark in several different
ways: look-through earnings, return on equity, or margin of
safety, for example. When you buy or sell a company in your
portfolio, you have either raised or lowered your economic
benchmark. The job of a portfolio manager who is a long-term
owner of securities, and who believes future stock prices eventually match with underlying economics, is to find ways to raise
the benchmark. For your own investments, that manager might
well be you.

If you step back and think for a moment, the Standard &
Poor's 500 Index is a measuring stick. It is made up of 500
companies, and each has its own economic return. To outperform the S&P 500 Index over time—to raise that benchmark—
we have to assemble and manage a portfolio of companies with
economics that are superior to the average weighted economics
of the index. The process of assembling and managing such a
portfolio is what this book is all about.

Tom Murphy, who ran Capital Cities/ABC before merging
it with The Walt Disney Company, understood economic
benchmarks perfectly. Inside Cap Cities was a group of media

188

companies that, on a combined weighted basis, produced an economic return for shareholders. Murphy knew that, to increase the value of Cap Cities, he had to find companies that could raise the existing economic benchmark. "The job of manager," Murphy once said, "is not to find ways to make the train longer but to find ways to make it run faster."[35]

You should not be lulled into thinking that just because a focus portfolio lags the stock market on a price basis from time to time, you are excused from the ongoing responsibility of performance scrutiny. With the advent of economic benchmarks, you will, despite the vagaries of the market, still have to defend your individual picks. Granted, a focus manager should not become a slave to the stock market's whims, but you should always be acutely aware of all economic stirrings of the companies in your portfolio.

TWO GOOD REASONS TO MOVE LIKE A SLOTH

Focus investing is necessarily a long-term approach to investing. If we were to ask Buffett what he considers an ideal holding period, he would answer "forever"—so long as the company continues to generate above-average economics and management allocates the earnings of the company in a rational manner. "Inactivity strikes us as intelligent behavior," he explains. "Neither we nor most business managers would dream of feverishly trading highly profitable subsidiaries because a small move in the Federal Reserve's discount rate was predicted or because some Wall Street pundit has reversed his views on the market. Why, then, should we behave differently with our minority positions in wonderful businesses?"[36]

Of course, if you own a lousy company, you require turnover. Otherwise, you end up owning the economics of a subpar business for a long time. But if you own a superior company, the *last* thing you want to do is to sell it.

This slothlike approach to portfolio management may appear quirky to those accustomed to actively buying and selling stocks on a regular basis, but it does have two important economic benefits, in addition to growing capital at an above-average rate:

1. It works to reduce transaction costs.
2. It increases after-tax returns.

Each advantage by itself is extremely valuable; their combined benefit is enormous.

Reduced Transaction Costs

On average, mutual funds generate turnover ratios between 100 percent and 200 percent each year. The turnover ratio describes the amount of activity in a portfolio. If a portfolio manager sells and rebuys all the stocks in the portfolio once a year, the turnover ratio is 100 percent. Sell and rebuy twice a year, and you have 200 percent turnover. But if a manager sells and rebuys only one-tenth percent of the portfolio in a year (implying an average ten-year holding period), the turnover ratio is a lowly 10 percent.

In a review of 3,560 domestic stock funds, Morningstar, the Chicago-based researcher of mutual funds, discovered that funds with low turnover ratios generated superior returns compared to funds with higher turnover ratios. The Morningstar study found that, over a ten-year period, funds with turnover ratios of less than 20 percent were able to achieve returns 14 percent higher than funds with turnover rates of more than 100 percent.[37]

This is one of those commonsense dynamics that is so obvious it is easily overlooked. The problem with high turnover is that all that trading adds brokerage costs to the fund, which works to lower your net returns.

Aftertax Returns

Low-turnover funds also have another important economic advantage: the positive effect of postponing capital gains tax. Ironically, turnover, which is supposed to increase your returns in a fund, also increases your current tax liability. When a manager sells a stock and replaces it with another stock, he or she does so in the belief that the move will enhance the fund's return. But because selling a stock means that a capital gain is realized, each new pick has the anchor of outperforming the capital gains tax associated with the stock it replaced.

If you own an Individual Retirement Account (IRA) or a 401(k) plan, you do not pay taxes on their earnings or gain until the time of withdrawal, and gains in a Roth IRA are completely tax-free. But if you own a mutual fund in your personal account, any realized capital gains generated in the fund will be passed down to shareholders, triggering a capital gains tax for you. The more stocks are sold from the fund, the more tax liability you may face.

Even when the year-end performance of a mutual fund shows a competitive return, by the time you have paid the taxes on the gains realized, your net aftertax return may very well be below average. Savvy shareholders are starting to ask whether the return provided by their actively managed fund is high enough to pay the taxes owed and still generate a return higher than index funds, which are by their nature very tax-efficient.

Except in the case of nontaxable accounts, *taxes* are the biggest expense that investors face—higher than brokerage commissions and often higher than the expense ratio of running a fund. In fact, taxes have become one of the principal reasons why funds generate poor returns. "That is the bad news," according to money managers Robert Jeffrey and Robert Arnott. They are the authors of "Is Your Alpha Big Enough to Cover Its Taxes?," an article that appeared in the well-respected *Journal of Portfolio Management* and generated extensive discussion in the investment world. "The good news," they write, "is that there are trading strategies that can minimize these typically overlooked tax consequences."[38]

In a nutshell, the key strategy involves another of those commonsense notions that is often underappreciated: the enormous value of the unrealized gain. When a stock appreciates in price *but is not sold,* the increase in value is unrealized gain. No capital gains tax is owed until the stock is sold. If you leave the gain in place, your money compounds more forcefully.

Overall, investors have too often underestimated the enormous value of this unrealized gain—what Buffett calls an "interest-free loan from the Treasury." To make his point, Buffett asks us to imagine what happens if you buy a $1 investment that doubles in price each year. If you sell the investment at the end of the first year, you would have a net gain of $.66 (assuming you're in the 34 percent tax bracket). Let's say you reinvest the $1.66 and it doubles in value by year-end. If the investment continues to double each year, and you continue to sell, pay the tax, and reinvest the proceeds, at the end of 20 years you would have a net gain of $25,200 after paying taxes of $13,000. If, on the other hand, you purchased a $1 investment that doubled each year and was not sold until the end of 20 years, you would gain $692,000 after paying taxes of approximately $356,000.

A cold look at the numbers makes a couple of observations clear: First, you end up with a great deal more profit if you don't take your gain each year but just let the money compound. Second, your lump-sum tax bill at the end of 20 years will take your breath away. That may be one reason people seem to instinctively feel it's better to convert the gain each year and thereby keep the taxes under control. What they fail to appreciate is the truly awesome difference in return that they are missing out on.

The Jeffrey-Arnott study concluded that to achieve high after-tax returns, investors need to keep their average annual portfolio turnover ratio somewhere between 0 and 20 percent.

ON COMPOUNDING

Start with a $1 investment that doubles in value every year. From there you have two options:

1. *Sell the investment at the end of the year, pay the tax, and reinvest the net proceeds. Do the same thing every year for 20 years. End up with $25,200 clear profit.*

Or

2. *Don't sell anything. At the end of 20 years, end up with $692,000 after-tax profit.*

What strategies lend themselves best to low turnover rates? One possible approach is a passive, low-turnover index fund. Another is a focus portfolio. "It sounds like premarital counseling advice," say Jeffrey and Arnott, "namely, to try to build a portfolio that you can live with for a long, long time."[39]

Today, portfolio managers run the risk of losing clients and offending consultants if their performance deviates too far away from the market return. The fear of "tracking error"—performance that is too far away from the market's return—has, according to Charlie Munger, "hobbled the industry."

We have spent a good deal of this section of the chapter on the ups and downs of mutual funds. We did so, you will recall, because mutual funds are familiar and therefore an easy example. But do not imagine for one minute that the erroneous thinking is limited to managers of mutual funds. They are used here merely to exemplify the broad trends that thread their way through the entire investment world. By observing what these mutual fund managers do and how they think, you can learn much about what you should do and how you should think.

We have learned that strong short-term performance does not necessarily identify superior portfolio managers any more than poor short-term performance excludes them. The time horizon we use to measure ability is simply too short to draw any meaningful conclusions. However, using alternative economic benchmarks such as look-through earnings may be a way for you to gauge your progress when price deviates from expected returns. We also learned that low turnover translates to higher returns in two simple, obvious ways. Fewer transactions means lower trading costs. Finally, don't overlook the value of unrealized capital gains. With the exception of passive index funds, focus investing gives you the best opportunity to compound this unrealized gain into major profits.

FAIR WARNING LABEL

Before you put this book down, it is critically important that you think seriously about what is said next. It has been suggested that writing about focus investing gives investors something like an owner's manual for a high-performance racecar. But if you took the wheel of a car capable of speeds in excess of 200 miles per hour, you would have a responsibility to drive it safely. You would be wise to not only read the operator's manual but to follow closely any information under a boldface **Warning** heading. Similarly, if you are ready to strap on a focus portfolio, I have five warnings for you:

1. Do not approach the market unless you are willing to think about stocks, first and always, as part-ownership interests in a business.

2. Be prepared to diligently study the businesses you own, as well as the companies you compete against, with the

194

idea that no one will know more about your business or industry than you do.

3. Do not even start a focus portfolio unless you are willing to invest a minimum of five years. Longer time horizons will make for a safer ride.

4. Never leverage your focus portfolio. An unleveraged focus portfolio will help you reach your goals fast enough. Remember, an unexpected margin call on your capital will likely wreck a well-tuned portfolio.

5. Accept the need to acquire the right temperament and personality to drive a focus investor. Never forget: There is a difference between investment and speculation.

As a focus investor, your goal is to reach a level of understanding about your business that is unmatched on Wall Street. You may protest that this is unrealistic, but, considering what Wall Street promotes, it may not be as hard as you think. Wall Street sells short-term performance emphasizing what may happen quarter to quarter. Business owners, on the other hand, are more interested in the long-term competitive advantages of the companies they own. They use periodic price changes, often caused by Wall Street's myopic view, to accumulate the shares of great companies at great prices. If you are willing to work hard at studying businesses, you will likely get to know, over time, more about the company you own than the average investor, and that is all you need to gain an advantage.

Warren Buffett's approach is deceptively simple. There are no computer programs to learn or two-inch-thick investment banking manuals to decipher. There is nothing scientific about valuing a business and then paying a price that is below this business value. "What we do is not beyond anybody else's competence," says Buffett. "It is just not necessary to do extraordinary things to get extraordinary things to get extraordinary results."[40]

You do not have to become an MBA-level authority on business valuation to profit from the focus approach. It does, however, require you to commit your time to studying the process. As Buffett says, "Investing is easier than you think but harder than it looks."[41] Successful investing does not require you to learn highbrow mathematics stuffed with Greek symbols, but it does require you to undertake a serious investigation of the businesses you own.

Some investors would rather chatter about "what the market is doing" than bother to read an annual report. But, believe me, a "cocktail conversation" about the future direction of the markets and interest rates will be far less profitable than spending 30 minutes reading the last communication provided by the company you own.

As everyone knows who has ever done it, making a change is difficult. Even if you are convinced intellectually that your new course is the right one, actually implementing it often involves some emotional or psychological adjustment. Thus, even though you may fully accept the scientific and mathematical arguments for focus investing, and even though you see that other very smart people have been successful with it, you may still feel some residual hesitation. After all, we are talking about your economic well-being, and that is a very serious matter indeed.

Perhaps you will find it useful to learn more about the complicated intersection of emotions and finances. Money matters are about the most emotional issues of all, and that will never change. But, at the same time, you need not be constantly at the mercy of those emotions, to the point where sensible action is handicapped. The key is to keep the emotions in appropriate perspective, and that is much easier if you understand something of the basic psychology involved. Which brings us to the next chapter.

CHAPTER 7

THE EMOTIONAL
SIDE OF MONEY

Despite computer programs and black boxes, people—human beings—still make markets. The stock market is nothing more, and nothing less, than the aggregate decisions of individual human beings. One thing we must always keep in mind is that, in all areas of life, people tend to make decisions on the basis of emotions, and emotions are stronger than reason.

When it comes to money, the two emotions that drive decisions most profoundly are fear and greed. Motivated by fear or greed, or both, investors frequently buy or sell stocks at foolish prices, far above or below a company's intrinsic value. To say this another way, investor sentiment has a more pronounced impact on stock prices than a company's fundamentals.

Anyone who hopes to participate profitably in the market, therefore, must not fail to allow for the impact of emotion. It's a two-sided issue: keeping your own emotional profile under control as much as possible, and being alert for those times when other investors' emotion-driven decisions present you with a golden opportunity.

To properly weight the impact of emotion in investing, the first step is to understand it. Fortunately, good information is at hand. In recent years, psychologists have turned their attention to studying how established principles of human behavior play out when the dynamic is money. This fairly new field, known as behavioral finance, draws on some well-established ideas that have been around for a while.

THE TEMPERAMENT OF A TRUE INVESTOR

Ben Graham, as we know, fiercely urged his students to learn the basic difference between an investor and a speculator. The speculator, he said, tries to anticipate and profit from price changes; the investor seeks only to acquire companies at reasonable prices. Then he went further. A successful investor, he said, is often a person who has achieved a calm, patient, rational temperament. Speculators have the opposite temperament: anxious, impatient, irrational. Their worst enemy is not the stock market, but themselves. They may well have superior abilities in mathematics, finance, and accounting, but if they cannot master their emotions, they are ill suited to profit from the investment process.

Graham understood the emotional quicksand of the market as well as any modern psychologist—maybe better. His notion that true investors can be recognized by their temperament as well as their skills holds as true today as when first expressed. Let's explore three key traits.

1. *True investors are calm*. They know that stock prices, influenced by all manner of reasonable and unreasonable forces, will fall as well as rise. When the prices of their stocks fall, they react with equanimity; they know that as long as the company retains the qualities that attracted them as investors in the first place, the price will come back up. In the meantime, they do not panic.

On this point, Buffett is blunt: Unless you can watch your stock holdings decline by 50 percent without becoming panic-stricken, you should not be in the stock market. In fact, he adds, as long as you feel good about the businesses you own, you should welcome lower prices as a way to profitably increase your holdings.

At the opposite end of the spectrum, true investors also remain calm in the face of what we might call "the mob influence." When one stock or one industry or one mutual fund suddenly lands in the spotlight, the mob rushes in that direction. The trouble is, when everyone is making the same choices because "everyone" knows it's the thing to do, then no one is in a position to profit. In remarks reported in *Fortune* at the end of 1999, Buffett talked about the "can't-miss-the-party" factor that has infected so many bull-market investors.[1] His caution seems to be: True investors don't worry about missing the party; they worry about coming to the party unprepared.

2. *True investors are patient.* Rather than being swept along in the enthusiasm of the crowd, true investors wait for the right opportunity to appear. They say no more often than yes. Buffett recalls that when he worked for Graham-Newman, analyzing stocks for possible purchase, Ben Graham turned down his recommendations most of the time. Graham, Buffett says, was never willing to purchase a stock unless all the facts were in his favor. From this experience, Buffett learned that the ability to say no is a tremendous advantage for an investor.

*D*on't be afraid to say no. Evaluate all opportunities as if you could make only 20 investment decisions in your entire lifetime.

Buffett believes that too many of today's investors feel a need to purchase too many stocks, most of which are certain to be mediocre, rather than wait for the few exceptional companies. To reinforce Graham's lesson, Buffett often uses the analogy of a punch card. "An investor," he says, "should act as though he had a lifetime decision card with just twenty punches on it. With every investment decision, his card is punched, and he has one fewer available for the rest of his life."[2] If investors were restrained in this way, they would be forced to wait patiently until a great investment opportunity surfaced.

3. *True investors are rational.* They approach the market, and the world, from a base of clear thinking. They are neither unduly pessimistic nor irrationally optimistic; they are, instead, logical and rational.

Buffett finds it odd that so many people habitually dislike markets that are in their best interests and favor markets that continually put them at a disadvantage. They feel optimistic when market prices are rising and pessimistic when prices are going down. If they take the next step and put those feelings into action, what do they do? Sell at lower prices and buy at higher prices—not the most profitable strategy.

Undue optimism rears its head when investors blithely assume that somehow the fates will smile on them and their stock choice will be the one that really takes off. It is especially prevalent in bull markets, when unrealistically high expectations are commonplace. Blind-faith optimists see no need to do the fundamental research and analysis that would illuminate the real long-term winners.

Undue pessimism, whether directed at one company or the market in general, motivates investors to sell at exactly the wrong time. In Buffett's view, true investors are pleased when the rest of the world turns pessimistic, because they see it for what it really is: a perfect time to buy good companies at bargain prices. Pessimism, he says, is "the most common cause of low prices. . . . We want to do business in such an environment, not because we like pessimism but because we like the prices it produces. It's optimism that is the enemy of the rational buyer."[3]

In 1979, Buffett wrote an article for *Forbes* entitled "You Pay a Very High Price in the Stock Market for a Cheery Consensus." At the time, the Dow Jones Industrial Average was selling slightly below book value; stocks were earning, on average, 13 percent on equity; and interest rates on bonds were fluctuating between 9 and 10 percent. Yet most pension managers purchased bonds over stocks.

In his article, Buffett offered one possible explanation for this illogical choice: Perhaps portfolio managers felt that as long as the immediate future was unclear, it was best to avoid equity commitments. Such a mentality, says Buffett, must acknowledge that "the future is never clear," and that "you pay a very high price for a cheery consensus."[4]

An investor's level of optimism or pessimism is, of course, a statement of what that investor thinks about the future. Forecasting what is going to happen next is tricky at best, and downright foolish when optimism (or pessimism) is based more on emotion than on research. Buffett, who once remarked that "the only value of stock forecasters is to make fortune tellers look good," makes no attempt to anticipate the periods in which the market is likely to go up or down.[5] Instead, he keeps an eye on the general emotional tenor of the overall market, and acts accordingly. "We simply attempt," he explains, "to be fearful when others are greedy and to be greedy only when others are fearful."[6]

Introducing Mr. Market

To show his students how powerfully emotions are tied to stock market fluctuations, and to help them recognize the folly of succumbing to emotion, Graham created an allegorical character he named "Mr. Market." Buffett has frequently shared the story of Mr. Market with Berkshire's shareholders.

Imagine that you and Mr. Market are partners in a private business. Each day, without fail, Mr. Market quotes a price at which he is willing to either buy your interest or sell his interest to you. The business that you both own is fortunate to have stable economic characteristics, but Mr. Market's quotes are anything but, because Mr. Market is emotionally unstable. Some days, he is cheerful and enormously optimistic, and sees only brighter days ahead. On these days, he offers a very high price for shares in your business. At other times, Mr. Market is discouraged and terribly pessimistic. Seeing nothing but trouble ahead, he quotes a very low price for shares in your business.

Mr. Market has another endearing characteristic, Graham said: He does not mind being snubbed. If his quotes are ignored, he will be back again tomorrow with a new quote. Graham warned his students that it is Mr. Market's pocketbook, not his wisdom, that is useful. If Mr. Market shows up in a foolish mood, you are free to ignore him or take advantage of him, but it will be disastrous if you fall under his influence.

"The investor who permits himself to be stampeded or unduly worried by unjustified market declines in his holdings is perversely transforming his basic advantage into a basic disadvantage," Graham wrote. "That man would be better off if his stocks had no market quotation at all, for he would then be spared the mental anguish caused him by other persons' mistakes of judgment."[7]

To be successful, investors need good business judgment and the ability to protect themselves from the emotional whirlwind that Mr. Market unleashes. One is insufficient without the other. One very important factor in Buffett's success is that he has always been able to disengage himself from the emotional forces of the stock market. He credits Ben Graham and Mr. Market with teaching him how to remain insulated from the silliness of the market.

Mr. Market, Meet Charlie Munger

It was more than 60 years ago that Ben Graham introduced Mr. Market, 60 years since he began writing about the irrationality that exists in the market. Yet, in all those years, there has been little apparent change in investors' behavior. Investors still act irrationally. Foolish mistakes are still the order of the day. Fear and greed still permeate the marketplace.

We can, through numerous academic studies and surveys, track investor foolishness. We can, if we follow Warren Buffett's lead, turn other people's fear or greed to our advantage. But to fully understand the dynamics of emotion in investing, we turn to another individual: Charlie Munger.

The range of topics that Munger is interested in, and the breadth and depth of his knowledge, are legendary. He speaks eloquently about his concept of a latticework of mental models, in which core concepts from many fields combine to produce true wisdom. For the moment, we are interested in just one of those fields: psychology.

Munger's understanding of how psychology affects investors, and his insistence that it be taken into account, have greatly influenced the operations of Berkshire Hathaway. It is one of his most profound contributions.

In particular, he stresses what he calls the psychology of misjudgment: What is it in human nature that draws people to make mistakes of judgment?

MUNGER'S TWO-STEP ANALYSIS

1. *Look at the facts: rational expectations and probabilities.*
2. *Carefully evaluate the psychological factors.*

Munger believes a key problem is that our brain takes short-cuts in analysis. We jump too easily to conclusions. We are easily misled and are prone to manipulation. To compensate, Munger has developed a mental habit that has served him well. "Personally, . . . I now use a kind of two-track analysis. First, what are the factors that really govern the interests involved, rationally considered? And second, what are the subconscious influences where the brain at a subconscious level is automatically doing these things which by and large are useful, but which often misfunction?" (OID)[8]

Behavioral Finance

In many ways, Charlie Munger is a genuine pioneer. He was thinking about, and talking about, the psychological aspects of market behavior long before other investment professionals gave them serious attention. But that is beginning to change. In the past few years, we have seen what amounts to a revolution—a new way of looking at issues of finance through the framework of human behavior. This blending of economics and psychology, known as behavioral finance, is just now moving down from the universities' ivory towers to become part of the informed conversation among investment professionals.

Ironically, the best academic work on this subject comes from the economics department at the University of Chicago, an institution known more for Nobel prize winners who postulate the efficient market theory of rational investors. However, Richard Thaler, a former Cornell University economist, joined the economics department at Chicago with the sole purpose of questioning the rational behavior of investors.

Behavioral finance is an investigative study that seeks to explain market inefficiencies by applying psychological theories. Observing that people often make foolish mistakes and illogical assumptions when dealing with their own financial affairs, academics, including Thaler, began to dig deeper into psychological concepts to explain the irrationalities in people's thinking. In this relatively new field of study, what we are learning is fascinating, as well as eminently useful to smart investors.

Overconfidence

Several psychological studies have pointed out that errors in judgment occur because people in general are overconfident. Ask a large sample of people how many believe their skills at driving a car are above average, and an overwhelming majority will say they are excellent drivers—which leaves open the question of who the bad drivers are. Another example can be found in the medical profession. When asked, doctors state that they can diagnose pneumonia with 90 percent confidence. In fact, they are right only 50 percent of the time.

Confidence per se is not a bad thing. But *over*confidence is another matter, and it can be particularly damaging when we are dealing with our financial affairs. Overconfident investors not only make silly decisions for themselves but also have a powerful effect on the market as a whole.

Investors, as a rule, are highly confident that they are smarter than everyone else and can pick winning stocks—or, at the very least, they can pick smarter money managers who, in turn, can beat the market. They have a tendency to overestimate their skills and their knowledge. They typically rely on information that confirms what they believe, and they disregard contrary information. In addition, their minds work to assess whatever information is readily available rather than to seek out information that is little known.

Overconfidence explains why so many money managers make wrong calls. They take too much confidence from the information they gather, and they think they are more right than they actually are. If all the players think their information is correct and they know something that others do not, the result is a great deal of trading.

Overreaction Bias

Thaler points to several recent studies that reveal how people put too much emphasis on a few chance events, thinking that they have spotted a trend. In particular, investors tend to fix on the most recent information they have received, and they extrapolate from it; the most recent earnings report thus becomes, in their minds, a signal of future earnings. Then, believing that they see what others do not, they make quick decisions based on superficial reasoning.

Overconfidence is at work here, of course; people believe they understand the data more clearly than others and can interpret it better. But there is more to it. Overconfidence is exacerbated by overreaction. The behaviorists have learned that people tend to overreact to bad news and to react slowly to good news. Psychologists call this *overreaction bias*. Thus, if the short-term earnings report is not good, the typical investor's response is an abrupt, ill-considered overreaction, which has an inevitable effect on stock prices.

Thaler describes this overemphasis on the short term as investor "myopia" (the medical term for nearsightedness) and believes most investors would be better off if they didn't receive monthly statements. In a study conducted with other behavioral economists, he proved his idea in dramatic fashion.

Thaler and colleagues asked a group of students to divide a hypothetical portfolio between stocks and Treasury bills. But first, they sat the students in front of a computer and simulated the returns of the portfolio over a trailing 25-year period. Half the students were given mountains of information, representing the market's volatile nature with ever-changing prices. The other group was given only periodic performance data measured in five-year time periods. Thaler then asked each group to allocate its portfolio for the next 40 years.

The group that had been bombarded by lots of information, some of which inevitably pointed to losses, allocated only 40 percent of its money to the stock market; the group that received only periodic information allocated almost 70 percent of its portfolio to stocks. Thaler, who lectures each year at the Behavioral Conference sponsored by the National Bureau of Economic Research and the John F. Kennedy School of Government at Harvard, told the group, "My advice to you is to invest in equities and then don't open the mail."[9]

Thaler is well known for another study that demonstrated the folly of short-term decisions. He took all the stocks on the New York Stock Exchange and ranked them by performance over the preceding five years. He isolated the 35 best performers (those that went up in price the most) and the 35 worst (went down the most), and created hypothetical portfolios of those 70 stocks. Then he held those portfolios for five years, and watched as "losers" outperformed "winners" 40 percent of the time. In the real world, Thaler believes, few investors would have had the fortitude to resist overreacting at the first sign of a price downturn, and would have missed the benefit when the "losers" began to move in the other direction.[10]

These experiments neatly underscore Thaler's notion of investor myopia—shortsightedness leading to foolish decisions. Why does myopia provoke such an irrational response? Part of the reason is another bit of psychology: our innate desire to avoid loss.

Loss Aversion

According to behaviorists, the pain of a loss is far greater than the enjoyment of a gain. Many experiments, by Thaler and others, have demonstrated that people need twice as much positive to overcome a negative. On a 50/50 bet, with precisely even odds, most people will not risk anything unless the potential gain is twice as high as the potential loss.

This is known as asymmetric loss aversion: the downside has a greater impact than the upside, and it is a fundamental bit of human psychology. Applied to the stock market, it means that investors who feel good when they pick a winner feel twice as bad when they lose money. This line of reasoning can also be found in macroeconomic theory. During boom times, consumers typically increase their purchases by an extra three and half cents for every dollar of wealth created. But during economic slides, consumers reduce their spending by twice the boom-time amount (six cents) for every dollar lost in the market.

Their aversion to loss makes investors unduly conservative, at great cost. We all want to believe we made good decisions, so

207

we hold onto bad choices far too long, in the vague hope that things will turn around. By not selling our losers, we never have to confront our failures. But if you don't sell a mistake, you are potentially giving up a gain that you could earn by reinvesting smartly.

Mental Accounting

One final aspect of behavioral finance deserves our attention. Psychologists call it *mental accounting*. It refers to our habit of shifting our perspective on money as surrounding circumstances change. We tend to mentally put money into different "accounts," and that determines how we think about using it.

A simple situation will illustrate. Imagine that you have just returned home from an evening out with your spouse. You reach for your wallet, to pay the baby-sitter, but discover that the $20 bill you thought was there, is not. So, when you drive the sitter home, you stop at an ATM machine and get another $20. The next day, you discover the original $20 bill in your jacket pocket.

If you're like most people, you react with something like glee. The $20 in the jacket is "found" money. Even though the first $20 and the second $20 both came from your checking account, and both represent money you worked hard for, the $20 bill you hold in your hand is money you didn't expect to have, and you feel free to spend it frivolously.

Once again, Richard Thaler has provided an interesting academic experiment to demonstrate this concept. In his study, he started with two groups of people. Each person in the first group was given $30 in cash and two choices: (1) pocket the money and walk away, or (2) gamble on a coin flip; a win would yield $9 extra, and a loss would cause a $9 deduction. Most of the first group (70 percent) took the gamble because they figured they would at the very least end up with $21 of found money.

Each member of the second group was offered a different choice: (1) try a gamble on a coin toss—a win would earn $39 and a loss would earn $21; or (2) get an even $30 with no coin toss. More than half (57 percent) decided to take the sure money. Both groups of people stood to win the exact same amount of money with the exact same odds, but the situation was perceived differently.[11]

The implications are clear: To fully understand the markets and investing, we must also understand our own irrationalities. The study of the psychology of misjudgment is every bit as valuable to an investor as the analysis of a balance sheet and income statement. You can become proficient in the art of valuing companies, but if you don't take the time to understand behavioral finance it will be very difficult to improve your investment performance.

> *Understanding the irrationalities inherent to human nature is every bit as important as understanding how to read a balance sheet and an income statement.*

Risk Tolerance

In the same way that a strong magnet pulls together all the nearby pieces of metal, investors' level of risk tolerance pulls together all the elements of the psychology of finance. The psychological concepts are abstract, but they get real in the day-to-day decisions that you make about buying and selling. And the common thread in all those decisions is how you feel about risk.

In the past dozen or so years, investment professionals have devoted considerable energy to helping people assess their risk tolerance. At first, it seemed a simple task. By using interviews and questionnaires, they could construct a risk profile for each investor. The trouble is, people's tolerance for risk is founded in emotion, and that means it changes with changing circumstances. When the market declines drastically, even investors with an "aggressive" profile will become very cautious. In a booming market, both aggressive and supposedly conservative investors add more stocks.

One other factor is at work, a factor that takes us back to the idea of overconfidence. In our culture risk takers are greatly admired, and investors are subject to the very human tendency to think themselves more comfortable with risk than they actually are. They are acting out what psychologist D.G. Pruitt calls the "Walter Mitty effect."[12]

In the 1930s, James Thurber, one of America's greatest humorists, wrote a delightful short story called "The Secret Life of Walter Mitty," later made into a memorable movie starring Danny Kaye. Walter, a meek, mouselike fellow, was completely intimidated by his overbearing, sharp-tongued wife. He coped by constructing daydreams in which the mild-mannered Mitty was magically transformed into a courageous, dashing hero who was always there to save the day. One minute, he was in an agony of fear that he had forgotten his wife's errand; the next, he was a fearless bomber pilot undertaking a dangerous mission alone.

Pruitt believes investors react to the market like Walter Mitty reacted to life. When the stock market goes up, they become brave in their own eyes, and take on additional risk. But when the stock market goes down, investors scramble for the doors, flee, and then stay out of sight.

How do we overcome the Walter Mitty effect? By finding ways to measure risk tolerance that, as much as possible, account for the richness of the phenomena; and by looking below the surface of the standard assessment questions and investigating issues driven by psychology. A few years ago, in collaboration with Dr. Justin Green of Villanova University, I developed a risk analysis tool that focuses on personality as much as on the more obvious and direct risk factors. After studying the risk tolerance literature, both theoretical and substantive, we abstracted important demographic factors and personality orientations that, when taken together, might help people more accurately measure their risk tolerance.

WHO IS COMFORTABLE WITH RISK?

- *People who believe they have control over their lives.*
- *People who set goals to guide their actions.*

We found that risk-taking propensity is connected to two demographic factors: gender and age. Older people are less willing to assume risk than younger people, and women are typically more cautious than men. There appears to be no distinction for wealth; having more money or less money does not seem to have any effect on risk tolerance.

For me, one of the most interesting findings involved personality traits. We found that two characteristics in particular are closely related to risk tolerance: personal control orientation and achievement motivation. Personal control refers to people's sense that they can affect both their environment and the life decisions they make within this environment. According to our research, people who believe they have this control have a high propensity for taking risk. The second personality factor, achievement motivation, describes the degree to which people are goal oriented. We found that risk takers are also goal oriented, even though a strong focus on goals may lead to sharp disappointments.[13]

To unlock the real relationship between these personality characteristics and risk taking, we realized that investors need to think about how they view the environment in which the risk is taking place.[14] Do they think of the stock market as (1) a

211

game in which the outcome depends on luck or (2) a contingency dilemma situation in which accurate information combined with rational choices will produce the desired results?

According to our research, the investor with a high degree of risk tolerance will be someone who sets goals and believes he or she has control of the environment and can affect its outcome. This person sees the stock market as a contingency dilemma in which information combined with rational choices will produce winning results.

Does that remind you of anyone?

Everything we have learned about psychology, risk tolerance, and investing comes together in the person of Warren Buffett. He puts his faith in his own research, rather than in luck. He processes information into rational choices. He believes he has control of his environment and, by his decisions, can affect outcomes. His actions derive from carefully thought-out goals, and he is not swept off course by short-term events. He understands the true elements of risk, and accepts the consequences with confidence.

Long before behavioral finance had a name, it was understood and accepted by a few renegades like Warren Buffett and Charlie Munger. Buffett has often remarked that one of the most valuable things he learned from Ben Graham is the importance of having a true investor's attitude toward the stock market. "If you have that attitude," Buffett says, "you start out ahead of 99 percent of all the people who are operating in the stock market. It's an enormous advantage." (OID)[15]

Developing the investor's attitude, Graham said, is a matter of being prepared, both financially and psychologically, for the market's inevitable ups and down. Not merely knowing, intellectually, that a downturn will happen, but having the emotional ballast needed to react appropriately when it does. In Graham's view, the appropriate reaction for an investor is the same as a business owner's response when offered an unattractive price: Ignore it.

WHEN A PRICE DROPS SUDDENLY

1. *Don't panic; don't rush to sell out.*
2. *Reassess the long-term economics of your business.*
3. *If the economics haven't changed, buy more.*

Lemmings and Mob Mentality

Lemmings, small rodents indigenous to the tundra region, are noted for their peculiar, self-destructive mass exodus to the sea. In normal periods, lemmings move about during their spring migration, searching for food and new shelter. Every three or four years, however, something odd begins to happen. Because of high breeding and low mortality, the population of lemmings begins to rise. As soon as their ranks swell, some of the lemmings begin an erratic movement under cover of darkness. Soon, this bold group begins to move in daylight. Others join the pack, until it becomes what we would, if referring to humans, call a mob. When they run into a barrier, the lemmings panic and rush through or over the obstacle, crushing some of the pack in the process. As this behavior intensifies, lemmings begin to challenge other animals they normally would avoid. Their restless drive continues, and although many lemmings die from starvation, predators, and accidents along the way, most reach the sea. There they plunge in and swim until they die from exhaustion.

People, it goes without saying, are not lemmings. But as every teacher since Aesop has known, animals can show us much about humans. In particular, watching the behavior of lemmings gives us a glimpse into the psychology of crowd behavior, a critical fact of life in the stock market.

Because financial markets are moved, dramatically, by moblike action, investment professionals have long been interested in the psychological theories of human behavior. Ben Graham offered a story to help illustrate the irrational behavior of certain investors. Buffett shared the story with Berkshire Hathaway investors in the 1985 annual report.

An oil prospector, moving to his heavenly reward, was met by St. Peter with bad news. "You're qualified for residence," said St. Peter, "but, as you can see, the compound reserved for oil men is packed. There's no way to squeeze you in." After thinking for a moment, the prospector asked if he might say just four words to the present occupants. That seemed harmless to St. Peter, so he agreed. The prospector cupped his hand and yelled, "Oil discovered in hell." Immediately, the gates to the compound opened and all the oil men marched out to head for the nether regions. Impressed, St. Peter invited the prospector to move in and make himself comfortable. The prospector paused. "No," he said, "I think I'll go along with the rest of the boys. There might be some truth to that rumor after all."[16]

It is perplexing to Buffett that, with so many well-educated, experienced professionals working on Wall Street, there is not a more logical and rational force in the market. In fact, stocks with the highest percentage of institutional ownership are often the most volatile in price. The wild swings in share prices, Buffett notes, have more to do with the lemminglike behavior of institutional investors than with the aggregate returns of the companies they own.

If you join the crowd, you have a much higher risk of being trampled.

The failure of most portfolio managers to exceed the major indexes is not a reflection of intelligence, says Buffett, but a symptom of the decision-making process. Most institutional decisions, he believes, are made by groups or committees that possess a strong desire to conform to generally accepted portfolio safeguards. The institution that compensates the money manager equates "safe" with "average." Adherence to standard diversification practices, rational or irrational, is rewarded over independent thinking.

"Most managers," said Buffett, "have very little incentive to make the intelligent-but-with-some-chance-of-looking-like-an-idiot decision. Their personal gain/loss ratio is all too obvious; if an unconventional decision works out well, they get a pat on the back and, if it works out poorly, they get a pink slip."

Buffett's conclusion is simple: to have the best chance of doing better than average, investors must be willing to go against the crowd, to not fall in with the rest of the lemmings. This is easier for individual investors, who are not bound by the same measures of success. As Buffett puts it, "Failing conventionally is the route to go; as a group, lemmings may have a rotten image, but no individual lemming has ever received bad press."[17]

CHAPTER 8

NEW OPPORTUNITIES, TIMELESS PRINCIPLES

Anyone who has studied Warren Buffett over the years has received a thorough education on the economics of banks, insurance, and financial service companies; beverage and razor blade businesses; and media and entertainment companies. His comments about those industries, and the results of his investments in them, are gobbled up by readers of Berkshire's annual reports because they know they are getting valuable lessons from a master teacher.

Careful readers of Berkshire's annual reports might also have noticed one important trend: Most of the businesses described there are large-capitalization, U.S.-based companies. Generally speaking, all of Buffett's major common-stock purchases in the past 20 years have been of this type. He has not had a strong presence in technology stocks, international companies, or small-capitalization businesses.

There is a reason for this consistency. Given the choice, Buffett has always preferred economic certainty, and he favors familiar and transparent accounting over the less detectable and opaque foreign standards. We should not be surprised, therefore, that he has avoided technology companies: Industries that are rapidly evolving do not readily provide the long-term economic certainty that Buffett requires. In the same way, we should not be surprised that he has committed scant resources to foreign companies whose accounting treatments differ from the General Accepted Accounting Principles practiced in the United States. We also know that Berkshire Hathaway's large capital base has forced Buffett to focus on larger companies that, in turn, can generate meaningful profits.

But because Buffett has not laid down a trail of bread crumbs for these three kinds of stocks, does that mean that you should avoid them also? Absolutely not. It is my firm belief that the Warren Buffett principles are an excellent roadmap for investments in *any* company, *any* industry, *any* market.

BEYOND BUFFETT

Whether or not you decide to pursue opportunities in any of these un-Buffetted areas is largely a matter of your investor temperament. The key issue seems to be, what level of certainty do you need before you are willing to proceed? Buffett, as we know, requires a great deal. He looks for companies that are virtually certain to grow earnings for the next 10 or 20 years; if the certainty is not there, he passes. That is a matter of his personal experience, his training under Ben Graham, and his individual psychological makeup.

Yours may be different. In fact, I suspect that every single investor has a slightly different threshold of certainty. The solution is to understand where you fall on this spectrum, and then to make the adjustments necessary to compensate if the purchase you are considering does not match your certainty zone.

Let's be clear: Buffett's two market tenets—determining the intrinsic value, and buying only at a discount—are nonnegotiable. But the remaining ten tenets give you room for negotiating with yourself. You may decide that you are comfortable moving forward and buying a stock when only nine of those tenets are satisfied, or eight, or whatever. No one is standing guard to dispute you; your decision must satisfy your personal comfort level.

When certainty is less than you would prefer, you have two ways to adjust:

1. Increase the margin of safety.
2. Decrease the weighting of this particular purchase.

The margin of safety, remember, comes from the discount at which you are able to buy the stock. The weighting refers to the proportion of your overall portfolio that this stock represents.

The lower the level of certainty, the greater the degree of adjustment needed. If you are intrigued by a certain stock but it satisfies, say, only eight out of the ten business, management, and financial tenets, you might decide to buy it if the margin of safety is greater than 25 percent, or 50 percent, or whatever percentage gives you the amount of certainty you require. In addition, your initial purchase should be a small percentage of your portfolio. On the other hand, if you are considering something that satisfies all ten tenets, your margin of safety could be much lower and you would be right to act boldly with a large purchase.

In this chapter, you will meet Bill Miller, Wally Weitz, and Mason Hawkins, three well-known and respected professional investors who have successfully applied Warren Buffett's approach, respectively, in technology, small-capitalization, and international stocks. Just as they learned much from Buffett, we have much to learn from their experiences.

HOW TO COMPENSATE
FOR LESS CERTAINTY

1. Insist on a greater margin of safety.
2. Buy less.

TECHNOLOGY STOCKS

Because Berkshire Hathaway does not own any technology companies, many people have assumed that technology companies as a group cannot be analyzed with any degree of confidence, or Buffett would have done so.

Not true.

Buffett easily admits that he doesn't feel competent to understand and value technology companies. At the 1998 Berkshire Hathaway annual meeting, he was asked whether he would ever consider investing in the technology group at some point in the future. "Well, the answer is no," he responded, "and it's probably been pretty unfortunate.

"I've been an admirer of Andy Grove and Bill Gates," he continued, "and I wish I'd translated that admiration into action by backing it up with money. But when it comes to Microsoft and Intel, I don't know what the world will look like ten years from now, and I don't want to play in a game where the other guy has an advantage. I could spend all my time thinking about the technology for the next year and still not be the 100th, 1,000th, or 10,000th smartest guy in the country analyzing those businesses. There are people who can analyze technology, but I can't."(OID)[1]

This thinking is echoed by Charlie Munger. "The reason we are not in high-tech businesses is that we have a special lack of aptitude in that area. The advantage of low-tech stuff is that we think we understand it fairly well. The other stuff we don't and we'd rather deal with what we understand."(OID)[2]

For years, money managers who pattern themselves after Buffett stayed away from technology companies because of his lack of activity in this area. Wrongly perceiving that they could not analyze this new industry, they now find themselves far behind the curve among a group of talented competitors. Another reason many value-oriented money managers avoided technology companies is that those companies exhibit traits usually associated with growth companies: high price-earnings ratios, high price to book value, and lack of dividend yield. Value investors favor stocks with low price-earnings ratios, low price to book value, and higher dividend yields; they tend to consider stocks with the opposite characteristics overvalued, and they say no thanks.

Both these reasons for avoiding technology stocks demonstrate a disturbing lack of knowledge about how investors should value stocks. Buffett reminds us that the value of any stock has nothing to do with its price-earnings ratio, or price-to-book ratio, or dividend yield. The only way to determine the value of a stock, or any other investment, is by discounting to present value all the future cash flow streams. Growth, he points out, is simply a part of the calculation that pertains to the cash flow. "In our opinion," says Buffett, "the two approaches [value and growth] are joined at the hip."[3]

The moral is clear: Labeling yourself "value" rather than "growth" is not sufficient reason to stay away from technology stocks. Neither is fearing that you cannot place a value on those particular stocks. All stocks are valued the same way: by using the Buffett tenets to determine future cash flow, and then discounting it back to the present. This is true whether you're talking about soft drinks or software.

Legg Mason's Bill Miller

Bill Miller is well known in the investment world. Morningstar named him Equity Manager of the Year in 1998, and Equity

Manager of the Decade in 1999. When *Business Week* profiled "The Heroes of Value Investing" in June 1999, only five people were described: Benjamin Graham, David Dodd, John Burr Williams (who introduced the dividend-discount model), Warren Buffett, and Bill Miller.

Miller has been credited with taking the concept of value investing and the teachings of Warren Buffett and successfully applying them to the New Economy in general and to technology stocks specifically. Bill's track record is impressive and we have much to learn from studying how he did it.

In 1982, Legg Mason, a Baltimore-based brokerage and money management firm, launched its flagship mutual fund, Value Trust. From 1982 until 1990, Value Trust was comanaged by Ernie Kiehne, the former head of research at Legg Mason, and a bright but untested Bill Miller.

Bill's pathway to the money management business was unusual. While his competitors were studying modern portfolio theory in business schools, Bill was studying philosophy at Johns Hopkins Graduate School. While other money managers-in-training were reading Markowitz, Sharpe, and Fama, Bill was reading William James and John Dewey. After graduate school, Bill served a brief time as a corporate treasurer, which helped him understand how companies work. From there, he moved to Legg Mason's research department, where he then joined Ernie Kiehne in managing Value Trust.

During the 1980s, Value Trust was an exercise in two disciplines. Ernie followed Ben Graham's approach to buying companies that were selling at low price-earnings ratios and discounts to book value. Bill took a different course. "My approach," he explained, "is more the theoretical approach that Graham talks about and that Warren Buffett has elaborated on, which is: The value of any investment is the present value of the future cash stream. The trick is to value that and thus value the assets rationally and buy them at a big discount."[4]

During 1990, Bill assumed full control of Value Trust and began to put the full weight of his investment approach into the fund. What happened next was not duplicated by any other general equity fund in the 1990s. For ten consecutive years (1991–2000), Value Trust outperformed the Standard & Poor's 500 Index.

"Bill takes big positions and takes the long view," said Eric Savitz, formerly of *Barron's*. "Over the long term, you can see how it has worked." Savitz, who followed Bill's success while writing the mutual fund column for *Barron's*, remembers Bill as very low-key. "He was nonpromotional. There were plenty of other money managers who jumped on CNBC and talked themselves up, but Bill is not that kind of person who trumpets his own success. Still, he was more insightful about the stocks than anybody I knew."[5]

Today, Bill manages over $20 billion in assets for Legg Mason Funds Management. He routinely keeps Value Trust in a narrow list of 30 to 40 names. It is not unusual to have half the assets in his portfolio invested in 10 names. "There are several parallels between Bill Miller and Warren Buffett," explains Amy Arnott, former editor of *Morningstar*. "He does have a very low turnover strategy and his portfolio is very concentrated compared to other equity funds. His method of valuing companies is similar to Buffett in that they both look at free cash flow as a measure of intrinsic value."[6]

Even though he is a value manager, Bill does not always show up in the "value" area of the style box—the shorthand summary of attributes used by several financial publications. If you look at traditional measures of value, including price to earnings and price to book, Bill does not always fall neatly into this mold. "We are trying to distinguish between companies that are deservedly cheap from those that are undeservedly cheap," he explains. "There are a lot of companies that trade at low valuations that are down in price and are not attractive. The trick is to separate the ones that are from those that aren't."[7]

"Most value investors use historical valuations to determine when stocks are cheap or expensive," he explains. "However, if investors use only historical models, their evaluation methodologies become context-dependent." In other words, historical valuation models work as long as the future looks very much like the past. "The problem facing most value investors is that the future is different from the past in many respects," says Miller, "and, importantly, one of the major differences is the role of technology in society.

"Actually, I think that, in many cases, technology lends itself especially well to the Warren Buffett Way template," he continues, "which is really just a tool kit for sharpening your analytical ability to select, out of the whole universe of potential investments, those that are likely to have the highest probability of giving you an above-average return over a long period."[8]

From that perspective, we can see that several technology companies exhibit the economic traits Buffett admires most: high profit margins, high returns on capital, the ability to reinvest the profits back into a fast-growing company, and management that acts in the interests of shareholders. The difficulty is estimating the future cash flows of the business so we can then discount back to the present and get some sense of intrinsic value.[9]

"The problem most people have with trying to value technology companies is that the picture of the future is so uncertain," explains Lisa Rapuano, Director of Research at Legg Mason Funds Management. "So you have to think about several outcomes rather than just one. This can create a greater variance—in the potential future payoff—from a long-term investment. However, if you really dig into the key aspects of the company you're looking at—the potential size of the market, its theoretical profitability, its competitive position—you can understand exactly what is driving the differences between one scenario and another, and that will reduce your uncertainty level. We still create cash flow valuations, but we often use several target values rather than a single one."

Furthermore, she says: "Since technology is a true driver of future economic growth, and since many winning technology companies generate outsize returns when they do work, we find that the extra level of analysis pays off. It can lead to returns far in excess of what we can find elsewhere, even taking the greater uncertainty into account."[10]

"It is important to remember," Miller points out, "that Buffett wants to minimize error. He is unwilling to make an investment unless he is absolutely convinced he is right. Thus, his error rate is low." In contrast, says Bill, "our certainty threshold is somewhat lower, particularly if we think the potential payoff could be very large." Most money managers who invest in technology face the probability of a higher error rate, so it becomes critical to recognize errors quickly and get rid of them. "The payoff for this strategy," he explains, "is that when you operate with a wider funnel of ideas, you get potentially more big winners that will more than pay for the smaller mistakes that naturally occur."[11]

We already know that one good strategy for tamping the risk of companies whose future is unclear (like technology firms) is to demand a higher margin of safety with each purchase. Another is reducing the weightings of each stock. Here is one additional strategy: Combine technology stocks with a portfolio filled with stable and highly predictable companies.

"It is like anything new," Bill reminds us. "You have to spend time to understand it. I think a lot of people approach technology with a thinking model that is defective. They believe technology is very difficult to understand, so they don't try to understand it. They have already made up their minds in advance." That narrow view of the world has one predictable outcome: it blinds people to what is actually occurring. "Yes, people are still buying Coca-Cola and Gillette razor blades, and using their American Express Card," explains Bill, "but they are also using America Online, and Microsoft software, and buying Dell Computers—and that's ubiquitous."[12]

Selected technology companies are the franchises of the twenty-first century.

The Franchise Factors

Warren Buffett teaches us that the best business to own, the one with the best long-term prospects, is a franchise—a business that sells a product or service that is needed or desired, has no close substitute, and yields profits that are unregulated. He has often said that the next great fortunes will be made by the people who identify the new franchises. "I believe technology companies are the modern-day equivalent of Buffett's franchise factor," says Bill Miller.

In Buffett's consumer products world, the factors that are important in a franchise are brand awareness, pricing power, and share of mind. In the technology world, the key franchise factors include network effects, positive feedback, lock-in, and increasing returns. These factors are very valuable additions to our investor's toolbox, for they give us an extra level of analysis for evaluating technology companies.

1. *Network effect.* A network effect exists when the value of a good increases as the number of people who use the network increases. Typically, people prefer to become connected to a larger network rather than a smaller one. If there are two competing networks, one with 5 million members and one with 1 million members, new members will tend to select the larger network because it is more likely to fulfill their need for connections to other members, more services, or whatever the network consists of.

For network effects to take hold, it is important to get big fast. This thwarts competition from getting established. The idea was originated by Bob Metcalfe, the inventor of the Ethernet

226

standard and the founder of 3Com Corporation, a networking company. Today, network effects are sometimes popularly known as "Metcalfe's Law."

2. *Positive feedback.* We can think of positive feedback as a variant of network effects. It is a behavioral component of human nature described by B.F. Skinner, a behavioral psychologist. Positive experiences give us pleasure or satisfaction, and we want to relive them. Someone who has a positive experience when using a technology product (or any product, for that matter) will have a tendency to return to the product. The net effect of positive feedback in businesses is that the strong get stronger and the weak get weaker.

Positive feedback is one reason the economics of a company follow an "S" curve phenomenon—a three-stage development. In the first stage, growth is relatively flat. In the second stage, there is a period of rapid growth, as positive feedback kicks in. When the market is saturated and growth levels off, the third stage has been reached. Investors need to be highly sensitive to the "elbow" stage of development—the upward curve between the end of stage one and the start of stage two. When sales and earnings start to take off dramatically, positive feedback is in place.

3. *Lock-in.* The term *lock-in* refers to both a mechanism and its result. It takes advantage of a piece of human psychology: When we learn one way of doing something, we have little interest in learning another way.

High-technology products—specifically, software—can be difficult to master. When users have become proficient using one product, they fiercely resist changing to another. Changing requires learning a completely new set of instructions, often very difficult instructions. This is true even if a competitor's product is deemed superior.

Every person who types on a keyboard is locked in to an inferior system. The *qwerty* keyboard (named for the topmost row of letters) was intentionally designed to be slow, in the days when the long metal typewriter keys were easily jammed by fast typists. It has been demonstrated in numerous experiments that other keyboard arrangements would permit improved typing speed, but everyone knows the current system and no one is willing to change.

Similarly, most engineers considered beta videotapes superior in quality to VHS tapes, but the VHS format quickly gained the dominant spot in the market. Because of that initial dominance, consumers browsing in video rental stores found many more choices available on VHS tapes than on beta tapes. The natural consequence was that many more VHS-format tape players were sold than beta-format machines. The producers of videotapes, not wanting to miss sales, brought out more and more new product in the VHS format. Eventually, the system was completely locked in.

Because switching costs are high, users of a product or service are usually easy customers for an upgraded version. Even if the issue is not one of superior performance, people will still stick with the same system, simply because they prefer it. In either case, lock-in (sometimes called *path dependence*) automatically leads to increasing returns.

4. *Increasing returns.* Think of increasing returns as the economic variant of positive feedback. A technology company enjoys increasing returns this way: First, there is substantial upfront cost in developing the product. Then, as sales increase (due to positive feedback and lock-in), there is a rapid acceleration of economic gains. Because little additional capital reinvestment is needed at this point, increasing sales come with negligible cost.

Think of a software product. It might cost hundreds of millions to develop initially, but after the product takes off, relatively minor capital reinvestment is needed. Compare this to a traditional manufacturer. To increase sales, the company has to build more factories, retool the equipment, retrain workers, and so on.

For most technology companies, none of this activity is needed. As positive feedback and lock-in yield millions of customers, the last few million customers are generating steadily increasing returns for the company.

America Online

The success of America Online (AOL) is largely attributed to its getting the Internet concept right, from the onset. Some Internet providers saw the Internet as a way to provide information (think library). AOL saw the Internet as a communication system (think phone system). From the start, AOL differentiated itself from its competitors, and because of this, it quickly moved into the number-one spot.

Bill Miller was one of the first fund managers to recognize this dominance and understand its significance. He has taken some criticism from value-investing purists for his purchases of technology stocks, especially AOL, but he is not dissuaded. He was confident in his original decision, and he has been proved right. If we take the case of AOL and array it against Buffett's tenets, and then against the technology franchise factors, it is easy to see why.

AOL and the Buffett Tenets

America Online is a strong company that does not align perfectly with all twelve tenets of the Warren Buffett Way, but Bill Miller saw enough compensating factors and went ahead unworried.

Lisa Rapuano, Legg Mason's director of research, summarized the thinking on AOL in relation to nine of Buffett's tenets.[13]

1. *Simple and understandable?* Yes and no. "In one sense, that particular kind of business had never been done before. So, for example, analyzing what the entry of a new competitor would mean was very difficult. On the other hand, in a pure sense, as a business it wasn't really new. There was a customer relationship, for which there was a monthly payment, and there was the opportunity for significant other payments such as e-commerce and advertising. The cost structure was easy to understand, so basically it was pretty easy to disaggregate the business and understand what the value drivers were. What was a little more difficult was forecasting, because we didn't have a clean example of how it was going to work out."

2. *Consistent operating history?* No. It was too new.

3. *Favorable long-term prospects?* "Absolutely," Lisa says. Not only was it already the largest Internet provider in the United States, by a considerable margin; it was only going to get larger relative to competitors.

4. *Rational management?* "They have been able to meet the competitive threats in the changing landscape, and in the changing technology, incredibly well. They have had to reposition a couple of times in order to maintain their lead." And once their lead was solid? "At that point the most rational thing to do was to allocate all of your capital to growing, because you had this tremendous opportunity. So that's what they did. They made good decisions."

5. *Resist the institutional imperative?* At a time when their main competitors, including CompuServe, were still using metered pricing, AOL made the bold switch to flat pricing. "It was a risk, but it was a question of: How can we pull ahead here? How can we really change the game? They went to flat-rate pricing when they needed to, they changed their technology when they needed to. They did exactly what they needed to do to get to where they are now."

6. *Candid management?* "They learned as they went," Lisa remembers. "When we first started with them, they were very candid. Then they went through a very tough period where they were not sure how much to tell you. And then when they finally got religion, they said, 'We are going to tell you whatever you want to know.'"

7. *Return-on-equity cash earnings?* After noting that there wasn't much return in the early years, Lisa quickly adds,

"But the interesting thing was that they were losing a lot less money than people thought they were. They were not actually making money because they were capitalizing their marketing, but they weren't losing as much money as people had forecast. But what was critical to understand is that there was a point at which you did not need to invest a whole heck of a lot more capital in the business, and the return would continue to escalate."

8. *High profit margins?* "Very. And the fastest growing part of the business was the advertising business, which is basically 90 percent."

9. *What is the value?* Lisa describes the Legg Mason multifactor approach. "We broke apart the economics and compared them to other businesses that have similar kinds of economics. First, there is a subscription-based model, which is basically the bulk of AOL's business. How did AOL compare to other subscription-based businesses, like cable? There was also the retail transaction business. Every time AOL customers made an e-commerce purchase, AOL received a percentage of the sale. So we could measure that. Then there was the advertising business, which we analyzed like any other advertising business. We just took each part—subscription, retail transactions, and advertising—valued them separately, and added them up."

In 1996, Bill Miller began buying AOL for the Legg Mason Value Trust. At the time, the company's market capitalization was approximately $4 billion, and the share price was approximately $40. Based on Legg Mason's multifactor model, the judgment was that AOL was worth more like $7.5 billion, or $75 a share. By that calculation, AOL was selling at a 46 percent discount. Even so, when Bill purchased AOL, he invested only 1.5 percent of his portfolio in the stock. Today, of course, with the Time Warner merger, AOL has become the world's largest media company, selling for $50 a share, and Bill Miller's original cost basis, split adjusted, is $1.75.

AOL and the Technology Franchise Factors

Part of Bill Miller's genius is seeing things before other people do. He knew, early on, that the Internet was going to be an enormous force in all parts of society, not just a passing fad. And in the specific case of AOL, he could see that the franchise factors were beginning to show up, even before the company's economics were obvious. Once he spotted those franchise factors, Miller knew it was only a matter of time before the economic factors would reflect them. Everyone else was looking for the economics, and when they didn't see them, they wrote AOL off.

1. *Network effect.* Because it saw itself as providing a complete communication system, AOL differentiated itself by the various communications channels it offered its members: e-mail, chat rooms, message boards, instant messaging. Because AOL had the right platform, it soon started experiencing network effects. People said, "I wanted to sign up for AOL because my best friend (brother, granddaughter, tennis partner) was on it." Very quickly, these connections began to multiply in a very forceful way, until AOL became so large that each new potential member overwhelmingly chose AOL over its competitors.

2. *Positive feedback.* Because AOL offered so many features that members wanted, most people had positive experiences with every usage and were eager to come back for more. Bill Miller was also able to measure individual usage, and he knew that AOL subscribers were spending more and more time on the site.

3. *Lock-in.* From a user's point of view, AOL's technology is not daunting, but the lock-in effect worked in the company's favor anyway. Members quickly became used to sending and receiving e-mail in a certain way and didn't care to change. Even if some other provider offered more bells and whistles, they were not interested in changing.

Even more interesting is what happened when the company switched to flat-rate prices. Hundreds of thousands of Internet users recognized that as a good deal, and the number of subscribers jumped astronomically, causing the system to become hopelessly jammed. Anyone trying to access the service heard nothing but constant busy signals. New customers were angry, old customers were furious. Media coverage of the situation was intensely negative, which only heightened users' frustration. But the question for stock analysts was: Did people change to another provider? The answer: No. Despite the busy signals and the negative publicity, membership continued to grow.

One special note: At Berkshire Hathaway's annual meeting in Omaha in 2000, Buffett discussed how he looks for companies that had endured great adversity and still survived. He mentioned American Express and the salad oil scandal, and he recalled what happened to Coca-Cola when it introduced New Coke. To that list, said Buffett, we can add AOL. "Customers were mad at the company, but still subscriptions rose. This was powerful."

4. *Increasing returns.* The original capital investment was large, but once it was made, AOL could add millions of new members without a corresponding amount of new capital. Remember Lisa Rapuano's astute comment: "There was a point at which you did not need to invest a whole heck of a lot more capital . . . , and the returns would continue to escalate."

SMALLER AND MID-CAPITALIZATION STOCKS

As portfolio managers become more successful, typically they are asked to manage more money. Great performance records attract more clients. Over time, these successful managers find themselves managing not millions but *billions* of dollars. Strange as it may seem on the surface, that creates a problem: Once their asset base reaches this level, managers are forced to focus only on large-capitalization stocks and to ignore the smaller companies.

Here's how it works. When you manage $100 million and you decide to allocate 5 percent of your portfolio into a company, you can easily invest that $5 million in either big- or smaller-capitalization stocks. If a small-cap company is worth $1 billion, your 5 percent portfolio stake would represent only one half of 1 percent of the company's market capitalization. But if you were managing $10 billion and wanted to buy a 5 percent stake in that same company, you would be buying half the company. (A 5 percent position in a $10 billion portfolio is $500 million.) Even if it were possible to buy half the shares of the company, it could take weeks, months, or even years to fill in the position. That is why larger money managers simply do not invest their time or money in smaller stocks.

Now think about Warren Buffett and Berkshire Hathaway. With $30 billion in investable cash, Buffett cannot easily navigate the smaller-cap market. He simply cannot buy enough shares of smaller-cap stocks to make a meaningful difference in Berkshire's return. Because of Berkshire's multibillion-dollar asset base, Buffett is forced to invest in larger and larger companies.

The interesting twist on this is that Buffett *does* buy small-cap companies when he can acquire the whole company. In fact, a study of Berkshire's private transactions over the years shows that these businesses were often small: Willey Home Furnishings, CORT Business Services, Jordan's Furniture, and Justin Industries, in addition to some of the well-known purchases outlined in Chapter 2. Sometimes the purchase price of these private wholly owned businesses has been less than $1 billion. In all these cases, Buffett looked at the business, its management team, its financials, and its purchase price—exactly the same methodology he used when he bought large-capitalization stocks like Coca-Cola and General Re Insurance.

We know that, given the choice, Buffett would prefer to own all of a company rather than a small percentage, because that puts him in the position of making all of the capital-allocation decisions. If he cannot buy all of a company, owning just a few hundred thousand shares of small-cap stock is not enough to add value to Berkshire's billion-dollar portfolio.

When the total number of shares outstanding for a company, and the average daily volume of shares traded, are too small for institutional managers with large sums of money, we refer to this as a lack of liquidity. The company is said to be "thinly traded." The important thing for individual investors to remember is that, occasionally, this lack of liquidity creates temporary mispricing of the shares. Then, if they are paying attention, they may find a wonderful opportunity.

Wally Weitz

In 1983, armed with $10 million under management, Wally Weitz launched his own investment advisory firm. Today, Wallace R. Weitz & Company manages over $5 billion for individuals, corporations, endowments, and foundations. At the heart of the firm are three well-known and highly successful mutual funds: Weitz Value Fund, Weitz Partners Value, and Weitz Hickory. The first two are mid-capitalization stock funds, the third invests primarily in small-capitalization stocks, and all of them have Morningstar's highest (five-star) rating.

Weitz and Buffett have a lot in common. Both work out of small offices in Omaha, Nebraska, and both take a businessperson's approach to studying stocks. Each time Weitz studies a stock, he tries to determine what a rational buyer would pay if that buyer had the opportunity to purchase 100 percent of the company. In determining the value of a stock, he looks at the earning power of the company and its asset values, and tries to discover whether the company has any enduring competitive advantage: Does the company have some special market niche, for example, or a franchise value?

Like Buffett, Weitz sticks with companies he understands; he seeks out businesses that generate more cash than they need to operate; and he looks for intelligent and honest managers

235

who treat their shareholders as partners in the business. If a company with these attributes is available in the market, at an attractive price and a big margin of safety, then Weitz is very interested in becoming an owner of the company.

Also like Buffett, Weitz likes to hold onto stocks for several years. His firm typically has a very low turnover ratio (between 20 and 30 percent annually). "I would love to hold a stock for 20 years," he said. "It's expensive to change, both in terms of transactions costs—commissions and the buy-sell spread—and in terms of the tax consequences. Warren Buffett says his favorite holding period is forever. That might be overstating it a bit, but I would like to hold for long periods of time."[14]

Wally Weitz started his investment career in 1970. For a short time, he worked as an analyst for a small securities firm in New York. One day, while pitching an idea to a portfolio manager, Weitz heard a tale about Warren Buffett. Years earlier, this same portfolio manager, so the story goes, had traveled to Omaha to try to sell Buffett on a stock idea. He presented the typical Wall Street pitch, but soon realized that Buffett knew more than he did about how the business worked. The portfolio manager told Weitz that, thinking back, it was the best education he ever received.[15]

Weitz never adapted to the fast-paced style of New York. To him, it was a city that bounced between extremes. He regarded the financial district as a casebook example of manic depression. Everyone was euphorically chasing the latest hot tip and dumping a favorite stock at the first hint of disappointment. In Omaha, the lifestyle was slower. Investors were favored over speculators, and holding a stock for years was considered the norm, not the exception. More important, a contrarian could find comfort in Omaha.

"After I moved here in 1973, some mutual friends introduced me to Warren Buffett," Weitz recalled. "I quickly came to respect his ability to identify, articulate, and focus on the critical variables. That impressed me, and I started to pay attention to Berkshire Hathaway." Weitz has owned Berkshire

Hathaway and has attended its annual meetings since the 1970s. In those early years, only a half-dozen shareholders would show up at the annual meetings. These lucky shareholders would spend the afternoon with Buffett, talking about Berkshire and other businesses. Since then, Weitz has watched, read about, and studied the movements of Warren Buffett.

Weitz explained, "What I came to learn is there are no simple formulas. To be successful at investing requires you think about the business. How does the business work? What makes it successful? What could make it unsuccessful? What is the nature of the 'moat'? Is there a legal franchise or do they possess an execution advantage? What makes Costco better than Kmart? These are specific questions that you need to ask, and each investment situation is going to be different."

The critical variable for any businessperson, Weitz believes, is judging a company's cash flow. That means looking past the general accounting principles and focusing on a company's discretionary cash flow. For example, a cable television company or a cellular telephone company that spends billions of dollars on infrastructure will later report huge depreciation and amortization charges that will, for a time, nullify reported earnings. Even though on an accounting basis the company reports no earnings, management has in fact huge cash flows to invest.

In the early 1990s, Weitz earned extraordinary returns by investing in both large and small cable companies. "The cable business was wonderful," he explained. "Even though there was always the threat of satellite delivery, the local cable company operated with an exclusive franchise. You had a measurable current subscriber base. You knew exactly what each subscriber was being charged. The revenues were right in front of you and were highly predictable over the next five years or longer. You could count on some increase in subscribers, you could count on the expansion of the number of channels and some price increases. Of course the market would rise and fall all during this period, and that gave investors some buying and selling opportunities."

Looking at these companies, Weitz and his colleagues would model out different scenarios of revenue increases, price increases, and new channel delivery. Because of the high infrastructure costs, there were also interest payments to pay on the debt. But all these variables were measurable and all were reasonably predictable. "We would sit down and run off different models, from the worst-case scenario to the best. Each time we would ask ourselves, 'Is this company worth owning if everything goes wrong?' And, in many cases, it was. Even the worst scenario would still give us an annual return of 15 percent or more."

Focusing on Small-Cap Companies

What are the challenges of investing in smaller companies as opposed to large companies? "In theory," says Weitz, "there shouldn't be any difference." He believes the analytical process of investing in small companies is exactly the same as investing in big companies. You look for the same variables: predictability, cash flow, and management capability. You focus on the same factors whether the market cap of the company is $100 million, $10 billion, or $100 billion.

"In practice, though," Weitz continues, "there are some differences when it comes to investing in small companies versus big companies." According to Weitz, larger companies typically have more layers of complexity. Their annual reports and their accounting statements are more complicated. You have to peel back more layers. In some big companies, the communication lines are more formalized, which can make the analytical job easier. On the other hand, with smaller companies you often get more chances to meet with management.

So why, over many recent years, has there been a greater disparity in the performance of big-cap stocks compared to small-cap stocks? Weitz believes the answer is largely linked to the growing asset base of most managers. As investment managers

SMALL-CAP COMPANIES

- *Until they have gained substantial market share, they are potentially greater economic risks.*
- *They tend to be less complex, less bureaucratic.*
- *Their managers are often more accessible.*

find themselves with more money to manage, they have to seek out stocks that allow them to more easily buy and sell large blocks of shares. "But, remember, this is an external market force," says Weitz, "that has little to do with the analytical differences in stocks."

Interestingly, Weitz never set out to invest solely in small- or mid-capitalization stocks. "The mid-cap classification is based on a snapshot of our portfolio," said Weitz, "not something that comes out of our charter. I would love to own huge companies so that liquidity was never an issue, but I am also willing to own very small companies. I have lots of patience accumulating positions in thinly traded stocks, and I am willing to own them a long time, so I don't have to worry about bouncing in and out of them."[16]

Weitz is able to invest larger sums in smaller companies because of his insistence on maintaining a low-turnover strategy in his portfolio. If he were a high-turnover manager who bought and sold large blocks every day, he would find it extremely difficult to operate in the small-cap market.

Where is Weitz shopping for stocks today? "Good ideas come in bunches," he says. "In the past, we made a lot of money in cable and cellular telephone companies, and at the time we invested a good portion of portfolio into this sector. But today, most of our money is invested in financials." The strong showing of the very large financial companies, with global operations and strong growth opportunities, has created a situation where the prices of the smaller companies are trading substantially below their intrinsic value. "They may not be growing very fast and a lot of people think they are boring stocks," Weitz explains, "but that doesn't mean they can't be a good investment at the right price. For example, small thrifts, all with single-family mortgages on garden-variety houses, selling at half of book value with management willing to buy in stock—that's like picking up dimes on the sidewalk. It may be slow, but it's worth doing."

INTERNATIONAL STOCKS

In 1990, Berkshire Hathaway made its first substantial investment in a foreign company. That year, Buffett purchased 31 million shares of Guinness PLC for $300 million. At the time, it was the world's largest alcoholic beverage company, with two principal operating units: United Distillers and Guinness Brewing. United Distillers produced Johnnie Walker, the world's best-selling scotch, along with other popular scotch brands, including Bell's (the best-selling scotch whiskey in the United Kingdom) and Dewar's White Label (the best-selling scotch whiskey in the United States). Guinness was the world's seventh largest brewer. Its premium brands included Guinness stout (the world's leading stout beer), Harp Lager, Cruzcampo Lager, Smithwick's Ale, and Kaliber.

According to Buffett, Guinness is very much the same type of company as Coca-Cola. Both companies earn the majority of their profits from international operations. "Indeed," Buffett explained, "in the sense of where they earn their profits, continent by continent, Coca-Cola and Guinness display strong similarities."[17] However, Buffett, who remains a devoted fan of Cherry Coke, is quick to point out that he will never get the drinks of these two companies confused.

Studying the Guinness purchase, it is easy to see how the company aligned with Buffett's investment tenets. Like Coca-Cola, it was a simple and understandable business with a long and consistent operating history. Although liquor consumption has basically been flat in mature markets like the United States, Great Britain, and northern Europe, demand for the company's products has been steadily growing in the developing countries. Guinness enjoyed high profit margins, cash earnings, and a high return on equity. Using very conservative growth rates of its cash earnings, it was clear that Buffett was buying Guinness at a considerable margin of safety.

Surprisingly, in the years that followed, Buffett made no other significant foreign purchase for Berkshire Hathaway. Guinness, which began as a $300 million purchase, never became a major investment for the company. In 1994, when Buffett listed only securities with a $300 million market value, Guinness was no longer included. The market value of the company had dropped to $270 million.

In 1999, Buffett stepped into the foreign markets again. He purchased 2.2 percent of Allied Domecq, a British spirits and food retailing giant that also owned Baskin-Robbins and Dunkin' Donuts.

Buffett is not against international investing. Given the choice, he would much prefer to own great U.S. companies at great prices, but there is no demarcation line that prohibits him from looking overseas. At the 1999 Berkshire Hathaway annual meeting, he made a point of emphasizing his willingness to invest in *any* good business as long as he can understand it and the price is right. He noted that, a few years previously, Berkshire had made an offer for a Japanese company but missed out on the purchase, and recently had made a written offer for a German company.

Still, because Berkshire's foreign investments have been so few and, dollarwise, so insignificant, Buffett has not given investors a long treatise on international investing to match his reasoning on domestic stocks. From his remarks, however, it is clear that the same investment tenets he follows for making U.S. purchases apply to international investing.

If you choose to venture across borders for your next investment, you can use the by-now familiar tenets of the Warren Buffett Way as a basic map for your journey. Even so, there is always some measure of comfort in observing explorers who have gone first. Fortunately, we have such an explorer, one who has been highly successful in applying Buffett's principles to international investing.

Mason Hawkins

In 1975, Mason Hawkins founded Southeastern Asset Management in Memphis, Tennessee. Today, the firm manages over $14 billion in assets for institutional accounts as well as four Longleaf Partners mutual funds: the celebrated Longleaf Partners Fund, Longleaf Partners Small Cap Fund, Longleaf Partners Realty Fund, and Longleaf Partners International Fund.

Mason Hawkins has no doubt about the reasons for his success. "Our success is greatly derived from the lessons taught by Ben Graham and Warren Buffett," he says.[18] Hawkins, like Buffett, likes to own good businesses that are understandable, have strong balance sheets that generate free operating cash flow (adjusted for working capital and capital expenditures), and demonstrate a competitive advantage in the marketplace. He also looks for strong capable managers who are shareholder-oriented and are good at allocating the capital of the business. He determines the intrinsic value of a company by calculating the present value of the future free cash flows. And, just as Ben Graham has taught a generation of investors, Hawkins demands a margin of safety with each purchase. His safety margin is very specific: He will buy a company only if it is selling at less than 60 percent of intrinsic value.

In 1998 Hawkins, along with Southeastern's other portfolio managers and analysts, was having a difficult time finding good U.S. companies that were also selling at the required margin of safety. However, abroad, many high-quality companies were selling at big discounts to their intrinsic value. Longleaf Partners Fund was, by prospectus, allowed to purchase foreign securities but only with 30 percent of its portfolio. Because the investment bargains overseas were so plentiful, Hawkins decided to launch an international fund that could invest a much larger percentage of the portfolio into foreign securities.

The Longleaf Partners International Fund is different from most other international funds. For one thing, Hawkins and his comanagers, G. Staley Cates and Andrew McDermott, wanted their fund to be registered as a nondiversified fund, which would allow it to make more concentrated investments.[19]

In addition, the team at Southeastern Asset Management decided the fund would be run strictly bottom-up. In other words, the fund does not begin with any geographical bias. The fund managers are looking for the best 20 international investments they can find, regardless of country weighting, sector weighting, or how the portfolio matches against an international index. As true business owners, they do not care how their portfolio corresponds to some named index. Instead, they ask: What are the economic returns of the companies we own? What prices did we have to pay to become shareholders?

Business owners of international companies must employ at least the same level of investigation as those who buy only U.S. companies. They must be able not only to understand the business but also to gauge the value of management and to decipher the balance sheet and income statement.

One common stumbling point for some international investors is the differences in accounting standards between countries. Hawkins believes that some dissimilarities must be reconciled. He acknowledges the differences in accounting disclosure between the U.S. standards and those used in the

United Kingdom, Western Europe, Japan, and Hong Kong, but his team of analysts has been able to uncover what is important to a business owner. "We never look at GAAP earnings," he claims. "We are interested in after-tax free cash flows available to owners once maintenance capital expenditures and working capital needs have been met."

According to Hawkins, most international companies have depreciation and amortization schedules that are adequately delineated. "We reconcile the various schedules to derive normal operating cash flows, and from normal operating cash flows we subtract required inventory, receivables, and replacement capital requirements. The data is standardly available in industrialized countries," explains Hawkins. "It is only in the emerging countries where you will find more difficulty in deciphering the accounting statements."

It is important to note here that all international investors must take one thing into account: *country risk*. Many emerging countries and new stock markets around the world are inviting

THE CHALLENGE OF FOCUSING ON INTERNATIONAL COMPANIES

- *They may have different accounting standards.*
- *There is a risk that the currency will decline relative to the dollar.*
- *It is more difficult to interview management.*
- *Political, social, and economic turmoil can ruin companies and swallow the expected gains.*

individuals and professionals to invest, but the economic and political uncertainty in these emerging nations may be much higher than investors want to assume. For example, heightened political risk could make it difficult to predict when a transfer of power in a country could monopolize private holdings. The country could be economically unstable, thereby making its currency too expensive to hedge. Or the accounting standards of a certain country may be incomplete by American standards, making it difficult for a thoughtful business owner to correctly gauge the economic value of a business based in that country. In any one of these cases, the analysts at Longleaf will simply refuse to make an investment. "We would certainly not attempt to invest in a company in a country where you wouldn't feel comfortable leaving your cash on deposit in a bank," explains Hawkins, quoting his associate, Andrew McDermott.

It is also important to note that Longleaf Partners International Fund is fully hedged. The total assets of the fund that are invested in any one country are hedged by selling short that country's currency against the U.S. dollar. This safeguards against another common, but frequently overlooked, risk in international investing.

Astute international investors have come to learn that they can get the economics of a foreign company right and still lose money if the foreign currency drops. When a foreign currency declines relative to the dollar, it takes more of that currency to purchase back U.S. dollars, which could potentially negate any economic gain that comes from owning a good-performing company. By shorting the currency of the countries they are invested in, individual investors can protect themselves from a potential loss in currency transactions.

Hedging can cost money and thus reduce the potential investment gain. But because of the volatility of international currencies, Mason Hawkins believes hedging is a prudent strategy to protect shareholders' money. "We build the cost of hedging into our appraisals," he explains. "You have to subtract the annual cost or add the benefit of hedging when you are looking at

the economic valuation of the company. So if your average holding period is going to be five years, you take into account the
net cost."

Do those interested in foreign countries need to alter their
discount rate to compensate for potential risk? No, according to
Hawkins. "If we are hedged back [on the currency], there is no
need to adjust the discount rate." Today, Longleaf uses a discount rate around 9.5 to 10.5 percent. "It is a big premium to
the long bond," Hawkins admits, "but we think it is the minimal requirement that an equity investor is going to demand to
be in a business."

In addition to deciphering slightly different accounting
statements and hedging a portfolio for currency risk, international investors who follow Warren Buffett's tenets have one
more challenge: interviewing management. Because business
owners are acutely interested in how management intends to
run the business and allocate the capital, there is an intense desire to connect with management. Owning foreign companies
can make this difficult. Not every investor is prepared to travel
overseas to meet with management, and even if such a meeting were possible, not every manager is prepared to sit down
and chat.

The professionals at Longleaf often get the opportunity to
meet with management, and they frequently find themselves
traveling the globe to conduct interviews. However, to cut
down on wasted trips, the analysts do their financial homework
ahead of time. Before they schedule a visit, they first determine
whether the company meets the minimum financial standards,
and then decide whether the share price is trading at a satisfactory discount to intrinsic value.

Meeting with the management of a foreign company, explains Hawkins, is not always necessary. Much of what is needed
is available on the Internet. "I think investors can get a tremendous amount of information about the company and its management team by reading proxy statements, the past five years'

worth of annual reports, and the interviews with management that are available in magazines and newspapers. And the company's Web site is usually stocked full of useful insights."

"I think Conrad Black, CEO of Hollinger International [a Canadian newspaper/media company] writes the best annual reports," says Longleaf comanager Andrew McDermott. "He explains share buybacks in layman's terms: 'It's like buying dimes for nickels on a grand scale.' "(OID)[20]

It has also been reported widely in the media that several Japanese managers have taken a rational approach to managing their companies. McDermott particularly points to president Ken Matsuzawa, at Nippon Fire & Marine Insurance Company. "He was the first Japanese CEO in Japan's non-life-insurance sector to grasp the importance of corporate governance, management compensation, and increasing returns for shareholders, not just employees and other customers," McDermott explained. "Matsuzawa has acted on this belief by repurchasing shares, executing an attractive merger with a smaller company, cutting costs, and reforming Nippon's investment process."(OID)[21]

The new SEC Rule 13F-D (fair disclosure) was enacted this past year to help level the playing field for all investors—individuals and professionals alike. Under the new rule, management of a publicly traded company cannot disclose pertinent information about the company to any analyst or institutional investor unless it simultaneously releases that information to all shareholders. Most observers believe that most companies will use the mass media and their own Web site as the mechanisms to communicate worldwide. They also believe that many foreign companies will adopt this new communication approach to reach not only their own shareholders but new shareholders who may be interested in the company.

Will this new rule hinder our ability to analyze companies according to the Warren Buffett tenets? According to Mason Hawkins, absolutely not. "It [Rule 13F-D] is going to disappoint the 99 percent of Wall Street that is worried about a company's quarterly financial results, and that will mean there is going to be more short-term price volatility. But it will also mean more great businesses will be inefficiently priced."

With great success, the analysts at Longleaf have taken one step beyond Warren Buffett. Not only have they aggressively invested in foreign countries, they have invested in an occasional technology company in foreign countries as well. As Longleaf's Staley Cates puts it, "Like every other industry group, technology gets down to business, people, and price. We have done technology and we will continue to do technology, but it has to be on our terms. Along the business/people/price model, we need to understand what they do. We need to understand their competitive advantage; we need to know and trust and like managers riding that technology, and, most importantly, we have to buy cheaply."(OID)[22]

One of Longleaf's international technology winners was Philips Electronics, Europe's biggest electronics company. The company's single biggest segment is semiconductors, but it wasn't special insight about semiconductors that attracted Longleaf. Instead, it was because a short-term change in the company's stock price was so dramatic that it offered an opportunity to pick up shares at prices lower than the net cash and marketable securities that were on the balance sheet. When the price of the company dramatically fell in one day, Longleaf was ready. No way would they pass up an opportunity to get $20 billion of semiconductors and other related electronic businesses for free. "For reasons we can never understand or figure out, entire countries, regions, and sectors fall in and out of favor on what seems like a weekly basis," McDermott explained. "And that provides us with fantastic opportunities because all we do is hang numbers on businesses."(OID)[23]

Today, Longleaf Partners International Fund is invested around the globe. It owns financial companies, industrial and services businesses, and retail companies in Canada, the United

Kingdom, Japan, New Zealand, South Africa, Bermuda, and the European Union. In every case, it is looking for the same thing Warren Buffet is looking for: Good businesses that generate great economics, are run by smart managers, and are available at cheap prices. Sometimes those companies are available in the United States, but often they are available overseas.

ESSENTIAL TO LOOK FOR— ANYWHERE, ANY TIME

Good businesses that generate great economics run by smart managers available at cheap prices.

Our world is changing every second of every day. New companies are being created. New industries are being formed. New technologies are being discovered. New governments are being born, and familiar countries are being reborn to take a different role on the international stage. Whether those changes are exciting or disconcerting is a matter of your own psychological makeup, your personal response to change. But there is no doubt that they represent opportunities for profitable investment.

You will have to make some effort. There is a learning curve to understanding new technology, for example, and translating foreign accounting statements may be awkward at first. But the payoff for that effort can be substantial.

Just as ecosystems change over time, so too will markets and economies continue to evolve and adapt. Our greatest challenge as investors is to remain flexible and open-minded, and to educate ourselves as fully as possible. Armed with Buffett's timeless principles, we need not fear these new challenges, but move forward with passion.

◼ LEARNING FROM THE BEST

The major goal of this book is to help investors understand and employ the strategies that have made Warren Buffett successful. It is my hope that, having learned from his experiences, you will be able to go forward and apply his methods. Perhaps in the future you will see companies that resemble some of his purchases and, knowing what Buffett might do in a similar case, you will be ready to profit from his teachings.

Buffett's success, I believe, is as much the failure of others as it is any innate superior ability he may possess. "It has been helpful to me," he explains, "to have tens of thousands [of students] turned out of business schools taught that it didn't do any good to think."[24] I do not mean to imply that Buffett is average. Far from it. He is unquestionably brilliant. But the gap between Buffett and other professional investors is widened by their own willingness to play a loser's game, a game Buffett chooses not to play. Readers of this book are given the same choice.

Success is the product of rational thinking.

The driving force of Warren Buffett's investment strategy is the rational allocation of capital. Determining how to allocate a company's earnings is the most important decision a manager will make; determining how to allocate one's savings is the most important decision an investor will make. Rationality—displaying rational thinking when making that choice—is the quality Buffett most admires. Despite its underlying vagaries, there is a line of reason that permeates the financial markets. Buffett's success is a result of locating that line of reason and never deviating from its path.

Buffett has had his share of failures and no doubt will have a few more in the years ahead. But investment success is not synonymous with infallibility. Rather, success comes from doing more things right than wrong. Adopting Warren Buffett's approach to investing is no different. Its success is as much a result of eliminating those things you can get wrong, which are many and perplexing (predicting markets, economies, and stock prices), as it is of getting things right, which are few and simple (valuing a business and paying a price for the business that is below its intrinsic value).

Over his lifetime, Buffett has tried different investment gambits. At a young age, he even tried his hand at stock charting. But his success was made possible, he believes, because of what he learned from others—by studying with Ben Graham, reading Phil Fisher, and working alongside Charlie Munger. This trio is considered by many to be the brightest financial minds in our recent history. "I don't think I have any original ideas," Buffett once said. "Certainly, I talk about reading Graham. I've read Phil Fisher. So I've gotten a lot of ideas myself from reading. You can learn a lot from other people. In fact, I think if you learn basically from other people, you don't have to get too many new ideas on your own. You can just apply the best of what you see."(OID)[25]

Over the past 45 years, through all the market's distractions, Buffett found his niche. A point where all things make sense: where investment strategy cohabits with personality. "Our [investment] attitude," Buffett says, "fits our personalities and the way we want to live our lives."[26] This harmony is easily found in Buffett's attitude. He is always upbeat and supportive. He is genuinely excited about coming to work every day. "I have all in life I want right here," he says. "I love every day. I mean, I tap dance in here and work with nothing but people I like."[27] "There is no job in the world that is more fun than running Berkshire, and I count myself lucky to be where I am."[28]

Gaining knowledge is a journey. Warren Buffett and Charlie Munger took much of their wisdom from people who came before them, shaped it into their own mosaic of understanding, and now generously offer it to others—that is, others who are

251

willing to do their own homework and learn all they can, with a fresh, vigorous, open mind.

Without question, the three very successful money managers profiled in this chapter have benefited from following the essentials of Buffett's philosophy. But theirs is not a blind copycat approach. Each of them, in his own way, applied Buffett's ideas in new and different directions. In the process, each added a fresh layer of knowledge and experience to the investment philosophy that is encapsulated by Warren Buffett.

Learning from the best is a dyadic process: it is both a privilege and a responsibility. We gratefully accept wisdom from those who have gone before us; it is our privilege. Then, with respect, we pass it on to those who follow; that is our responsibility.

Guided by timeless principles, our journey continues.

NOTES

Chapter 1 The Unreasonable Man

1. This quote was used to describe Warren Buffett in V. Eugene Shahan's article, "Are Short-Term Performance and Value Investing Mutually Exclusive?" *Hermes,* spring 1986.

2. Carol Loomis, "Inside Story on Warren Buffett," *Fortune,* April 11, 1988, p. 34.

3. Berkshire Hathaway Annual Report, 1996, p. 16.

4. Berkshire Hathaway Annual Report, 1987, p. 14.

5. Stephen Jay Gould, *Full House: The Spread of Excellence from Plato to Darwin* (New York: Crown, 1996), p. 116.

6. Peter Bernstein, "Where, Oh Where Are the .400 Hitters of Yesteryear?" *Financial Analysts Journal,* November/December 1998, p. 6.

7. Ibid., p. 11.

8. *Broadcasting Magazine,* June 9, 1996. Also see Simon Reynolds, *Thoughts of Chairman Buffett: Thirty Years of Unconventional Wisdom from the Sage of Omaha* (New York: HarperCollins, 1998).

9. Ronald Surz, "R-Squareds and Alphas Are Far from Different Alpha-bets," *The Journal of Investing,* summer 1998.

10. Berkshire Hathaway Annual Report, 1993, p. 16.

11. Ibid., p. 14.

12. Ibid.

13. Berkshire Hathaway Annual Report, 1997, p. 5.

14. Ibid.

15. John Maynard Keynes, *The General Theory of Employment, Interest, and Money* (Orlando, FL: Harcourt Brace, 1964).

16. Benjamin Graham and David Dodd, *Security Analysis* (New York: McGraw-Hill, 1951).

17. *Outstanding Investor Digest*, August 8, 1997, p. 14.

18. I am indebted to Larry Pidgeon for his thoughts on this subject.

19. *Outstanding Investor Digest*, March 13, 1998, p. 56.

20. *Outstanding Investor Digest*, August 8, 1997, p. 19.

21. George Johnson, *Fire in the Mind: Science, Faith and the Search for Order* (New York: Vintage Books, 1995), p. 104.

22. Andrew Kilpatrick, *Of Permanent Value: The Story of Warren Buffett* (Birmingham, AL: AKPE, 1998), p. 794.

23. Ron Chernow, *The Death of the Banker: The Decline and Fall of the Great Financial Dynasties and the Triumph of the Small Investor* (New York: Vintage Books, 1997).

24. Thomas S. Kuhn, *The Structure of Scientific Revolutions* (Chicago: The University of Chicago Press, 1970), p. 77.

25. Munger's idea is so intriguing to me, and so profoundly valuable to investors, that I felt it was worth a full book-length discussion. The result is *Latticework: The New Investing*, by Robert Hagstrom (New York: Texere, 2000).

26. *Outstanding Investor Digest*, May 5, 1995, p. 49.

27. Ibid.

28. Ibid.

29. *Outstanding Investor Digest*, August 8, 1997, p. 61.

30. Ibid., p. 13.

CHAPTER 2 The World's Greatest Investor

1. The Carson Group, a global capital markets intelligence consulting firm based in New York, released results of its survey on

November 22, 1999. For more information, contact the company at www.carsongroup.com or call 212/581–4000.

2. Carol J. Loomis, "The Inside Story of Warren Buffett," *Fortune,* April 11, 1988, p. 30.

3. Warren Buffett, "The Superinvestors of Graham-and-Doddsville," *Hermes,* fall 1984.

4. Warren Buffett, "The Security I Like Best," *The Commercial and Financial Chronicle,* December 6, 1951; reprinted in Andrew Kilpatrick, *Of Permanent Value: The Story of Warren Buffett,* rev. ed. (Birmingham, AL: AKPE, 2000), p. 302.

5. Berkshire Hathaway Annual Report, 1999, p. 9.

6. The purchase price is often quoted as $22 billion, and in a sense that is true. The two companies announced in June 1998 that Berkshire would acquire all General Re shares at a 29 percent premium over the closing share price, by trading an equivalent value in Berkshire stock. But six months passed before the deal finally closed, and by that time both share prices had declined. General Re shareholders received $204.40 for each share they owned, rather than the $276.50 value the shares had back in June. The actual purchase price was thus approximately $16 billion in Berkshire stock, rather than $22 billion.

7. Quoted in Kilpatrick, *Of Permanent Value,* p. 18.

8. Berkshire Hathaway Annual Report, 1999, p. 6.

9. Quoted in Kilpatrick, *Of Permanent Value,* p. 14.

10. Remarks at Berkshire Hathaway's 1997 annual meeting, quoted in Janet Lowe's biography of Charlie Munger, *Damn Right!* (New York, John Wiley, 2000).

11. Berkshire Hathaway Annual Report, 1999, pp. 13, 14.

12. Ibid., p. 14.

13. Kilpatrick, *Of Permanent Value,* p. 413.

14. Ibid., p. 452.

15. Ibid.

16. Howard Banks, "Flying Buffett," *Forbes,* September 21, 1988.

17. Berkshire Hathaway Annual Report, 1999, p. 10.

18. Berkshire Hathaway Annual Report, 1987, p. 22.

19. Berkshire Hathaway Annual Report, 1999, p. 3.

CHAPTER 3   Lessons from the Three Wise Men of Finance

1. Adam Smith, *Supermoney* (New York: Random House, 1972), p. 178.

2. *New York Times,* December 2, 1934, p. 13D.

3. Benjamin Graham and David Dodd, *Security Analysis,* 3d ed. (New York: McGraw-Hill, 1951), p. 38.

4. Ibid., p. 13.

5. "Ben Graham: The Grandfather of Investment Value Is Still Concerned," *Institutional Investor,* April 1974, p. 62.

6. Ibid., p. 61.

7. John Train, *The Money Masters* (New York: Penguin Books, 1981), p. 60.

8. Philip Fisher, *Common Stocks and Uncommon Profits* (New York: Harper & Brothers, 1958), p. 11.

9. Ibid., p. 16.

10. Ibid., p. 33.

11. Philip Fisher, *Developing an Investment Philosophy,* The Financial Analysts Research Foundation, Monograph Number 10, p. 1.

12. Fisher, *Common Stocks,* p. 13.

13. Fisher, *Developing an Investment Philosophy,* p. 29.

14. Andrew Kilpatrick, *Of Permanent Value: The Story of Warren Buffett,* rev. ed. (Birmingham, AL: AKPE, 2000), p. 89.

15. Andrew Kilpatrick, *Warren Buffett: The Good Guy of Wall Street* (New York: Donald I. Fine, 1992), p. 38.

16. Robert Lenzner, "Warren Buffett's Idea of Heaven: 'I Don't Have to Work with People I Don't Like,'" *Forbes,* October 18, 1993, p. 43.

17. Berkshire Hathaway Annual Report, 1989, p. 21.

18. L.J. Davis, "Buffett Takes Stock," *New York Times Magazine,* April 1, 1990, p. 61.

19. Berkshire Hathaway Annual Report, 1987, p. 15.

20. Berkshire Hathaway Annual Report, 1990, p. 17.

21. Benjamin Graham, *The Intelligent Investor,* 4th ed. (New York: Harper & Row, 1973), p. 287.

22. Warren Buffett, "What We Can Learn from Philip Fisher," *Forbes,* October 19, 1987, p. 40.

23. "The Money Men—How Omaha Beats Wall Street," *Forbes,* November 1, 1969, p. 82.

Chapter 4 Guidelines for Buying a Business: Twelve Immutable Tenets

1. Berkshire Hathaway Annual Report, 1987, p. 4.

2. Robert Lenzner, "Warren Buffett's Idea of Heaven: 'I Don't Have to Work with People I Don't Like,'" *Forbes,* October 18, 1993, p. 43.

3. *Fortune,* November 11, 1993, p. 11.

4. Berkshire Hathaway Annual Report, 1992, p. 15.

5. Berkshire Hathaway Annual Report, 1987, p. 7.

6. Berkshire Hathaway Annual Report, 1989, p. 22.

7. Berkshire Hathaway Annual Report, 1982, p. 57.

8. Lenzner, "Warren Buffett's Idea of Heaven."

9. Berkshire Hathaway Annual Report, 1991, p. 8.

10. Carol Loomis, "Inside Story on Warren Buffett," *Fortune,* April 11, 1988, p. 32.

11. "Cost of capital" equals cost of debt plus cost of equity, in proportionate measures. Cost of debt is simply the interest rate the company pays on borrowed money, adjusted for interest expense deductibility. Cost of equity is determined by the riskiness of the business, as measured by the CAPM. For more detailed discussion, see Robert Hagstrom, *The Warren Buffett Portfolio* (New York: John Wiley, 1999), pp. 91–93.

12. Berkshire Hathaway Annual Report, 1988, p. 5.
13. Berkshire Hathaway Annual Report, 1986, p. 5.
14. Berkshire Hathaway Annual Report, 1989, p. 22.
15. Ibid.
16. Linda Grant, "The $4 Billion Regular Guy," *Los Angeles Times,* April 7, 1991, Magazine Section, p. 36.
17. Lenzner, "Warren Buffett's Idea of Heaven," p. 43.
18. Berkshire Hathaway Annual Report, 1985, p. 9.
19. Berkshire Letters to Shareholders, 1977–1983, p. 17.
20. Berkshire Hathaway Annual Report, 1987, p. 20.
21. Ibid., p. 21.
22. Berkshire Hathaway Annual Report, 1984, p. 15.
23. Berkshire Hathaway Annual Report, 1986, p. 25.
24. Loomis, "Inside Story on Warren Buffett," p. 34.
25. Berkshire Hathaway Annual Report, 1990, p. 16.
26. Berkshire Hathaway Annual Report, 1982, p. 52.
27. Technically speaking, it is more correct to refer to "discount rate" rather than "interest rate." Whether we are valuing a bond or using the same concept to value future earnings flow, correctly applying a discount to data over a spread of years involves a complex mathematical formula. It is not a simple matter of summing the annual data and then multiplying by, say, 9 percent. Financial specialists rely on discount-rate tables to plug in the right numbers. For example, look at Table 4.2 in this chapter. The row labeled "Discount factor" shows the actual numbers used for the first ten years—0.9174, 0.8417, and so on—to accomplish a 9 percent discount rate.
28. Berkshire Hathaway Annual Report, 1989, p. 5.
29. Jim Rasmussen, "Buffett Talks Strategy with Students," *Omaha World-Herald,* January 2, 1994, p. 26.
30. Berkshire Letters to Shareholders, 1977–1983, p. 53.
31. Berkshire Hathaway Annual Report, 1996, p. 15.
32. Quoted in Berkshire Hathaway Annual Report, 1993, p. 14.

33. Andrew Kilpatarick, *Warren Buffett: The Good Guy of Wall Street* (New York: Donald I. Fine, 1992), p. 123.

34. Mark Pendergrast, *For God, Country and Coca-Cola* (New York: Scribner's, 1993).

35. Art Harris, "The Man Who Changed the Real Thing," *The Washington Post*, July 22, 1985, p. B1.

36. "Strategy for the 1980s," The Coca-Cola Company.

37. Ibid.

38. The first stage applies 15 percent annual growth for ten years. In year 1, 1988, owner earnings were $828 million; by year 10, they will be $4.349 billion. Starting with year 11, growth will slow to 5 percent per year, the second stage. In year 11, owner earnings will equal $3.516 billion ($3.349 billion × 5 percent + $3.349 billion). Now, we can subtract this 5 percent growth rate from the risk-free rate of return (9 percent) and reach a capitalization rate of 4 percent. The discounted value of a company with $3.516 billion in owner earnings capitalized at 4 percent is $87.9 billion. Since this value, $87.9 billion, is the discounted value of Coca-Cola's owner earnings in year 11, we next have to discount this future value by the discount factor at the end of year 10 $[1/(1 + .09)10] = .4224$. The present value of the residual value of Coca-Cola in year 10 is $37.129 billion. The value of Coca-Cola then equals its residual value ($37.129 billion) plus the sum of the present value of cash flows during this period ($11.248 billion), for a total of $48.377 billion.

39. Lenzner, "Warren Buffett's Idea of Heaven," p. 43.

40. Berkshire Letters to Shareholders, 1977–1983, p. 82.

CHAPTER 5 Focus Investing: Theory and Mechanics

1. Interview, Warren Buffett, August 1994.

2. Andrew Barry, "With Little Cheery News in Sight, Stocks Take a Break," *Barron's*, November 16, 1998, p. MW1.

3. Berkshire Hathaway Annual Report, 1993, p. 15.

4. Ibid.

5. Interview with Ken Fisher, September 15, 1998.

6. Interview with Warren Buffett, August 1994.

7. *Outstanding Investor Digest,* August 10, 1995, p. 63.

8. Ibid.

9. Peter L. Bernstein, *Against the Gods* (New York: John Wiley, 1996), p. 63.

10. Ibid.

11. Ibid.

12. *Outstanding Investor Digest,* May 5, 1995, p. 49.

13. Robert L. Winkler, *An Introduction to Bayesian Inference and Decision* (New York: Holt, Rinehart and Winston, 1972), p. 17.

14. Andrew Kilpatrick, *Of Permanent Value: The Story of Warren Buffett* (Birmingham, AL: AKPE, 1998), p. 800.

15. *Outstanding Investor Digest,* April 18, 1990, p. 16.

16. Ibid.

17. *Outstanding Investor Digest,* June 23, 1994, p. 19.

18. Robert G. Hagstrom, Jr., *The Warren Buffett Way* (New York: John Wiley, 1994).

19. Berkshire Hathaway Annual Report, 1990, p. 16.

20. Berkshire Hathaway Annual Report, 1993, p. 15.

21. Berkshire Hathaway Annual Report, 1990, p. 16.

22. Berkshire Hathaway Annual Report, 1993, p. 16.

23. Edward O. Thorp, *Beat the Dealer: A Winning Strategy for the Game of Twenty-One* (New York: Vintage Books, 1962).

24. I am indebted to Bill Miller for pointing out the J.L. Kelly growth model.

25. C.E. Shannon, "A Mathematical Theory of Communication," *Bell System Technical Journal,* vol. 27, no. 3, July 1948.

26. J.L. Kelly, Jr., "A New Interpretation of Information Rate," *Bell System Technical Journal,* vol. 35, no. 3, July 1956.

27. *Outstanding Investor Digest,* May 5, 1995, p. 57.

28. Andrew Beyer, *Picking Winners: A Horse Player's Guide* (New York: Houghton Mifflin, 1994), p. 178.

29. *Outstanding Investor Digest,* May 5, 1995, p. 58.

30. For a comprehensive and well-written historical recovery of the development of modern finance, see: Peter Bernstein, *Capital Ideas: The Improbable Origins of Modern Wall Street* (New York: The Free Press, 1992).

31. Ibid., p. 47.

32. Jonathan Burton, "Travels Along the Efficient Frontier," *Dow Jones Asset Management,* May/June 1997, p. 22.

33. Bernstein, *Capital Ideas,* p. 86.

34. Ibid., p. 13.

35. *Outstanding Investor Digest,* April 18, 1990, p. 18.

36. Berkshire Hathaway Annual Report, 1993, p. 13.

37. "Intrinsic value risk" is a term first coined by John Rutledge of Rutledge & Company, Greenwich, CT; *Forbes,* August 29, 1994, p. 279.

38. Berkshire Hathaway Annual Report, 1993, p. 13.

39. *Outstanding Investor Digest,* June 23, 1994, p. 19.

40. Berkshire Hathaway Annual Report, 1993, p. 12.

41. *Outstanding Investor Digest,* August 8, 1996, p. 29.

42. Berkshire Hathaway Annual Report, 1988, p. 18.

43. Ibid.

44. *Outstanding Investor Digest,* August 8, 1996, p. 29.

CHAPTER 6   Managing Your Portfolio:
            The Challenge of Focus Investing

1. Benjamin Graham, *The Memoirs of the Dean of Wall Street* (New York: McGraw-Hill, 1996), p. 239.

2. The speech was adapted as an article in the Columbia Business School's publication *Hermes* (fall 1984), with the same title. The remarks directly quoted here are from that article.

3. Warren Buffett, "The Superinvestors of Graham-and-Doddsville," *Hermes* (Fall 1984). The superinvestors Buffett presented in the article include Walter Schloss, who worked at Graham-Newman Corporation in the mid-1950s, along with Buffett; Tom Knapp, another Graham-Newman alumnus, who later formed Tweedy-Browne Partners with Ed Anderson, also a Graham follower; Bill Ruane, a former Graham student who went on to establish the Sequoia Fund; Buffett's partner Charlie Munger; Rick Guerin of Pacific Partners; and Stan Perlmeter of Perlmeter Investments.

4. Quoted in Berkshire Hathaway Annual Report, 1991, p. 15.

5. Jess H. Chua and Richard S. Woodward, "J.M. Keynes's Investment Performances: A Note," *The Journal of Finance,* vol. 38, no.1, March 1983.

6. Ibid.

7. Ibid.

8. Buffett, "Superinvestors."

9. Ibid.

10. Ibid.

11. Sequoia Fund Annual Report, 1996.

12. Solveig Jansson, "GEICO Sticks to Its Last," *Institutional Investor,* July 1986, p. 130.

13. Berkshire Hathaway Annual Report, 1986, p. 15.

14. Berkshire Hathaway Annual Report, 1995, p. 10.

15. The research described here is part of a larger research study I conducted with Joan Lamm-Tennant, PhD, Villanova University, and presented in a monograph titled "Focus Investing: An Alternative to Active Management versus Indexing."

16. It is important to note that when the benchmark return is higher than the median return of the broadly diversified portfolios, the probabilities of outperforming the benchmark rise to the degree the portfolio manager is willing to reduce the number of stocks in the portfolio. If the benchmark return is less than the median return of the broadly diversified portfolio, this relationship does not hold. In other words, a group of concentrated portfolios

under this circumstance would not have more probabilities of outperforming the benchmark, compared to a group of broadly diversified portfolios. However, the group of concentrated portfolios still gives the potential for higher returns when compared against a group of broadly diversified portfolios.

17. Warren Buffett, "Superinvestors."

18. Joseph Nocera, "Who's Got the Answers?" *Fortune,* November 24, 1997, p. 329.

19. Ibid.

20. Eugene Shahan, "Are Short-Term Performance and Value Investing Mutually Exclusive?" *Hermes* (spring 1986).

21. Sequoia Fund, Quarterly Report, March 31, 1996.

22. Mark Carhart, "On Persistence in Mutual Fund Performance," *Journal of Finance,* vol. 52, no. 1, March 1997; Burton G. Malkiel, "Returns from Investing in Equity Mutual Funds, 1971 to 1991," *Journal of Finance,* vol. 50, no. 2, June 1995.

23. Darryll Hendricks, Javendu Patel, and Richard Zeckhauser, "Hot Hands in Mutual Funds: Short-Run Persistence of Relative Performance, 1974–1988," *Journal of Finance,* vol. 48, no. 1, March 1993.

24. Stephen J. Brown and William N. Goetzmann, "Performance Persistence," *Journal of Finance,* vol. 50, no. 2, June 1995.

25. Widely quoted remark.

26. Berkshire Hathaway Annual Report, 1987, p. 14.

27. Ibid.

28. Ibid.

29. Berkshire Hathaway Annual Report, 1981, p. 39.

30. Benjamin Graham and David Dodd, *Security Analysis* (New York:
McGraw-Hill, 1951).

31. Berkshire Hathaway Annual Report, 1987, p. 15.

32. Berkshire Hathaway Annual Report, 1991, p. 8.

33. Ibid.

34. *Outstanding Investor Digest,* August 10, 1995, p. 10.

35. Widely quoted remark. Murphy uses the train metaphor to describe how to manage a holding company.

36. Berkshire Hathaway Annual Report, 1996.

37. Carole Gould, "The Price of Turnover," *New York Times,* November 21, 1997.

38. Robert Jeffrey and Robert Arnott, "Is Your Alpha Big Enough to Cover Your Taxes?" *Journal of Portfolio Management,* spring 1993.

39. Ibid.

40. Carol Loomis, "Inside Story on Warren Buffett," *Fortune,* April 11, 1988, p. 28.

41. A frequently quoted statement from Warren Buffett.

Chapter 7　The Emotional Side of Money

1. Carol Loomis, Ed., "Mr. Buffett on the Stock Market," *Fortune,* November 22, 1999.

2. Mark Hulbert, "Be a Tiger Not a Hen," *Forbes,* May 25, 1992, p. 298.

3. Berkshire Hathaway Annual Report, 1990, p. 17.

4. Warren Buffett, "You Pay a Very High Price in the Stock Market for a Cheery Consensus," *Forbes,* August 6, 1979, pp. 25–26.

5. Berkshire Hathaway Annual Report, 1992, p. 6.

6. Berkshire Hathaway Annual Report, 1986, p. 16.

7. Benjamin Graham, *The Intelligent Investor: A Book of Practical Counsel* (New York: Harper & Row, 1973), p. 107.

8. *Outstanding Investor Digest,* May 5, 1995, p. 51.

9. Brian O'Reilly, "Why Can't Johnny Invest?" *Fortune,* November 9, 1998, p. 73.

10. Jonathan Burton, "It Just Ain't Rational," *Fee Advisor,* September/October 1996, p. 26.

11. Fuerbringer, "Why Both Bulls and Bears Can Act So Bird-Brained," *New York Times,* March 30, 1997, section 3, p. 6.

12. D.G. Pruitt, "The Walter Mitty Effect in Individual and Good Risk Taking," *Proceedings of the 77th Annual Convention of the American Psychological Association* (1969), pp. 425–436.

13. J.W. Atkinson, R. Bastian, W. Earl, and G.H. Litwin, "The Achievement Motive and Goal Setting, and Probability Preference," *Journal of Abnormal and Social Psychology,* 60 (November 1960), pp. 27–36. J.W. Atkinson and G.H. Litwin, "The Achievement Motive and Test Anxiety Conceived as a Motive to Avoid Failure," *Journal of Abnormal and Social Psychology,* 60 (November 1960), pp. 52–63.

14. L.W. Littig, "Effects of Skill and Chance Orientation on Probability Preferences," *Psychological Reports, 10,* 1962, pp. 72–80.

15. *Outstanding Investor Digest,* August 10, 1995, p. 11.

16. Berkshire Hathaway Annual Report, 1985.

17. Berkshire Hathaway Annual Report, 1984, p. 14.

Chapter 8   New Opportunities, Timeless Principles

1. *Outstanding Investor Digest,* September 24, 1998, p. 48.

2. *Outstanding Investor Digest,* March 13, 1998, p. 55.

3. Berkshire Hathaway Annual Report, 1992, pp. 13–14.

4. "Will the Real Ben Graham Please Stand Up?" *Forbes,* December 11, 1989, p. 30.

5. Interview with Eric Savitz, December 2, 1998.

6. Interview with Amy Arnott, December 2, 1998.

7. Adam Shell, "Bill Miller: Beating the Market Is Routine," *Investor's Business Daily,* November 7, 1997.

8. Interview with Bill Miller, December 1, 1998.

9. A book that Bill Miller often cites as an aid to the process of understanding technology companies is Jeff Moore's *The Gorilla Game: An Investor's Guide to Picking Winners in High Technology* (New York: HarperCollins, 1998).

10. Interview with Lisa Rapuano, December 2, 1998.

11. Interview with Bill Miller, October 2, 2000.

12. Interview with Bill Miller, December 1, 1998.

13. Interview with Lisa Rapuano, Legg Mason Research Director, October 16, 2000; unless otherwise cited, all quotes from Ms. Rapuano in this section were taken from this interview.

14. "Fund Manager Interview: Wallace R. Weitz, Weitz Series Value Funds," *AAII Journal,* April 1998.

15. The story was told to me by Wally Weitz in an interview conducted September 29, 2000. Unless noted otherwise, all quotes from Weitz in this section of the chapter are from this interview.

16. *AAII Journal,* April 1998.

17. Berkshire Hathaway Annual Report, 1991, p. 15.

18. Interview with Mason Hawkins on October 5, 2000. Unless otherwise noted, all quotes from Hawkins in this section of the chapter are from this interview.

19. The SEC allows nondiversified funds to invest 24.9 percent of the portfolio into any one security as long as half the portfolio is restricted from purchasing more than 5 percent of its assets in any one security. So, theoretically, a nondiversified fund could own, at purchase, two 24.9 percent positions and ten 4.9 percent positions.

20. *Outstanding Investor Digest,* July 31, 2000, p. 11.

21. Ibid., p. 12.

22. Ibid.

23. Ibid., p. 11.

24. Linda Grant, "The $4 Billion Regular Guy," *Los Angeles Times Magazine,* April 7, 1991, p. 36.

25. *Outstanding Investor Digest,* August 10, 1995, p. 21.

26. Berkshire Hathaway Annual Report, 1987, p. 15.

27. Robert Lenzner, "Warren Buffett's Idea of Heaven: 'I Don't Have to Work with People I Don't Like,'" *Forbes,* October 18, 1993, p. 40.

28. Berkshire Hathaway Annual Report, 1992, p. 6.

ACKNOWLEDGMENTS

To begin, I wish to express my deep gratitude to Warren Buffett for his teachings and for allowing me to use his copyrighted material. I have never hesitated to admit that the success of my earlier books is first and foremost a testament to Warren Buffett. He is, without question, the most successful investor in modern history, and he stands out as the most important role model any individual investor can select. His wit, charm, and intellect have captivated investors worldwide.

I would like to also thank Charlie Munger for his intellectual contributions to the study of investing. His ideas on the "psychology of misjudgment" and the "latticework of mental models" are extremely important and should be examined by all. My appreciation to Charlie also includes thanks for his thoughtful conversations and his kind words of support.

Over the years, I have had countless opportunities to talk about Warren Buffett, and investing, with many bright individuals. Whether they realized it or not, they gave me important additional insights that ultimately found their way into this book. With genuine gratitude, I would like to thank Chuck Akre, Al Barr, David Braverman, Jamie Clark, Bob Coleman, Chris Davis, Charles Ellis, Phil Fisher, Bob Goldfarb, Ed Haldeman, Ajit Jain, Michael Levitan, Michael Mauboussin, Larry Pidgeon, Bill Ruane, Tom Russo, Alice Schroeder, Lou Simpson, Ed Thorp, Dale Wettlaufer, and David Winters.

In particular, my thanks to both Wally Weitz and Mason Hawkins for sharing their valuable time with me and describing

Acknowledgments

how they have applied the Warren Buffett tenets in their successful funds.

I count myself extremely fortunate to be able to work with Bill Miller. He is a gifted teacher. His patience, his generosity of spirit, and his ability to explain abstract concepts with clarity and flair have helped me in many ways and, particularly for this book, have showed me how Warren Buffett's teachings can be applied to technology. Thank you, Bill. I am also fortunate to work in an environment that supports and promotes a Warren Buffett approach to investing. For their intellectual support, I would like to thank all my colleagues at Legg Mason Funds Management, and a very special thank you to Lisa Rapuano, Research Director, for her insight, her valuable time, and her thoughtful consideration. I am especially grateful to Cathy Coladonato and Ericka Peterson for their hard work and dedication at Legg Mason Focus Capital.

Thanks also to Andy Kilpatrick, author of *Of Permanent Value: The Story of Warren Buffett* and to Roger Lowenstein, author of *Buffett: The Making of an American Capitalist*. I often turn to both of these books for my research. In my judgment, Andy is the official historian of Berkshire Hathaway, and Roger has written the definitive biography of Warren Buffett.

I was also fortunate to work with Joan Lamm-Tennant, PhD, at Villanova University as we both intensely studied the concept of focus investing. Thanks also to Pat Shunk for his computer programming assistance, and to Professor Justin Green for his research investigation and assistance in studying risk tolerance.

All investors, and all readers of this book, owe special thanks to Henry Emerson, editor of *Outstanding Investor Digest* (OID). Henry covers the Berkshire Hathaway annual meetings and the occasional lectures given by Warren Buffett and Charlie Munger, and presents them in his publication. With Henry's permission, I have included numerous quotations from *Outstanding Investor Digest* in this book.

Acknowledgments

My relationship with John Wiley & Sons has been a pleasure. I appreciate very much the care and attention they provide for my books on Warren Buffett. A special thanks to Joan O'Neil, publisher and editor for this book.

As always, I feel fortunate indeed to have Laurie Harper at Sebastian Agency as my agent. Laurie is, in a word, awesome. Not only does she act with dignity, class, and good cheer, she is always willing to go the extra mile to ensure our work is first rate.

With all the appreciation I have given above, none could match the thanks I owe my writing partner, Maggie Stuckey. Maggie is collaborator, editor, and cheerleader. This is the fifth book we have written together, and, as usual, she has dedicated 100 percent of herself to the project. Although she works in Oregon and I work in Pennsylvania, it often feels like she is sitting across the desk with me. We easily step from one idea to the next, from one chapter to the next, searching for the very best way to structure the material and articulate the concepts. I as the author and you as the reader are very fortunate that Maggie has been willing to share her many talents with us.

Anyone who has sat down to write a book knows that it means countless hours spent alone, working on the details. Those are, inevitably, hours taken away from one's family. Writing requires certain sacrifices from the author, but even more from the author's family. I dearly love and appreciate my children, Kim, Robert, and John, and I am forever dedicated to my wife Maggie, who never wavers in her support for me and for our family. Her constant love makes all things possible. Even though they come last in this list, Maggie, Kim, Robert, and John are forever first in my heart.

For all that is good and right about this book, you may thank the people mentioned above. For any errors or omissions, I alone am responsible.

R.G.H.

INDEX